Uncle Sam's War of 1898
and the Origins of Globalization

Uncle Sam's

A FAIR FIELD AND NO FAVOR!

UNCLE SAM: "I'M OUT FOR COMMERCE, NOT CONQUEST!"

War of 1898

and the

Origins of Globalization

⚜

Thomas Schoonover

☙

Foreword by Walter LaFeber

THE UNIVERSITY PRESS OF KENTUCKY

Publication of this volume was made possible in part
by a grant from the National Endowment for the Humanities.

Scholarly publisher for the Commonwealth,
serving Bellarmine University, Berea College, Centre
College of Kentucky, Eastern Kentucky University,
The Filson Historical Society, Georgetown College,
Kentucky Historical Society, Kentucky State University,
Morehead State University, Murray State University,
Northern Kentucky University, Transylvania University,
University of Kentucky, University of Louisville,
and Western Kentucky University.
All rights reserved.

Editorial and Sales Offices: The University Press of Kentucky
663 South Limestone Street, Lexington, Kentucky 40508-4008
www.kentuckypress.com

05 06 07 08 09   5 4 3 2 1

Frontispiece: "A Fair Field and No Favor." Uncle Sam restrains
aggressive, militaristic European treatment of China in order to
promote an open door to commercial and investment opportunity
(China holds a train). (*Harper's Weekly,* November 18, 1899)

Library of Congress Cataloging-in-Publication Data

Schoonover, Thomas David, 1936–
Uncle Sam's War of 1898 and the origins of globalization /
Thomas Schoonover ; foreword by Walter LaFeber
p.   cm.
Includes bibliographical references and index.
ISBN 0-8131-2282-1 (hardcover : alk. paper)
1. Spanish-American War, 1898. 2. United States—Territorial
expansion. 3. World politics—19th century. 4. Globalization—
Political aspects—United States. I. Title.
E715.S36 2003
973.9'91—dc21   2003011379
Paper ISBN 0-8131-9122-X

Manufactured in the United States of America

  Member of the Association of
American University Presses

Dedicated to my son, Paco, who died on 23 July 2000.
He knew about this project.
He read an article containing many of its themes,
and we discussed the project.
My heart and soul are heavy and sad
because he will not be able to read the final form.

Contents

List of Illustrations   vii

Foreword by Walter LaFeber   viii

Preface   xi

Introduction   1

1. Exploration and New Territories, 1780s–1850s   9

2. The Great Powers in the Caribbean Basin, 1800–1890s   18

3. The Great Powers in East Asia and the Pacific,
       1840s–1890s   35

4. U.S. Domestic Developments and Social Imperialism,
       1850s–1890s   53

5. Three Crises: The 1893 Depression, China, and Cuba   65

6. The War of 1898 in the Pacific Basin   88

7. The Legacy of the Crises of the 1890s   102

Notes   123

Selected Bibliography   153

Index   165

List of Illustrations

Maps

Gulf-Caribbean Basin   xiv
Pacific Ocean and East Asia   xv

Figures

1. "Le Gâteau Chinois"   71
2. "Gâteau des Rois et des Empereurs," *Le petit journal*   72
3. "Uncle Sam to the European Powers," *Boston Globe*   77
4. "Knocking at the Door," *Chicago Tribune*   78
5. "Uncle Sam and Liberty Enjoy Their Good Deed," *St. Louis Globe-Democrat*   80
6. "Ha! Ha!" *Los Angeles Times*   81
7. "Shelling the Enemy," *Judy*, London   82
8. "John Bull," postcard, 1900   89
9. "Off to War Parade, Denver"   90
10. "Hospital in the Philippines"   93
11. "Chinesische Spottkarte. Chinese verjagt Europa"   107
12. "Chinese Boxer Troops"   108
13. "War in China," postcard, 1900   109
14. "Entrance of Chinese Empress Dowager, Cixi," postcard   110

Foreword

Walter LaFeber

⊰ In 1904, Halford Mackinder arose to present a paper before the Royal Geographical Society in London. Extraordinarily learned, lengthy, and dry, the paper turned out to be one of those few documents that helped unlock the dynamics of twentieth- and twenty-first-century international relations. "The Geographical Pivot of History," as Mackinder immodestly but accurately titled his paper, argued that Central Asia held the key to the control of global events. Whoever held that region, stretching roughly from the oil-rich Caspian Sea through Afghanistan to western China, would be able to control the entire Eurasian landmass, he concluded. It was thus necessary for British interests, Mackinder warned, to ensure that Russia could never consolidate a hold on that region. Later, during World War II, Soviet, British, and U.S. policy aimed to deny this region to Hitler's forces, an objective the Russians barely but historically achieved in 1941–42, thereby helping to fix the course of the Nazis' destruction. Between 1999 and 2003, the U.S. superpower for the first time established military bases in Central Asia so it could secure an area that, in Washington's eyes, continued to be a "pivot" of world affairs.

Thomas Schoonover's book redefines Mackinder's epochal approach by placing it in a different, but equally important, framework of historical movement. The American scholar differs from his British counterpart by locating the "pivot of history" not in Europe but in the Caribbean–Central American region that for over four centuries linked European and then U.S. expansionism to the quest for control of Asia, especially Asian markets—"the chief theatre of events in the world's great hereafter," as Asia was termed by William Seward, Lincoln's secretary of state and one of American history's more accurate prophets. To rephrase, while Mackinder saw history's "pivot" as land-based, Schoonover emphasizes that the key to centuries of European and now U.S.

power can be found in the control of the sea, especially the Panamanian route between two great oceans.

With its sweep and extraordinary research, Schoonover's argument brings together succinct stories of European and then U.S. expansionism, explains why the United States became an overseas imperialist power in the 1890s, demonstrates how it and other imperialist nations viewed and fought over the Caribbean–Central American region, then traces the effects of this imperial competition on the evolution of not only Central America, but the vast Pacific Ocean–East Asian area. By using the Caribbean–Central American region in this way, this book presents a fresh, highly important perspective on the West's expansionism and its several centuries of effects on Seward's "chief theatre of events." The bookends of this story, Schoonover neatly suggests, are Christopher Columbus and Mao Zedong.

Schoonover's is a perspective that, while focusing on the critical question of how the United States made the historic leap in the 1890s to become a great power, moves beyond the American scene to examine the dynamics of Western Europe, Central America, and East Asia. Schoonover is superbly (it is tempting to say uniquely) qualified to tell this story. For nearly forty years he has exploited diplomatic and other archival materials in Germany, France, Great Britain, Spain, and Central America, as well in the United States. He has mastered the West European as well as the American secondary literature. His own books and articles on how, and why, Europeans and Americans competed in the Western Hemisphere have been critical in shaping the perspectives from which scholars and journalists have viewed that centuries-long imperial competition and its effects on the global arena.

Trans-national and trans-cultural histories are now popular approaches, especially among some historians who understand much about culture but little about either power or the archives of the most powerful nations. Schoonover not only utilizes those archives, and he not only appreciates the importance of an approach that takes in the many important players, but he knows that the events that climaxed in the 1890s and whose results shaped the next century have to focus especially on dominant U.S. power. As Henry Adams once phrased it, the central question of 1901, as in 1801, was how, and whether, Washington (that is, the government representing the American people's interests) could control New York City (that is, the hub of U.S. economic power). Schoonover understands what Adams was saying, and his analysis is as important for the early twenty-first century as it is for the late nineteenth. It is especially worth reflection when he notes some of the components of this U.S. power, not least its incredible technology and its often destructive religious-missionary motivations.

On 11 March 2003, China's official newspaper, *People's Daily*, published a remarkable overview of four hundred years of American history. The analysis not only revealed how a new Chinese leadership viewed the centuries-long motivations of U.S. foreign policy, but how, from Beijing's perspective, that history would now shape the future of Chinese-U.S. relations. The authors broke the era down into four eras: continental expansion that stretched from the first settlements to the 1890s; overseas expansion lasting from the 1890s to about 1945; a struggle for global hegemony during the late 1940s through 1991; and, finally, a post-1991 move toward world domination. The origins and effects of the last two — post-1940s — eras will long be argued over. But for the first two eras, Schoonover has moved across both continents and centuries to provide a compelling argument that demonstrates why the 1890s and the Caribbean–Central American region were and are so pivotal in understanding these two eras.

During a time when Americans speak all too glibly about their "empire," it is necessary to understand where they took the fork in the road to that empire, how their last empire turned out (that is, badly), and how we should think about American empires. Schoonover does all this masterfully, succinctly, and in a broad historical context that is as instructive as it is imaginative.

Preface

⫷ In early 1996, Walther Bernecker and Thomas Fischer of the University of Erlangen-Nürnberg, Germany, invited me to address a special conference of the Latin American Section of the Central Institute planned for June 1997. The conference's title, "1898: The Year that Marked an Epoch," set me to analyzing the meaning of the 1890s. Other opportunities to talk on 1898 at St. Antony's College, Oxford, in June 1997; at "The Crucible of Empire" conference organized by the University of New Orleans's Eisenhower Center in February 1998; at a panel discussion with Walter LaFeber, Robert Beisner, Kristin Hoganson, and Joseph A. Fry at the Society for Historians of American Foreign Relations (SHAFR) meeting in June 1998; at the University of Cologne in July 1998; and at the Pacific Coast Branch of the American Historical Association meeting in San Diego in August 1998 encouraged my quest for greater understanding of 1898.

My graduate training in the U.S. Civil War and Reconstruction and in U.S. military history started under T. Harry Williams. During the early years of the Vietnam War, I discovered U.S. foreign relations. The writings of Walter LaFeber, Thomas McCormick, Hans-Ulrich Wehler, David Horowitz, and, of course, William A. Williams persuaded me to study foreign relations rather than military history. Later, the work of French scholar Fernand Braudel, U.S. sociologist Immanuel Wallerstein, and others drew me to the larger meaning of history.

The scholarship and friendship of Walt LaFeber, Louis Pérez Jr., Ralph Lee Woodward, Jürgen Buchenau, Tom McCormick, Kinley Brauer, Akira Iriye, and Robin Winks aided me at various turns. I owe these scholars and friends all a debt of gratitude. The debt I owe Walt as a friend and colleague is special. He discussed this book with me over several years, read the whole manuscript very closely in an advanced stage, and agreed to write the fore-word. Several colleagues at the University of Louisiana at Lafayette have en-couraged and supported my work: Dean David Barry, former Academic Vice-President Gary Marotta, and two recently retired colleagues, Jim Dormon and Gloria Fiero. A glance at my interpretation of the international military and diplomatic events of the nineteenth century and 1898 reveals the debt to them and to scores of others.

Much of the argument and evidence in this book comes from colleagues who may not agree with my reworking and synthesizing of their work. An-other part of the evidence is borrowed from my research in fifteen countries over the past thirty-five years. Rather than burden the endnotes with extensive (and repetitive) citations of archival items, I have cited my essays and books as a shorthand device to direct the reader to places with full reference to the archives and scholarship which have influenced me on these matters.

This project amplifies and expands on ideas advanced in the various talks mentioned in the first paragraph and published, in a revised version, in Walther Bernecker, ed., *1898: su significado para Centroamérica y el Caribe. Cesura, Cambio, Continuidad?* (Frankfurt: Vervuert, 1998), and in the *SHAFR News-letter* 28:3 (Sept. 1997). I thank the following presses for permitting me to draw upon my prior writings: Purdue University Press, from the essay "Napo-leon Is Coming! Maximilian Is Coming!: The International History of the Civil War in the Caribbean Basin," in *The Union, the Confederacy, and the Atlantic Rim*, ed. Robert E. May (W. Lafayette, Ind.: Purdue Univ. Press, 1995); the University of Alabama Press, from *Germany in Central America: Competi-tive Imperialism, 1821–1929* (Tuscaloosa, Ala.: Univ. of Alabama Press, 1998); and Scholarly Resources, from *The French in Central America: Culture and Commerce, 1820–1930* (Wilmington, Del.: Scholarly Resources, 2000).

I opted for a selected bibliography, which lists items cited several times in the notes or that were vital to my education about the meaning of 1898 in U.S. history. The translated quotations from German, Spanish, and French are my work. Colleagues at UL Lafayette, Guiliang Feng, Ke Lan, and Haiyan Tian, graciously guided me to the modern Pinyang spelling of Chinese personal and place names (the older Wade-Giles form is placed in parentheses at the first use). Various friends and colleagues have helped me locate and acquire the photos and images—I wish to thank all of them heartily: Louis A. Pérez Jr., Dr. Georg Mondwurf (Bremerhaven, Germany), Iris Engstrand, Jean-Michel Granger (Paris, France), and Michael Bolln (Wedel, Germany). My colleague Robert Carriker worked with me (and taught me) to make the maps.

I owe a debt of gratitude to John Ziegler, Gena Henry, Derik Shelor, and David Cobb, whose diligent labors helped convert my manuscript into a book. My closest collaborator, however, on this as on my previous writing projects, has been my wife, Ebba Wesener Schoonover.

The United States and the Caribbean

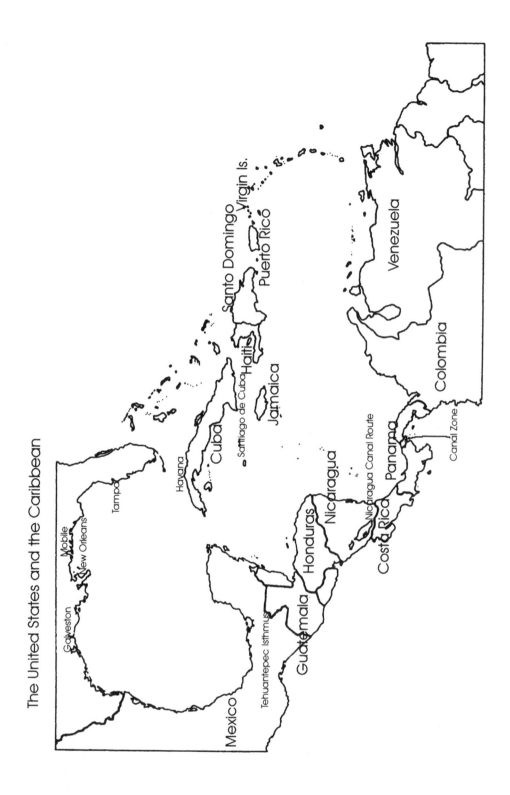

Galveston
New Orleans
Mobile
Tampa
Havana
Cuba
Santiago de Cuba
Haiti
Jamaica
Santo Domingo
Virgin Is.
Puerto Rico
Tehuantepec Isthmus
Mexico
Guatemala
Honduras
Nicaragua
Nicaragua Canal Route
Costa Rica
Panama
Canal Zone
Colombia
Venezuela

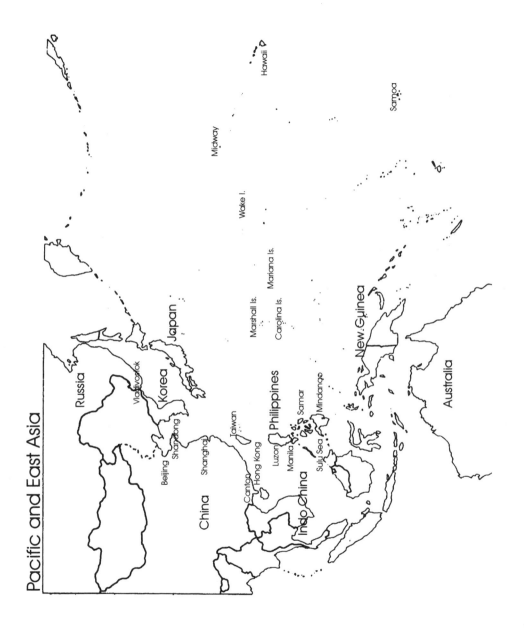

Pacific and East Asia

Russia

Vladivostok

Korea

Japan

China

Beijing

Shandong

Shanghai

Taiwan

Canton

Hong Kong

Luzon

Manila

Philippines

Samar

Mindango

Sulu Sea

Indo China

Hawaii

Samoa

Midway

Wake I.

Mariana Is.

Marshall Is.

Carolina Is.

New Guinea

Australia

Introduction

⁂ Over a decade ago, historian Peter Novick in *That Noble Dream: The "Objectivity Question" and the American Historical Profession* described one central quandary that confronted me in writing this book. Novick addressed the tension between the general and the specific in doing history. He examined specific historians in his search for a general description and analysis of "objectivity" in the historical profession: "The price I pay for emphasizing breadth of coverage is that I am unable to offer rounded and nuanced treatments. . . . I have, of course, attempted to avoid misrepresenting . . . or overinterpreting . . . , but I am less likely to have succeeded in this attempt than a scholar who has made an intensive study of one or a few individuals. Scholarship, like all of life, is full of trade-offs."[1]

The quandary in this project revolves around the relationship of specific events, people, and states engaged for over 125 years in the United States, the Gulf-Caribbean basin, Oceania, and East Asia to the broader understanding of long-term historical processes. This book does not try to tell the precise, detailed history of events, but strives to present a clear argument to encourage further study, more questions, and additional debate about broader themes in U.S. history. Ernest May, in *American Imperialism: A Speculative Essay*, described his objectives: he "meant to provoke rather than to satisfy. The sooner it becomes obsolete, the more successful it will have been."[2] My goal is a clear, pointed argument that is suggestive and argumentative and not in any way "definitive."

When I began this project, I adopted a temporary title: "An International History of the War of 1898: Columbus, Technology, and the Rise of Mao Zedong." Since the last three terms might jar (or amuse) the readers at first, I changed the title to the present one: "Uncle Sam's War of 1898 and the Origins of Globalization." Christopher Columbus represented Europe's (later the North Atlantic community's) quest for a westward route to the wealth and products of Asia. In the second half of the nineteenth century, technology was evident in the engineering for the Suez and Panama Canals, submarine cable networks, iron steamships, mass production rooted in iron, steel, coal, and lubricants, and expanded contact between the North Atlantic communities and the Pacific basin. The conflux of rapid technological change, an aggressive and expansive U.S. political economy, and resistant, traditional states in Spain and China ended in conflict. The Spanish-American War, however, is a misdirected name (the conflict is more aptly called the War of 1898), but even more troubling, the traditional name describes the war inappropriately. The European, U.S., and Japanese fighting in China and other parts of East Asia provoked nationalist responses throughout East Asia. Mao Zedong (Tse-tung), who began his rise to power in the 1910s, symbolized the Asian nationalist and anti-foreign reaction to the sharp rise in European and North American activity in the Pacific and East Asia, linked to the partial division of China in 1897–1898, the War of 1898, and the Panama Canal. The War of 1898 and its aftermath transferred the leadership (unwillingly on the part of Spain, most of Europe, and Japan) in that quest for wealth in Asia and the Pacific to the United States.

This passage of power to Americans occurred within the context of nineteenth-century U.S. society and its competitive relationship with other states in the North Atlantic and in the Caribbean and Pacific basins. The Pacific and Caribbean basins required close attention. Since the seventeenth century, North Americans had struggled to hinder detrimental developments and to shape events positively. Protestant North Americans considered their religion, security, commercial activity, and culture challenged by the Catholic colonies to the south and west and by all the non-Christian areas of the Pacific basin. Western missionary demands, merchant objectives, and the use of military technology contributed to the defeat of the Chinese in two wars, 1839–1842 and 1856–1858, and then defined the expanded role of western merchants, sailors, and missionaries in the remodeled Chinese society. Nineteenth-century U.S. development and competition with foreign merchants, missionaries, and officials around the world explain much of the U.S. intervention in the internal Spanish colonial conflicts of the late nineteenth century. U.S. confrontation with foreign powers also sheds light on U.S. intervention in the Caribbean, Mexico, Central America, Asia, and Oceania (the Pacific islands of Melanesia, Polynesia, Micronesia, the Malay Archipelago, New Zealand, and Australia). Finally, this study analyzes the role of U.S. officials, military leaders, missionaries, and entrepreneurs (all descendants of European emigrants to the New World) who belatedly fulfilled the Columbus-European vision.

The surge of U.S. activity in the Gulf-Caribbean and on the Central American isthmus in the late nineteenth and early twentieth centuries was motivated in large part by the same vision, greed, competitiveness, and curiosity that drove the European adventurers who quested for a route to Asia in the fifteenth century. Columbus's vision had stimulated numerous European statesmen, merchants, monarchs, religious leaders, and adventurers. Later, North Atlantic travelers sought not only to extract wealth and value from Asian resources and labor, but also to make the Asian societies more compatible with the dominant western cultures. These European travelers assumed that Asians, once transformed, would benefit materially and spiritually, and that westerners would find comfort, profit, and safety in Asian lifestyles shaped by western morals, ethics, culture, and outlook. Western businessmen in Asia recognized that they profited from Asia's cultural adjustment. Over time, however, ever more Asians, Pacific islanders, and people in the circum-Caribbean responded to the political, economic, and cultural pressures with nationalist, anti-imperialist, and anti-capitalist movements. The Chinese Revolution (1910–1919), in which Mao had a role, can be interpreted as a dramatic end marker for the international history of the War of 1898.

The War of 1898 lies along the line between Columbus's vision and the acceleration of Asian and Latin American anti-foreign reactions to unwanted intrusions. Cuban and Philippine insurgents caused much of Spain's distress in 1895–1898, and their efforts encouraged U.S. military action against Spain. U.S. officials had little control over the crisis in China in the 1890s. That crisis threatened to divide the vast China market among the imperial powers of Europe and Japan, and greatly increased pressure upon U.S. officials to act to preserve U.S. access to trade and investment. In fighting Spain, the U.S. government expected the support of the Cuban and Philippine insurgents, but without a commitment for insurgent self-rule. Once the U.S. government established its authority, its racial and class biases rejected the insurgents' appeals for self-government. The Spanish and U.S. governments paid a high price for ignoring popular, anti-imperial Cuban and Philippine nationalist movements.[3] The western powers and Japan then paid dearly for underestimating Chinese nationalism and anti-imperialism. Later, in the 1930s and 1940s, the Japanese slogan "Asia for the Asians" would appeal to anti-western, anti-imperial sentiments throughout Asia.

Norman A. Graebner, a prominent U.S. diplomatic historian, opened *An Uncertain Tradition*, a book about U.S. secretaries of state in the twentieth century, with an illustrative, poignant story: "At the turn of the century a foreign ambassador in Washington observed that, although he had been at his post only a brief time, he had seen two different countries—the United States before the war with Spain and the United States after that war. In this picturesque remark, the diplomat recognized what some thoughtful Americans had already sensed—that 1898 was a turning point in the history of the Republic.[4] "That splendid little war" of 1898, as Secretary of State John Hay called it, and its aftermath scarred the societies of the Caribbean and Pacific basins as well as the United States and Spain.

The War of 1898 was not an aberration (a phantom event inconsistent with U.S. historical development), a psychic crisis, an artifact of the historical processes and circumstances, a mission, an obligation, a humanitarian and democratic duty, or something thrust upon the U.S. government. Nor was it a false path followed for several decades before the country recovered its senses, ideals, and purpose and did the right thing. The U.S. policies of the late nineteenth and early twentieth centuries had specific political objectives. The U.S. role in the crisis of 1898 was the consequence of a century of dreams and expansion. Intervention abroad, with extensive political, economic, or military power, has continued to mark U.S. relations for over a century since the 1890s.

The War of 1898 integrated almost all the main themes of U.S. history. The crises and conflicts of the 1890s involved westward expansion, discovery and exploration, maritime activity, labor exploitation, violence, racism, class conflict, idealism, missionary activity, security issues, the Monroe Doctrine, Manifest Destiny, and aspirations in the Gulf-Caribbean and Pacific basins. Nineteenth-century U.S. growth encompassed economic, geopolitical, and missionary ties to the Pacific basin. Merchants, missionaries, fur traders, whalers, and other groups repeatedly claimed a vital role for that basin in the prosperity and well-being of U.S. society. The War of 1898 reflected U.S. society during the century before the conflict.

Nineteenth-century liberal development through industrialization, technology, and mass production and distribution accelerated material accumulation. Industrial development, however, dislocated human and material values and added urgency to the national and international competition for scarce factors of production, such as land, labor, capital, and distribution. Improved communications impacted every nation's expansion in the nineteenth century. From the late nineteenth century until World War II, the world communicated by telegraph, telephone, and radio. Before the construction of telegraph lines to

Asia in the 1840s, a response to a message from London to India took about two years. Early telegraph technology reduced that to about thirteen hours in the 1860s, but disruptions made this contact unreliable. In the 1890s, a response to a message from London to New York arrived in less than ten minutes, and from Bombay in less than ninety minutes. And these cables were more reliable. Telegraph technology implemented a more meaningful reduction in communications time than the Internet of the late twentieth century. By 1900, governance, military security, and economic activity operated in a different world.[5]

The consequences of the new technology rapidly changed power, wealth, and status. This process affected the North Atlantic world directly and most of the rest of the world indirectly. National political leaders and businessmen, who revved up economies to incredible productivity, competed to secure commercial routes, resources, labor, and capital, while the accumulated power, wealth, and status of the new liberal bourgeoisie, bankers, and speculators protected a narrow distribution of gain. In the mid and late nineteenth century, commercial steam vessels — regular, fast carriers of bulk and weight — drove sail vessels off the seas. Huge increases in production capacity and effective access to sites with large quantities of raw material and extensive consumer markets only worked meaningfully when the transportation network could handle large weights and volumes speedily and reliably.[6]

Large-scale production and worldwide distribution created the conditions for immense accumulation of wealth. Impatient, greedy accumulators of wealth employed coercion and bribery to induce people to work beyond the necessities and comforts. Various forms of coerced labor — slavery, serfdom, peonage, and prison labor — had existed for millennia, but these forms did not foster high productivity. Increasing productivity required convincing workers that they shared in the benefits of production and bribing them with an apparent sharing of economic, political, social, and cultural power. If challenged, the military technology of the North Atlantic states — smokeless powder; repeating, breech-loading rifles; machine guns; and exploding anti-personnel artillery shells — commonly resolved the disputes.[7]

The global depression between 1873 and 1898 transformed the world's economy and politics. This depression had three troughs in the United States: from 1873 to 1878, from 1882 to 1885, and from 1893 to 1898. The crisis of 1893 had a magnified impact because of the residual damage from the preceding downturns. The crises surrounding the War of 1898 — world depression, Cuban revolt, Philippine revolt, and the threatened division of China — were related to the high value which laissez-faire liberalism placed upon material accumulation. At the end of the nineteenth century, the industrialized and industrializing powers (roughly ten European states, the United States, and Japan) encouraged external expansion in an effort to control the demand of their political economy (the management of the resources of a people and its government) for increasing resources and distribution to supply ever higher profits, wages, and standards-of-living.

The industrialized powers looked for surplus factors of production chiefly in the unincorporated or poorly incorporated regions of the world because their business and governmental leaders, who espoused liberal ideologies, lusted for material accumulation, which they labeled "progress." The uncontrolled rapid economic growth created grave socio-economic problems. Some U.S. leaders responded to the disorder with social imperialism—external activity to reduce domestic disorder that grew from the social consequences of the free markets. These leaders were convinced that access to the assets in other countries, an "open door," was necessary for domestic order, well-being, and security. U.S. supervision of other areas, peoples, and strategic locations assured secure access to the factors of production and distribution. This course conflicted with the national ideology of freedom and liberty. It required antidemocratic, aggressive, and violent conduct; these characteristics are in conflict with the national self-image of a democratic, Christian, benevolent people.[8]

Social imperialism differs from most other imperialisms in one important way. Most imperial explanations see the less-developed (or peripheral in world system's terms) regions as sources of opportunity for members of a given developed country (called core or metropole in world system's terminology).[9] Social imperialism rests upon a vision of imperial expansion that is related closely to internal metropole affairs. Social imperialism thus elevates metropole domestic matters to the sphere of international problems. Under social imperialism, domestic problems of any kind can be converted into matters linked to any part of the world.

The common argument that foreign trade creates domestic jobs seems to function for advanced technological and manufacturing economies, but not commonly for peripheral societies. There, foreign trade transfers internal social tensions to politicians and workers less able (materially) to respond to the increased burden. The peripheral states in the circum-Caribbean and Asian basins possessed limited resource bases, smaller and less-educated populations, and less capital, communications, and technological development—yet they were supposed to bear some of the burden of metropole unemployment and social disorder in addition to their own. This social disorder abroad could easily trigger metropole intervention because metropole well-being is defined in part in terms of access to periphery resources. To give just one of hundreds of examples: Standard Oil marketed kerosene in China. U.S. workers were employed to supply this export market, but tens of thousands of Chinese farm families that produced vegetable oils for lighting and cooking lost their livelihood. As a result, a U.S. firm essentially exported U.S. unemployment, social misery, and potential social disorder to China (or to other states on the periphery).

The social imperial relationship relied on the dependent status of the peripheral societies. Metropole development in the competitive world economy required the underdevelopment of the periphery. If the periphery ever became developed, the option to exploit and extract accumulation from it—to resolve or ameliorate metropole domestic crises—would end. Social imperialism sheds light on the impulses operating within the metropole states, and dependency theory illuminates the international ties of the metropole-periphery relationship and the consequences of metropole intrusions into the peripheral states.

The search for more stuff to feed the mass production machinery and the workers who tended the machinery led industrializing states abroad; this transferred ever more of the competitive activity to the less-regulated international stage. The major powers in the late nineteenth and early twentieth centuries envisioned but scarcely implemented effective world courts, governing bodies, and executive authority. Initially, the attraction of the world's less-developed areas was precisely that weakness of courts, police, law and rules, and regulations; in short, these areas lacked supervising authority (they were closer to the law of the jungle). Examples of the strong substituting for the weak can be found in extraterritoriality in China from about 1830 to 1950, or the prevalence of English language, coinage, and judicial customs along the north coast of Nicaragua and Honduras. The weaker, less-experienced civil and military authorities facilitated "deals," concessions or paper thefts of resources, property, or labor value. This process, however, also left disputes in dangerous areas where force more readily ruled. Rebellions, regional conflicts, and ultimately world wars would settle disputes where police or judicial power was ineffective.

Well before 1898, the U.S. government assumed a Columbus-like mission in its westward journey. Westward expansion in U.S. history is commonly treated as a quest for land and freedom in a Jeffersonian agrarian world. But between the 1780s and 1806, Thomas Jefferson worked with John Ledyard, Meriwether Lewis, and George Rogers Clark to open the continent to the Pacific coast and to use land and water routes to tie the United States and the North Atlantic to Asia and the Pacific basin in pursuit of Columbus's dream.

The U.S. stake in the Pacific basin increased with exploration and westward migration. The U.S. government nudged the country relentlessly—the Louisiana Purchase, the War of 1812, the John Quincy Adams–Luis de Onís

Treaty, the Willamette Valley, the Mexican War, the Oregon Settlement, the 1849 gold rush, the free soil land policy, and Indian wars—toward the Pacific. North Americans engaged in merchant, whaling, fur gathering, and lumbering activity on the west coast of the North American continent, among the islands of the Pacific, and in East Asia.[10]

It was neither accidental nor odd that U.S. entrepreneurs and officials leapt to the west coast and established ties with the Pacific islands, China, and Japan before the west was settled. The sea was a cheaper and faster means of transportation from coast to coast than land. The west coast served the whaling industry with processing sites and lumber for ship repairs, barrel staves, and trade goods in Hawaii, Australia, and other places in the Pacific. Both Ledyard and John Jacob Astor expected to sell highly valued furs in commerce with China and Russia. The west and northwest supplied goods and services to the Pacific and East Asia.[11]

In the 1490s and the 1890s, fame and great wealth awaited the opening of a cheaper, quicker route to Asia and the whole Pacific basin. Whereas the sixteenth-century adventurers sought primarily luxury goods and souls to save, nineteenth- and twentieth-century visionaries and businessmen sought souls to save, luxury goods, raw materials, investment opportunities, and markets for manufactured products. Early maritime adventurers took considerable risks to reach Asia. Four hundred years later, U.S. expansion across the isthmus and into the Pacific basin entailed less personal and physical risk, but considerable strategic and political risk from great power competition.[12] The age of discovery gave way to an age of diversified economic, religious, strategic, and political ventures and conflict. The fruits of Columbus's vision included conflicts throughout the nineteenth century and even more intensive and bloody conflicts in the twentieth century.

Walter LaFeber's recent book, *Michael Jordan and the New Global Capitalism,* underlines the bogeyman hidden in the expansion of the U.S. political economy and culture. One story illustrates the concerns of late nineteenth- and early twentieth-century Asian nationalists. *New York Times* reporter Nicholas Kristof expected, before long, that Asian families would stop at their U.S. bank on their way to Wal-Marts to fill their Fords with Fritos and Snickers before going to a Disney film at a U.S.-owned cinema and, upon returning home, would check their U.S. mutual funds on America Online using Microsoft software in their IBM computer. And of course, the whole family would know English and would have visited Hawaii, if not the continental United States. Emilio Aguinaldo, Mao Zedong, and Ho Chi Minh and other Asian nationalists had perceptive visions, not aberrations, of such a future.[13]

CHAPTER I

Exploration and New Territories, 1780–1850s

꒯   Throughout the era of exploration, discovery, and colonization of the New World, expeditions searched for water or land routes to Asian wealth. The quest had always had plural objectives: China, Japan, Southeast Asia, Australia, New Zealand, and the Pacific islands. The chief problems in the Pacific region related to the geographical vastness; the inadequate navigational charts; the complexity of dealing with numerous, distinct indigenous populations; and the tense relations among adventurers, settlers, merchants, sailors, and missionaries from various imperial states. In the late eighteenth and early nineteenth centuries, various sea and land explorers—for example, Louis Antoine de Bougainville, Jean François de la Perouse, James Cook, C.A. Vincendon-Dumoulins, Charles Wilkes, John Ledyard, John Jacob Astor, Meriwether Lewis, and George Rodgers Clark—and a multitude of whalers and sealers supplied information and generated curiosity about access to the Pacific and about the Pacific basin.[1]

John Ledyard, who sailed in the 1770s with James Cook, the great British Pacific explorer, had noticed how eagerly the Chinese traded for furs. In the 1780s, he planned to return to China for a fur-trading venture, but in Paris, U.S. minister Thomas Jefferson enlisted him to cross Russia, sail the northern Pacific to Nootka Sound, and finally cross the U.S. continent from west to east. The scheme collapsed when Ledyard was arrested in Siberia and sent back to Europe.[2] But increasing numbers of dreamers, adventurers, and entrepreneurs hoped to link the New World to Asia.

Increasingly after the sixteenth century, explorers sought a canal route or a waterway that would cut the continent in two (such as Mexico's Tehuantepec Isthmus, Nicaragua's San Juan River, or Colombia's Atrato River). Proposals for transisthmian roads and, even more enthusiastically, railroads attracted investors and engineers in the nineteenth century. By the mid-nineteenth century, as historian Charles Vevier so aptly describes, U.S. geopoliticians had incorporated part of North America, the Caribbean basin, northern South America, and the isthmus into projects that aimed to open up the Pacific basin. Such ideas persisted until the Panama Canal was completed in the early twentieth century.[3]

Land expansion served an agrarian folk in the first instance, but successful farmers on rich lands needed markets to absorb their large harvests and to acquire the production of others to enhance rural life. Initially, the source of imported goods and the market for surplus production were across the water in Great Britain. Later, the routes from the east coast area to Asia went on water, over land, or via some combination of the two. Historian Foster Rhea Dulles observed that the "ambition to win the mastery of the Pacific and control its rich commerce runs persistently through the entire history of the United States . . . first awakened by the old China traders."[4]

The importance of water in early North American history has been obscured. Since the 1890s, Frederick Jackson Turner and other historians have emphasized the westward movement and diverted attention to land in the first three centuries of European settlement in North America. Water was not just an essential dietary component; it offered transportation, nourishment, and recreation. Many colonists lived from shipbuilding, fishing, and maritime activity.

Novelist Herman Melville captured the power of the Pacific Ocean's image in the mid-nineteenth century: "This serene Pacific . . . rolls the mid-most waters of the world, the Indian Ocean and the Atlantic being but its arms. The same waves wash the moles of the new-built Californian towns, but yesterday planted by the recentest race of men, and lave the faded but still gorgeous skirts of Asiatic lands, older than Abraham; while all between float milky-ways of coral isles, and low-lying, endless, unknown Archipelagoes, and impenetrable Japans. Thus this mysterious, divine Pacific zones the world's whole bulk about; makes all coasts one bay of it; seems the tide-beating heart of earth." His imagery reflected the aspirations of Columbus and the inspiration of the geopoliticians of the nineteenth century.[5]

The Hawaiian islands, the inhabited island group closest to the west coast of North America, were an early objective in the Pacific for U.S. expansionists. Explorers and seafarers knew this island group well since Cook visited them in 1778. The discovery of Japanese sperm whale fields in the 1810s boosted Hawaii's utility, and Hawaii became the principal base for whaling in the Pacific. The Hawaiian islands served about six-sevenths of the whaling industry for decades and attracted missionaries and merchants.[6]

One historian labeled the initial western contact with the Pacific islands "Resource Raiding." Since the islands had no gemstones or spices, and gold and silver were elusive, the newcomers hunted for whales, bêche-de-mer (trepang or sea cucumber), shells, and sandalwood. Once an island was stripped of resources and yielded little valuable cargo, it became a navigational hazard. While western captains and ships gathered the products of Oceania, all these products, except for whale oil, went to the China market. Another historian of U.S.-Asian relations described the consistency in U.S. policy in the Pacific basin: "We are now no less concerned than we were during the nineteenth century with the protection of our trade routes in the Pacific and our commerce in the Orient." He found this "motive behind every advance we made in the days of expansion and it remains the key to our present policy."[7]

Oceania was one of the last regions in the world that the imperial powers divided up. The French, more than the British, extended political control over Pacific islands. Initially, France was a reluctant participant in the exploration and exploitation of Oceania. Then French leaders decided that the naval and scientific information, the missionary activity, and the commercial benefits made the effort worthwhile. Once France entered the region, it sought competitive advantage. In the first half of the nineteenth century, the French government maintained a large squadron in Valparaiso, Chile, the center for French merchant operations. The South Pacific islands were the next logical area for trade or whaling. By the 1830s, French missionaries landed on several islands. French commerce had revived; its little whaling fleet, much smaller than the U.S. fleet, rivaled Britain in the Pacific, and its merchants had the largest share of west coast South American trade.[8]

Increased French economic activity encouraged thoughts of colonies. French missionaries and merchants acted energetically. In 1837, the French government, alleging an anti-French policy and the denial of religious practices, negotiated a treaty with Hawaii to protect the rights of Frenchmen. Since French Catholic priests and missionaries continued to complain, in 1839 a French naval vessel compelled an agreement to protect Catholic worship. The 1839 treaty brought extraterritoriality to Hawaii. Under its terms, Frenchmen would be tried by a jury of foreign residents rather than native Hawaiians. The French government also created a network of Pacific naval stations. In 1842, French admiral Abel Dupetit-Thouars proclaimed annexation of the Marquesas Islands, the major island group closest to South America. The French government, unwilling to hesitate before the British and facing an enthusiastic French public reaction, agreed to supervise (not annex) the islands. Napoleon III's restored French empire annexed New Caledonia in 1853. Later, in anticipation of a Panama canal, the French government formally annexed the Marquesas in 1880.[9]

The U.S. vision of expanding territory, commerce, and security interests, and an ill-defined civilizing mission, were rooted in the European heritage and by no means unique. Like the French, U.S. society entered the Pacific basin after the British, Spanish, Portuguese, and Dutch, but it quickly developed major economic activities there. And it soon stretched its western border to the Pacific. Many within U.S. society persistently strove to reach the Pacific. Among these motivations were visions of wealth from conquests, purchases, settlements, various exploratory expeditions, the tension between materialism and idealism, public policies of encouragement (such as the Homestead Act), the technological benefits of the telegraph and railroads, and continual U.S. activity in the Pacific basin. The Caribbean, economically and strategically valuable itself, also facilitated transit to Asia.[10]

From the late eighteenth to the mid-nineteenth century, three powerful maritime economic activities—merchant commerce, whaling, and sealing— stimulated U.S. businessmen to covet the western part of the continent with regard to utilizing the Pacific islands and Asia. In 1784, the first U.S. merchant vessel, *The Empress of China*, left for China. When it returned a year later, its 30 percent profit on capital ensured that other merchants would follow. The 1780s depression drove early U.S. trading interests to eye a China (Asian) market, just as the 1890s depression later revived strong interest in Asian trade. West coast lumber was another early trade product linking the North American continent to the Pacific islands and East Asia. The trade began around 1800 and became a significant commercial contact after 1830.[11]

Of the other two ocean activities, sealing was secondary to whaling. Sealing was a fur-gathering activity done sometimes by land-based trappers and more often by ocean ships. Furs supplied the principal cold-climate winter clothing. Whaling remained a major U.S. economic activity until the 1860s. By the end of the eighteenth century, the Atlantic whales were greatly depleted, so the whalers drifted into the South Pacific. The whaler *Amelia*, with a Nantucket, Massachusetts, crew, left London in 1787 for the Pacific. It returned with a profitable cargo of whale oil. In 1791 seven whalers left for the Pacific, six with crews from Nantucket and one with a New Bedford crew.[12] Pacific whaling and sealing grew steadily from testing business opportunities to significant enterprises.

The whalers departed from Massachusetts, but Hawaii became the center of whaling. Until the last third of the nineteenth century, whale oils lubricated and lit home and workplace. Highly valued sperm whale oil supplied light without smoke and was a fine lubricant. Certain whalebone (called baleen) supplied the stays for men's and women's clothes in Europe and the United States. The first whalers visited Hawaii in 1819; by 1822 over sixty whalers visited. By the 1830s, Honolulu and Lahaina (Maui) in Hawaii, San Francisco, Apia in Samoa, and the northwest coast became centers for provisions, repairs, whaling supplies, and rest and recreation, as whaling vessels remained in the Pacific for years to avoid the long and hazardous return voyage. Hawaiians served as crew replacements; in the peak years, about three thousand Hawaiians served on whalers.[13]

The United States initially had competition in the whaling industry because the whale oils and baleen were used widely in Europe. But the British essentially abandoned whaling in the late 1820s. By 1830 the Stars and Stripes had become the principal flag in the whaling industry. French and Germanic whalers competed for a distant second position, and many other nations engaged at least one whaling vessel, but U.S. whalers dominated.[14]

The peak of U.S. whaling occurred from 1830 to 1861. In 1836, most of the 460 U.S. whaling vessels operated in the Pacific. By the mid-1840s, the 650 U.S. whaling ships measured about 200,000 tons, with a value of $20 million. In the late 1840s, a historian of whaling noted: "No fewer than 722 of the world's 900 whalers were American flagged vessels, while a few of the others were owned or operated by expatriated Nantucketers." In the 1840s, the harvest averaged about $7 million annually in whale oil and baleen. At that time, the value of the whaling fleet and one year's harvest was roughly equal to the national budget. From 1843 to 1860, Honolulu and Lahaina received visits from about 425 whaling vessels per year. Whaling was a large-scale economic activity and a cultural icon visible in Herman Melville's *Moby Dick*, *Typee*, and *Billy Budd* as well as James Fenimore Cooper's dozen novels of sea life, whaling, and seal hunting.[15]

In the decades after 1861, whaling shrank in size and value as petroleum products displaced whale oil as illuminator and lubricant, and steel replaced whalebone stays in clothing. Yet, even late in the nineteenth century, whalers could be the gold diggers of the sea. In April 1890, the *Mary D. Hume* sailed from San Francisco and returned in seventeen months with $400,000 in cargo. In the peak years of the 1850s, over 400,000 barrels of whale oil were taken; in 1910, even using modern methods, the world only harvested 340,000 barrels.[16] While whaling survived as a niche industry, it peaked between 1830 and 1861.

The great powers used four activities—exploration, whaling, trade, and missionary work—to compete for influence, wealth, and local power in the Pacific. The people from the great powers in the Pacific basin commonly engaged in overlapping and intertwined activities. Whaling had ties to exploration and discovery experiences as well as economic history. Lewis, Clark, Astor, and naval officer Charles Wilkes combined commercial, scientific, territorial, and military explorations, which served U.S. objectives. Naval officers, fur trappers, and whalers desired protected deep-sea ports for new whaling and fur-gathering operations and to enhance security.[17]

The great U.S. Exploring Expedition from 1836 until 1842, one of the most productive exploration expeditions of the nineteenth century, served westward territorial expansion, whaling, commerce, and U.S. exploration in the Pacific basin. The idea for a scientific expedition had surfaced in public discussion in 1812, received congressional action in 1828, and then lay dormant until the mid-1830s. Personal political antagonisms shrouded the expedition from inception to completion. President John Quincy Adams initiated a Pacific scientific expedition, but his archenemy and successor, Andrew Jackson, delayed the implementation.

Finally, President Martin Van Buren overcame cabinet resistance and ordered the preparation for the expedition from 1836 to 1838. Naval Lieutenant Charles Wilkes first gathered charts and instruments for the undertaking in England, then headed the expedition. It had two public missions—to further whaling and commercial activity and to conduct scientific explorations. It was the first U.S. expedition to combine naval and civilian scientists. Van Buren underscored the importance assigned the expedition when he took several cabinet members to Norfolk to wish Wilkes and the venture well. In 1838, six naval vessels and several large launches began almost four years of crisscrossing, exploring, and charting the Pacific basin.[18]

Wilkes sailed an unusual route. Once around Cape Horn, he explored and charted in Antarctica and the South Pacific before sailing to the Oregon country. Then he visited Hawaii, and finally East Asia, Columbus's objective. Throughout its voyage, the expedition engaged in broad maritime tasks. Although the U.S. government only had a claim to the land north of the forty-second parallel, Wilkes's secret instructions charged him to determine whether the Columbia River offered an all-season, deep-water naval and commercial port and to survey the region from the Oregon country to the San Francisco Bay area to establish the possibilities for settlement and fur production.[19]

Wilkes investigated the great northwest with respect to, as he put it, "global policy and safe harbors on the Pacific shores." His navigational charts and an extensive report on the northwest revealed that treacherous sand bars at the Columbia River's mouth disqualified it as a good harbor. Wilkes found that the Juan de Fuca Straits further north offered excellent harbors for world trade: "Nothing can exceed the beauty of these waters, and their safety: not a shoal exists within the Straits of Juan de Fuca, Admiralty Inlet, Puget Sound, or Hood's Canal, that can in any way interrupt their navigation by a seventy-four gun ship. . . . there is no country in the world that possesses waters equal to these." He was convinced that, north of San Francisco, only Puget Sound could serve merchants, fur gathering, settlement, whaling communities, and the Navy adequately. Wilkes also sent a land party to explore and describe the backcountry south to the port of San Francisco.[20] Wilkes's glowing secret report impressed Presidents John Tyler and James Polk and stiffened Polk's resolve to demand the forty-ninth parallel. The acquisition and settlement of the Pacific Northwest owed much to Wilkes and the whalers and sealers from Nantucket. These adventurers had stimulated the imagination about the northwest and about Asian wealth.

Generally, the explorers, merchant crews, and whaling industry had a profound effect upon the indigenous populations of the Pacific. Wilkes typified the U.S. ethnic and cultural disparagement of inferior societies. He was bellicose toward the indigenous peoples in the Pacific. Historian of the west William Goetzmann saw that "behind this bellicosity was the feeling that since American traders, whalers, and . . . missionaries had increasing 'business' in this land of 'savages,' the natives had better be taught to respect and even fear them. Wilkes unabashedly put his scientific expedition to the service of white, Anglo-Saxon Protestant imperialism."[21]

Midshipman William Reynolds, a crew member for the expedition, confided to his diary: "I could not help thinking, how much better it would be to let them [the natives] go their own way, but No, No! We must have all the world like us, if we can." After more conflict, Reynolds noted: "Our path through the Pacific is to be marked in blood."[22] U.S. relations with indigenous peoples on the islands of the Pacific were similar to those on the continental mainland.

Wilkes fulfilled his commercial and scientific charge with agreements and charts. Novelist (some say the first U.S. novelist) and naval historian James Fenimore Cooper praised Wilkes for concluding a treaty with the "piratical" Sultan of Sulu, in which the sultan "engaged to afford full protection to the commercial vessels of the [United States], and all privileges granted to the most favored nations, and also to afford aid to the shipwrecked vessels of any nations."[23] Even more than the treaties, Wilkes served commerce and whaling with charts of the islands. Before the great U.S. Exploring Expedition, whalers had crudely charted about 400 islands. Wilkes replaced many of these drawings with excellent surveys of 280 islands and another 180 charts. Some proved remarkably durable. Wilkes's grandson, a graduate of the U.S. Naval Academy, used his grandfather's charts on his maiden voyage in the Pacific in the early twentieth century. The British navy used his charts until well into the twentieth century, and the U.S. Navy used Wilkes's charts for the invasion of Tarawa in 1943 and other World War II activities.[24]

One scholar noted that when the expedition returned in the summer of 1842, its "accomplishments were overwhelming. In addition to circumnavigating the globe, the Expedition identified Antarctica as a continent, surveyed many islands in the Pacific for the first time, and collected specimens in all branches of the natural sciences."[25] Commercial treaties and a magnificent scientific labor marked the apparent successful fulfillment of the expedition's charge.

Severe personal and factional politics, however, buried the scientific accomplishments of the U.S. Exploring Expedition. President John Tyler, who despised Van Buren, court-martialed Wilkes for insubordination and dereliction of duty. The court-martial was a fiasco, so the Tyler administration, unable to injure Van Buren's reputation, ignored the expedition's scientific and geographical labors. The collection of specimens and data found no home, nor were they offered adequate storage and preservation. The expedition's accomplishments would shine on Van Buren, so Tyler attempted to shove them into obscurity.[26]

The principal students of the U.S. Exploring Expedition gave the project very high grades. Several scholars labeled Wilkes "America's Captain Cook" to highlight the expedition's accomplishments. The vessels of Wilkes's expedition, in Goetzmann's calculation, had "sailed nearly ninety thousand nautical miles . . . charting hundreds and hundreds of islands, reefs, straits, harbors, and coastlines. They produced a stupendous array of charts for Antarctica and the Pacific Ocean, created the structures of modern anthropology, and contributed enormously to the institutionalization of science in the United States government."[27] Additionally, Wilkes's expedition played a significant role in the Oregon settlement and whaling and commercial arrangements in the Pacific.

The scientists of the expedition gathered 160,000 noted specimens. The specimens overwhelmed the national scientific community and the government for several generations. By 1856, the Smithsonian "Castle on the Mall" was built in Washington, D.C., to house part of the collection.

The magnificent and costly instruments of the expedition were not properly cared for and remained largely unused in subsequent decades. The first permanent astronomical observatory was created to utilize some of them. By 1874, when government funding stopped, the expedition's officials and scientists had published twenty-three volumes and atlases. The scientific material remained underutilized, however. Eighty years after Wilkes's ships returned, scientists were still sorting through the expedition's specimens and publishing work on new species.[28]

The most thorough historian of Wilkes's mission concluded that "the Expedition was a logistical and scientific triumph" that contributed "to the development of the naval sciences, notably navigation, cartography, and hydrography." This scientific expedition trained midshipmen and young officers and "served as a model for some fourteen subsequent naval exploring expeditions before the Civil War." At least eight participants became admirals, one oversaw the laying of the first transatlantic cable, and another commanded the North Pacific Exploring Expedition.[29]

Many who have written on the U.S. penetration of the Pacific have overlooked Wilkes's expedition, as naval historians generally prefer tales of military exploits. Wilkes's expedition engaged in some military action, but it was principally an exploratory, charting, and commercial venture.[30] Despite the commercial, whaling, navigational, and exploring roots of U.S. activity in the Pacific basin, naval historians commonly analyze this history through a distorted reliance upon naval engagements.

The work of the expedition marked the history of U.S. and western relations with Oceania and East Asia. It was also important to the settlement of the west, especially the decision to acquire Oregon, San Francisco Bay, and northern California, and to the history of maps, charts, biology, and ethnography of the Pacific basin. The expedition's enormous scientific success survived even the destructive inattention given it because of the Van Buren–Tyler political squabble. From commerce, whaling, and furring, U.S. interests competed with other great powers to measure and mark the Pacific basin and to extract a variety of products from the region to enhance domestic wealth, well-being, and security. The principal gap to full exploitation of the Pacific basin's resources and opportunities remained the inadequate transport between oceans. The North Atlantic states needed effective interchange between the half-globes.

CHAPTER 2

༒

The Great Powers in
the Caribbean Basin,
1800–1890s

ᴝ Throughout the colonial period and in the early decades of U.S. independence, North Americans and Europeans had clashed repeatedly in the
Caribbean area. The British, Spanish, French, Dutch, Swedes, and Danes
had all established Caribbean colonies to support trade, to find gold or a passage to Asia, to acquire cane sugar and other tropical products, and to trade
slaves. In the 1810s and 1820s, Spain lost its mainland colonies, but dreamt of
launching the reconquest of imperial glory from its islands. Meanwhile Mexico,
Colombia, several European states, and the United States lusted after Cuba
and Puerto Rico. Jealousy and competitive attitudes, however, helped Spain
retain its islands. The quest to reach Asia was common to Europeans and
North Americans. The route to the Pacific basin would pass through the Caribbean and across the isthmus. Leaders in most circum-Caribbean countries
and colonies expected to profit from that region's geography.[1]

While Mexico, Cuba, and Gran Colombia (modern Columbia, Venezuela, and Ecuador) had been principal centers of the Spanish New World empire, Central America had been a minor area with a long history of non-Spanish
imperial activity—Great Britain exercised authority in Belize, the Bay Islands,
and the north coasts of Honduras and Nicaragua. After the wars of independence, other industrial and commercial powers—France, Belgium, Germany,
and the Netherlands—sought influence, a business base, and investment opportunities in the Caribbean basin. Only about mid-century did the U.S. government and American entrepreneurs move forcefully to gain preeminence
in the area. The rise in U.S. power and activity became a cause for grave
concern among Caribbean and isthmian leaders.

Most Caribbean islands remained colonies of European powers, but Gran

Colombia, Mexico, and the Central American states obtained independence in the 1820s. These states had to protect their sovereignty at a time when the North Atlantic political economies were industrializing under classical liberalism (or the free market economic system), which taught a growth or decay dichotomy. Some of the turbulence in Gran Colombia, Mexico, and Central America in the mid-nineteenth century related to U.S. and European agents pursuing transit routes between the Atlantic and Pacific. The metropole and semi-peripheral powers sought cooperation with isthmian political factions that would grant control of land for colonies or transit. The foreigners also needed local land and labor for development, permission to extract raw materials and export crops, and conditions to facilitate commerce in the world markets. Such advantages would support their lifestyle, stability, and expansion.

The Caribbean islands, except for Hispañola (Haiti and Santo Domingo), remained colonies. Several colonies—the Virgin Islands and Cuba—entered the whirlpool of great power competition. The rising sugar production and disputes about authority in Spanish Cuba drew U.S. (and Mexican and Colombian) attention before the 1890s. The heightened expectations of a canal on the isthmus invigorated German and U.S. interests in potential naval stations in Haiti, Santo Domingo, the Virgin Islands, and Cuba after mid-century.

Mexican society suffered for generations from the long, bloody, bitter, and costly war of independence that was simultaneously a civil and international conflict. After more than two decades of fighting, the war sputtered to a pause in the 1830s, more from exhaustion than resolution of differences. The fractured and impoverished Mexican society had experienced the destruction of its agricultural and commercial capital. Mexico's farm lands had returned to wilderness, its tools and equipment were destroyed, its planting seeds were consumed, its animals had been neglected, its work force had suffered death, injury, and disruption, and its buildings, bridges, and roads had deteriorated. The chaotic decades had allowed many leaders to exercise greed, self-serving conduct, and to pursue personal rather than social objectives. Civil-religious disputes remained fundamental—at stake was control of education, public records, wealth, and property—as reformers tried to convert church wealth into social wealth.

The value of the Caribbean colonial empires eroded in the nineteenth century. The islands supplied markets for fish, lumber, flour, and cheap textiles (slave clothing) and were a source of slaves, sugar, molasses, rum, and other tropical agricultural products, but the anti-slavery movements disrupted the labor force and the profitability of the plantations. When sugar cane production increased and European science developed beet sugar, the value of cane sugar decreased. And after 1808 slave trade with the U.S. south became an illegal activity, so even the wealth from the slave trade eroded.

North Americans had long had a variety of interests in the Caribbean and recognized that their well-being was related to the Caribbean–Central American region. British and U.S. officials considered Spanish and French possessions in the Caribbean and on the mainland as potential religious or military threats. U.S. leaders, mostly Protestant, worried about papal plots as they contemplated a Roman Catholic power lying across the entrances to the ports on the Gulf of Mexico. These ports were the outlet for production from western Pennsylvania through the midwest to the continental divide, as well as much of the south. After the acquisitions of the trans-Mississippi and Florida (via the Louisiana Purchase [1803] and the Adams-de Onís Continental Treaty [1819]), the Caribbean islands dominated the U.S. commercial outlets from Brownsville, Texas, to Miami, including Galveston, New Orleans, Mobile, and Tampa. Later, as U.S. officials and entrepreneurs nurtured interoceanic transit plans, command of the eastern entry to transisthmian transit increased the value of the Caribbean islands.[2]

In the nineteenth century, entrepreneurs and investors from Europe's rapid industrialization looked to the Caribbean for raw materials, cheap labor, investment opportunities, and a cheaper, quicker route to the Pacific. European scientists and inventors developed land and submarine cable technology, coal and petroleum technology, steamship transportation, and the inexpensive, high-quality steel needed to run mass production machinery. Steam engines and other technology sped up production, thereby raising demand for raw materials, foodstuffs for the growing urban population, and wider distribution of the goods produced. Steamships promised more effective mass distribution, but they required coaling stations. A European influx in the circum-Caribbean challenged U.S. security and jeopardized the success of U.S. economic and territorial expansion.

The European metropole activity troubled U.S. officials and businessmen. Several policy statements expressed Washington's concern and defined a sphere of influence. In the 1790s, U.S. officials mentioned the "no transfer" principle (no New World possession of an Old World power could be transferred to another Old World state), and in the 1820s, President James Monroe pronounced a special U.S. mission in the New World. The Monroe Doctrine protected U.S. security and economic interests by preserving the political and territorial status quo in the New World from European powers (but not from the ambitions of the U.S. government). The Europeans rejected the Monroe Doctrine, but normally they avoided direct confrontation with the United States.

The competition among the industrial powers sharpened in the nineteenth century, and the widening club of industrialized powers increased the pressure on the limited factors of production (land, labor, capital, and distribution opportunities) that create and transport the raw materials and foodstuffs. Rising productivity moved people from rural to urban-industrial areas and thus decreased labor for food production as it increased urban demand for food. In the process, industrialization also removed land from production to build cities — residences, stores, public buildings, roads, and factories — and diverted land use to the procurement of industrial raw materials rather than food. In sum, there were fewer food producers and a reduction of agricultural land in the industrial countries, yet rising demand for food and agricultural raw materials.

Nevertheless, agricultural technology and investment increased production so quickly that prices fell. Politically constructed comparative advantages (tariffs, preferences, quotas, colonies) shifted some food production abroad. Meanwhile, U.S. officials and entrepreneurs competed, tensely at times, with European states to control or to share the factors of production on the west coast of the New World, in South America, and throughout the circum-Caribbean.[3] The North Atlantic commercial and industrial nations — Great Britain, France, Belgium, the United States, Germany, Holland, and Italy — desired to alleviate internal crises, and they were apprehensive about the alternatives of a newly industrializing competitive world — growth or death — that intellectuals and theorists, from Thomas Robert Malthus to Brooks Adams and Otto Spengler, found so threatening and ominous.

The Caribbean and Pacific basins offered amazing opportunities. The Central American societies had had limited contact with European or North American governments or entrepreneurs during the Spanish colonial years and the era of the Central American Federation (1823 to 1847). Before the 1840s, Central America had provided few products for the world market, and the metropole states had not begun determined competition for transit. When metropole competition for land, opportunities, and authority matured into the imperialism of the late nineteenth and early twentieth centuries, some foreign penetration was welcome and some was not. The opening of markets for local products in Europe and North America was welcome; the grasping for control of the best land, mining sites, and transportation routes was not. Imperial activity in Central America and the Caribbean became more intense, disruptive, and intrusive in the last quarter of the nineteenth and early twentieth centuries.[4] Entrepreneurs and adventurers from the liberal, industrializing states sought to extract value from isthmian agriculture and transit, often in accord with local officials or factions.

Two developments of the mid-nineteenth century left enduring marks upon isthmian history. Interoceanic transit projects, direct descendants of Columbus's vision of access to Asia, involved isthmian leaders, foreign governments, and foreign entrepreneurs. Mexico, Central America, and New Granada each negotiated several unfulfilled interoceanic transit contracts between 1820 and 1846. Then, around 1849, two major interoceanic concessions (both exploited by U.S. citizens) transformed the isthmian area. In Nicaragua, Cornelius Vanderbilt's Accessory Transit Company provided transit along the San Juan River and over Lake Nicaragua to the Pacific. Southern pro-slavery filibusterer (a private military adventurer) William Walker conquered Nicaragua in the 1850s to convert it into a slave plantation society and to control the transit route. And a New York group built a railroad across the Panamanian isthmus. Central America had experienced its first major foreign intrusions since the conquistadors. The Panama Railroad and Accessory Transit Company did not satisfy the transit needs of the metropole economies, but merely whetted their appetites. Since neither option offered convenient, cheap transfer of bulk cargoes, demands for a canal increased in the next half-century. Central America's second important role in the world economy began when some Costa Ricans opted for coffee production in the 1830s. By 1850 coffee was Costa Rica's major export crop. Within two decades, El Salvador and Guatemala had also introduced large-scale coffee production.[5] By the 1870s, transit and coffee had stamped the economic and political life of the isthmus.

The chief powers in Europe sought transit options and railroads on the isthmus, and support points in the circum-Caribbean. The Dutch obtained the first canal concession in 1830. Belgians operated a large colonization project near Santo Tomás in Guatemala in the late 1830s and 1840s. Britain bolstered its strong position on the Caribbean coast of Central America. Spain and France sought to use the area to revive past grandeur. German and Italian states, each moving toward unification, expected wealth and prestige from new trade and colonization activities. Numerous development proposals and get-rich schemes peppered the Caribbean basin landscape. Until the mid-nineteenth century, Europeans dominated the commercial, investment, colonization, and security interests in the circum-Caribbean. Certainly the expanding industrial powers wanted to stake a claim to isthmian transit.[6] But it was not a case of the more the merrier.

Even before the Monroe Doctrine, U.S. geopoliticians, businessmen, and military leaders considered Latin America their special preserve. U.S. interest in this region grew from U.S. domestic development as much as from external events, however. From the independence era, a bitter contest raged in the U.S. political economy between the remnants of a paternalistic and mercantilistic agrarian order (the slave plantation economy) and liberalism's system of industrial capitalism and agrarian staple crop production. Southern planters needed land to sustain the slave plantation order, while northern merchant-capitalists looked for markets, investment opportunities, and shipping connections over the isthmus to the west coast of the New World, Oceania, and Asia. Each perspective supported colonization and filibustering schemes to control Caribbean or isthmian territory. Both viewpoints illustrated the social imperialist belief that the Caribbean basin could relieve internal U.S. disorder.[7]

Historians have captured the romance, adventure, and dangers of the expansionism of southerners, some northern merchants, and western settlers. These adventurers plunged into railroad, mining, and canal agreements. They invaded Mexico, Central America, and Cuba. Some southern planters wanted access to new lands to relieve the pressure upon their way of life. One historian has described how the filibusterers pursued "Southern dreams of a Caribbean empire" in order to expand the slave plantation system. In the 1840s and 1850s, some northern entrepreneurs, merchants, and shippers supported filibustering ventures that promised to gain transisthmian access to the Pacific basin. Northerners and southerners schemed jointly in "manifest design."[8]

The traditional surpluses in agricultural products and the increasing production of some manufactured goods prompted the more farsighted geopoliticians and Manifest Destiny advocates to urge securing harbors in the Pacific trade basin. Admittedly, the U.S. economy had little capital to export. Much of that limited export capital, however, was invested in transoceanic communications in the Caribbean–Central American region—the Panama railroad, the Nicaragua transit route, and steamship lines. And laying the groundwork for U.S. expansion into the Pacific basin busied U.S. officials in the nineteenth century. Important actions in Oceania and Asia included Edmund Roberts's diplomatic mission to Asia (1831–1832), Lieutenant Charles Wilkes's U.S. Exploring Expedition (1838–1842), the Treaty of Wangxia (Wanghia) with China (1844), Commodore Matthew C. Perry's mission to Japan (1853–1854), and the missionary, whaling, and merchant activities. U.S. well-being and progress envisioned connections of the industrial and commercial centers of the northeast and mid-Atlantic states with the Pacific basin.

The geopolitical ideas of prominent thinkers and entrepreneurs in the 1830s to 1850s encompassed trade, colonization, and investment activity that linked the Mississippi, Ohio, and Platt River valleys; the Caribbean; the Central American isthmus; and the Amazon River basin with the North Atlantic and Pacific basin. Thus, even before the Mexican War, the secretary of the Navy declared: "The object of the United States is . . . to possess itself entirely of Upper California." Many U.S. leaders expected to acquire one or more prime harbors on the west coast—San Diego, San Francisco, and a northwest harbor—to serve development in the Pacific basin. The whaling, sealing, land acquisitions, and fur, lumber, and provisions trade had grown interrelated in the early and mid-nineteenth century.[9]

For many geopoliticians, military leaders, and entrepreneurs, the isthmus figured in their plans for communications between the Atlantic and the Pacific and East and Southeast Asia. Vigorous diplomatic activity in Central America—for example the [John M.] Clayton–[Henry L.] Bulwer Treaty (an 1850 U.S.-British agreement which neutralized competition for a Central American canal)—linked the circum-Caribbean and the Pacific basin. Beginning around 1850, the Panama Railroad Company advertised combined isthmian railroad and steamship services as a transit to California (the gold fields), Oceania, and East Asia. The early, successful Pacific Mail Steamship Company (PMSS) initiated a regular steamer service between Panama and San Francisco in the 1850s, and the Pacific islands and East Asia in the late 1860s (so the Panama Railroad could compete more effectively with the Central Pacific–Union Pacific line after it was completed).[10]

Access to the Pacific drew all great powers. In the early and mid-nineteenth century, France and then the German states followed U.S. maritime interests into Oceania from the southwest coast of the New World. In reality, German, French, and U.S. sailors were following Columbus's vision to sail west from the Atlantic to reach Asia. After the Napoleonic wars, the numerous German states, a new center of economic growth and political unification in Europe, anticipated opportunities in the Caribbean-isthmian region. Leaders in Prussia and the Hansa cities expected to expand their interests in Latin America. Since the 1820s, Hansa, Rhine, and Ruhr entrepreneurs used the local economies of the Caribbean region as a sponge to absorb small but growing surpluses in textiles, iron wares, capital, and population (German emigrants), and as a supplier of raw materials and consumption items to improve German lifestyles. Members of the traditional aristocratic, military, and bureaucratic classes gradually realized that foreign expansion could help combat the problems of an industrializing economy.[11]

These German leaders hoped that some of the outspoken unemployed and discontented people could be sent abroad. They also expected cheap foodstuff and raw materials to lower the domestic cost of living and thus undermine support for socialists. Foreign markets and investment would consume surplus capital, manufactured goods, and technology. Exportation would preserve jobs. And any policy that reduced unemployment, boosted the standard of living, and weakened social agitation and protest was assumed to have a dampening effect upon crime and social discontent. About 1851, Prussian privy councilor Franz Hugo Hesse advised the Prussian king that "German business activity and production are in the midst of irresistible growth, yet if this growth is to become a blessing and not a curse, Germany needs markets which could still be found in the Middle American states." Unfortunately, German emigrants often adopted other citizenship and were lost to the fatherland. Hesse aimed to preserve the allegiance of the emigrants, to build a powerful position near a future interoceanic canal, and to supply markets for German manufactures. He wanted "Prussia to turn full attention to the states of Middle America in the interest of German trade and . . . to protect German emigration and colonization."[12] In the 1850s, about two thousand Germans immigrated into Central America. In the 1860s, more arrived, building clubs and schools, engaging successfully in agricultural, commercial, and financial affairs, and permanently establishing German interests and culture in Central America.[13]

French leaders envisioned a great role for France. First, Napoleon's plan to rebuild the French empire in Haiti and Louisiana from the 1790s to 1803 failed, and then Napoleon III planned to resurrect French imperial glory and a liberal economic order in the 1850s and 1860s. Napoleon III's government sought acquisitions in the Caribbean, Mexico, Central America, Southeast Asia, Oceania, and North Africa. In the New World, it promoted "Latin" values to recruit allies to block Anglo-Saxon expansion. French propagandist and promoter Félix Belly claimed that Nicaragua, displeased with U.S. aid to filibustering, was ready to grant favorable transit and colonization concessions if Europe could assure its independence. He and Napoleon III argued that the weaker Latin American states looked to Europe, especially "Latin" France, to resist the Anglo-Americans.[14]

Not all European "Latin" states had good relations with their cultural relatives in the New World. Spain's relations with Mexico were strained, largely because Spanish royalists financed and encouraged the Mexican conservatives, who went down in defeat during "la guerra de la reforma" (an 1857–1860 war between Mexican conservatives and liberals). The Spanish government and church then aided the defeated Mexican conservative refugees and meddled in Santo Domingo on the side of conservative interests. Spanish royalists and religious leaders, unwilling to accept liberal rule in

Mexico, preferred a restoration of Spain's royal house.[15] Beginning with the New World's independence movements, Spanish leaders revealed little comprehension of the goals of Spain's colonial subjects.

The British remained the largest colonial, naval, and commercial power in the circum-Caribbean for most of the nineteenth century, but they had less interest in transisthmian transit. India was their target in Asia, and they already had access to India via the Suez Canal. While both France and Britain had invested in the Suez, the British had quickly gained control of the canal and co-opted a cheap, quick route to their possessions in South Asia. While Britain, the world's major investing nation, exercised political influence in the whole Caribbean region and participated in the search for interoceanic transit, its engineers were experienced railroad builders who distrusted canals. The British were thus reluctant even to see a competitive canal project completed. A second canal offered only costs to Britain and likely shipping advantages to its competitors. Nevertheless, all metropole countries expected their colonies in the Caribbean and in Oceania to benefit enormously if a canal were completed.[16]

U.S. officials responded at times to European challenges in the circum-Caribbean during the 1840s and 1850s with diplomacy. They negotiated the [Benjamin] Bidlack Treaty (an 1846 U.S.-Colombian canal pact that assured U.S. transit at Panama), the Clayton-Bulwer Treaty of 1850, and the [James] Gadsden Purchase (1854) of a narrow strip of Mexican territory on the Arizona border that was judged essential for the best southern railroad route to the Pacific coast. U.S. agents in Spain, Belgium, and France authored the Ostend Manifesto (1854) to induce Spain to sell Cuba.[17] Many northerners and southerners supported some of these initiatives to secure U.S. authority in the circum-Caribbean basin and to acquire the best interoceanic transit route.

Soon, though, the Civil War fixed U.S. attention inward and weakened the nation's capacity to resist encroachments in nearby areas. France, Spain, Britain, Austria, and Belgium took advantage of the war to initiate plans in Santo Domingo, Panama, Nicaragua, Costa Rica, Honduras, and Guatemala in addition to Mexico, thus testing the U.S. government's authority in the Caribbean basin. The Mexican intervention has attracted considerable attention because of its size, duration, and the illustrious personalities involved — French emperor Napoleon III, Archduke Maximilian of Hapsburg, Princess Carlotta of Belgium, U.S. president Abraham Lincoln, Confederate president Jefferson Davis, Secretary of State William H. Seward, General Ulysses S. Grant, and General William T. Sherman.

Despite the best efforts of Lincoln's administration to prevent the operation, Napoleon III cited "Latin" ties to justify French military support of the conservatives in Mexico. The French government, however, sought more than a "Latin"-oriented Mexican government. In 1862, Napoleon III outlined France's task in the New World to General Elie Forey:

> The prosperity of America . . . nourishes our industry and gives life to our commerce. We are interested in seeing the United States powerful and prosperous, but we have no interest in seeing that republic acquire the whole of the Gulf of Mexico, dominate from this vantage-point the Antilles and South America, and become the sole dispenser of New World products . . . and of the passage between two seas. . . . [But if successful in Mexico,] we shall have opposed an insuperable barrier to the encroachments of the United States, we shall have maintained the independence of our colonies in the Antilles . . . create[d] immense markets for our commerce, and will procure the materials indispensable to our industry.[18]

But the intervention in Mexico was only one instance of European opportunism during the American Civil War.

Napoleon III's plan to establish a foreign monarch for Mexico produced unexpected difficulties. Abraham Lincoln's government voiced grave displeasure. Spanish leaders had joined the intervention to reassert Spanish monarchical authority, but once it was clear that a Spanish prince would not govern Mexico, Spain withdrew and sought glory elsewhere. In 1862, Spanish forces reestablished order in civil-war-torn Santo Domingo, but they vacated the island after the U.S. Civil War. In 1863, Spanish forces searching for guano for fertilizer blockaded several ports in Peru and Chile and occupied one Peruvian island before retiring in 1866. Almost every Latin American state as well as the U.S. government protested Spain's role in Mexico, Santo Domingo, and Peru.[19]

The British government also withdrew from Mexico once it realized that Napoleon III intended to challenge U.S. security and political interests. A decade earlier, the British had decided to pursue economic benefits and interoceanic transit in the region without challenging U.S. security objectives whenever possible. They had no interest in building a puppet regime for Napoleon III and angering the United States. In the mid-1860s, British subjects pursued an interoceanic mail route and several transcontinental railroad projects on the isthmus.[20] But the British government refused to challenge U.S. security interests there.

Napoleon III's government, facing U.S. objections to the intervention in Mexico, wished to solidify its toehold in the Gulf of Mexico–Caribbean area. It therefore planned to reorganize Belgium's colony at Santo Tomás, Guatemala, one of Central America's better harbors, into a powerful naval station. France also pursued an interoceanic transit concession in Nicaragua as a further step to assure its power in the Gulf. The French cabinet recoiled, however, at a request for a French war vessel to carry decorations for eight Nicaraguans because the idea might suggest French protection, challenge the U.S. Accessory Transit Company, and provoke a new U.S. invasion of Nicaragua.[21]

Policies to emancipate the slaves in the United States were linked to securing the circum-Caribbean. In the 1860s, U.S. minister to Mexico Thomas Corwin, Postmaster General Montgomery Blair, Secretary of State William H. Seward, and others considered colonizing U.S. blacks in the Caribbean–Central American area. They expected black emigration to alleviate domestic racial tension and bolster U.S. strategic influence near potential interoceanic routes. But plans for black colonies in Mexico, British Honduras, Guatemala, Honduras, and Costa Rica collapsed when the American government insisted that the colonists retain U.S. citizenship.

Ultimately, a few hundred blacks settled on the isthmus or in the Caribbean, but not in U.S.-supervised colonies. After guided black colonies were rejected, Seward returned to the idea that investment, trade, and steamer services were more desirable than territorial expansion. He succinctly defined the more profitable view: U.S. leaders had learned to "value dollars more and dominion less."[22] In fact, a mix of both could serve U.S. interests best.

From the beginning, U.S. policymakers questioned the motivation behind the European intervention in Mexico. The intervention aided the conservative Mexicans and the Confederates, undercut U.S. influence in Latin America, and weakened liberal and republican institutions everywhere in the New World. President Benito Juárez, Mexico's dedicated liberal president who remains one of the nation's most popular, heroic figures, found moral and material support throughout Latin America and in the United States. U.S. and Latin American leaders, however, disagreed about the best means of challenging French intervention. Most Latin American states favored a Pan-American conference to determine cooperative, joint action, but the U.S. government refused to participate. U.S. opponents of French intervention organized numerous Monroe Doctrine leagues and Mexican clubs. The Lincoln administration did not assert the Monroe Doctrine by name, but it insisted upon the principles. European, Mexican, and U.S. pressure persuaded

Napoleon III to withdraw French forces.[23] In 1867, the conservative forces failed and Maximilian was executed in Querétaro.

Reducing European participation in the circum-Caribbean and augmenting the U.S. role were important goals for U.S. officials. U.S. industry had limited prospects for expanding sales in the highly industrialized and technologically advanced European markets. For U.S. leaders without the intelligence, courage, or moral values to use the domestic market to develop a just and humane society, Latin America and Asia offered promising opportunities to extract the wealth needed to sustain domestic material accumulation and well-being while generating only modest political and military resistance. Columbus's vision—trade with Asia—required cheap, quick communications across the isthmus. Since control of the circum-Caribbean assured access to the whole Pacific basin, European action in the Caribbean basin after the 1860s endangered the U.S. future in Asia and Latin America. Therefore, U.S. leaders needed to contain foreign inroads if the United States was to profit from an increasingly globalized economy.[24]

The defeat of Napoleon III's dream in the 1860s did not end Europe's expansionism. Italian economic and diplomatic activity increased, as did Italian migration to Central America. The British continued to trade and invest in the circum-Caribbean and worked to secure access to isthmian transit. The Spanish became even more active in commerce and investment. Ultimately, they turned to culture—the *hispanismo* movement of the late nineteenth century, which sought to revive pride in a shared language, history, and customs— as a strategy to preserve Spain's ties to Latin America in the face of the challenge of Pan-Americanism.[25]

Germany's economic and political activity on the isthmus grew in the nineteenth and early twentieth centuries. In the late 1860s, as Prussia unified Germany and fostered industrial and commercial growth, its navy, diplomats, and merchants searched for naval stations in Asia, the Pacific, and the New World. Chancellor Otto von Bismarck was attentive when Civil War general and speculator John C. Frémont offered to sell his "rights" to build a Costa Rican transisthmian railroad and a naval station at Puerto Limón to the Prussian government. Bismarck had Frémont and the site at Puerto Limón investigated, but premature publicity undermined any acquisition plans. Then, in 1878 the German government used a minor incident in Nicaragua (and related incidents elsewhere) as the excuse for a display of force to protect its honor and assure its opportunities. A half-dozen German vessels gathered off Nicaragua's coasts, and a landing party seized Corinto temporarily. Nicaragua bowed to a German ultimatum. By the 1890s, Germans controlled well over half of Guatemala's principal export, coffee. Germans were major merchants and investors in Guatemala, El Salvador, Costa Rica, Haiti, Mexico, and Venezuela.[26] To the alarm of the U.S. government, German ambitions in the region grew and prospered.

Napoleon III's Mexican mistake was not the end of France's Gulf-Caribbean ventures. Some French investors followed the organizer of the Suez Canal, Ferdinand de Lesseps, to a Panama canal project in 1878 that revived French commerce, migration, and investment in the Caribbean basin. The French also revived ties with Haiti and prepared their colonies — Martinique and Guadeloupe — to serve as naval and commercial stations for the canal venture. And a French military mission trained the Guatemalan army from 1886 until 1930, despite sporadic opposition from Spain and the United States. By the 1890s, France was the second largest investor on the isthmus and threatened Britain's leading position.[27]

The European powers recognized the value of the waist of the New World for extensive exploitation of the Pacific basin resources. The Suez Canal was not advantageous for North Europeans trading with East Asia, the west coast of the New World, and the Pacific islands. The Suez only offered special access to the east coast of Africa, the Red Sea area, and South Asia. By the 1860s, the center of European economic activity and wealth accumulation had drifted north and west from Spain and Italy toward Great Britain and northern Europe. The United States had also become a major economic power. This economic productivity in the North Atlantic made Panama rather than Suez the way to East Asia and Oceania. A Panama canal would bring Auckland, New Zealand, 500 miles closer to Liverpool than did the Suez.

In addition to frequently shortening the distance from the North Atlantic to parts of the Pacific basin, the Panama canal would offer a safer route than around the Magellan straits or across the Indian Ocean, where monsoons and typhoons endangered ship travel. The Panama route would make Wellington 1,600 miles closer to Liverpool than the Suez route. Panama could shorten the route from Liverpool to Valparaiso, Chile, by 1,500 miles, to Honolulu by 4,400 miles, and to San Francisco by 5,700 miles. A Panama canal would serve the principal U.S. ports very well. It would shorten the trip from New Orleans to Hong Kong, Manila, or Canton by about 2,000 miles. The savings in travel to Yokohama would be 5,700 miles, to San Francisco 8,900 miles, and to Sydney 5,400 miles. The voyages from New York to San Francisco could be shortened 7,900 miles, to Yokohama, Beijing, or Shanghai about 3,600 miles. Manila and Hong Kong would be roughly the same distance but generally safer over the Panama route.[28]

In the post–Civil War years, U.S. officials and entrepreneurs desired American-controlled interoceanic transit, so they opposed foreign presence in the region. The U.S. business community and politicians deeply resented de Lesseps's Universal Interoceanic Canal Company as a "foreign intrusion" in an area that they considered had a "special relationship" to U.S. society. In the 1880s, U.S. entrepreneurs, with some encouragement from the executive and legislative branches, obtained a canal concession in Nicaragua. But de Lesseps's reputation impressed even U.S. investors, so a U.S.-Nicaraguan canal drew little support from American financiers and politicians. Then, in 1889, de Lesseps's company went bankrupt. French and other European capitalists were not indifferent to the fate of the bankrupt canal company. The gross mismanagement of the project, however, poured cold water on various schemes to revive French or European financing. The project seemed dead.[29]

Great power conduct in the circum-Caribbean reflected competitive strategies. Frequently, however, the Caribbean–Central American nations suffered severely from great power competition. Leaders of the isthmian states adapted to the schemes of foreign penetration. Those who collaborated or were co-opted expected material benefit, security, and some role in shaping their societies, while the anti-foreign element encountered external political, economic, and military pressure that aimed to deny them control of their countries.

Leaders in the isthmian states expected great personal and national wealth from the transit projects. The states from Mexico to Colombia competed intensely for transit projects because, most likely, capitalists would only finance one canal and a few transisthmian railroads. Winning was the only thing; the other states could expect only crumbs. The French canal project failed, but the Costa Rican railroad, under the guidance of Minor C. Keith, a founder of the United Fruit Company, succeeded. After climbing from Puerto Limón to the east side of Costa Rica's Central Plateau (Mesa Central) by 1890, Keith decided not to extend his busy and profitable railroad to the Pacific. He feared that Costa Rican officials would take a livelier interest in his business activity if an efficient connection linked the Central Plateau to his empire on the Atlantic coast. In the early twentieth century, Costa Rica and Guatemala completed transisthmian railroads. Meanwhile, the U.S. government was concerned that the intensified economic activity in the Caribbean–Central American region would encourage a larger foreign presence, which in turn might threaten U.S. national well-being and security.[30] Keith's activity, however, reflected a worldwide surge of metropole activity in Africa, Asia, Oceania, and Latin America.

Isthmian leaders as well as metropole entrepreneurs competed for the

envisioned great wealth. Tension and conflict among the isthmian states related in part to the fights over interoceanic transit and in part to accession to
power on the isthmus. From 1870 to 1885, Guatemalan president Justo Rufino
Barrios's fixation upon a Central American union under his control generated
Mexican and Costa Rican resistance. Barrios distrusted projects in Nicaragua
and Panama that threatened to transfer the wealth and control of any canal to
non-Guatemalan or non-isthmian hands. His Guatemalan government became ambitious. It adopted land, labor, and tax policies to encourage "liberal" materialism (called "growth"). He planned to incorporate neighbors into
his vision, to prevent conservative backlash, to absorb Nicaragua and Costa
Rica into a Central American union in order to gain control of their transit
routes, and to deny Mexico access to a leading position in the area. Barrios
intended to preserve the region for Guatemala's "liberal" elites, especially him-
self, to exploit with the minimum necessary cooperation of U.S. and foreign
capital and technology. A Guatemalan-led Central American union in control of Nicaraguan canal revenues would triple the population and greatly
increase the financial resources available to Guatemala. Because such a union
might revive Guatemala's claim to the Mexican areas of Soconusco and
Chiapas, Mexico voiced significant resistance. Mexican leaders wanted to avoid
a powerful and unfriendly Guatemalan-led union on its southern border. U.S.
officials proclaimed neutrality in the Central American union plans, but they
opposed Guatemala's or anyone's compelling union by force.[31]

Several new capital-intensive, export-oriented activities developed on the
isthmus in the 1880s: first, banana plantations, and second, mining operations, such as the New York–Honduras Rosario Mining Company. Bananas, a
natural fruit on the isthmus, were traded irregularly before 1875. Keith began
systematic exportation of bananas in the late 1870s as a return cargo for vessels
carrying railroad workers and supplies to Costa Rica. Plantation production
soon displaced harvesting of free-growing bananas. In 1899, the United Fruit
Company was formed from about twenty existing fruit and steamship companies. Coffee, bananas, and minerals lay at the heart of Central American export activity from the late nineteenth century until after World War II. Other
export products—cotton, meat, hides, live cattle, and sugar—proved transi-
tory and secondary in producing exchange or attracting foreign capital.[32]

The small Central American states tried to play the metropole powers
against one another and thus create breathing space for themselves. In the
early nineteenth century, when Britain was especially dynamic and aggressive, they periodically sought U.S. aid. Later, when U.S. entrepreneurs and
investors became more aggressive, the isthmian states called upon France,

Austria, Prussia, Italy, Mexico, and even Britain for protection. Seduced by the competitive world system and the power of the industrializing states, the isthmian political leaders replaced subsistence agriculture designed to feed their own people with a plantation cash crop system to feed foreign markets.[33] Only after being incorporated into the world economy did they discover the severe limitations this change placed upon their sovereignty for self-government.

The aggressive U.S. role in Cuba and Panama disturbed many Latin Americans. Throughout the nineteenth century, Mexico and the Central American societies feared the idea of U.S. domination of the circum-Caribbean region. The concerns of Mexican leaders intensified in the 1890s as Washington officials discussed a civil war–torn Cuba. Mexican president Porfirio Díaz and many Central American leaders viewed the U.S. military involvement in Cuba in 1898 as an opening act to an imperialist drama in Mexico and Central America. Most Costa Ricans favored Cuban independence, but a larger number opposed any U.S. intervention in the dispute. Mexico reacted to the events of 1898 with what one historian labeled "'Cuba Shock': a sudden awareness of the danger of U.S. intervention in Latin America."[34]

Mexico, Colombia, and the isthmian states viewed a possible U.S. canal with feelings of opportunity and danger. They cooperated or opposed each other, but consistently worried more about a dominant U.S. involvement than about each other's role. Nicaraguans and Costa Ricans feared a U.S. isthmian canal because the U.S. defensive responsibility for the canal would threaten their independence. Mexican officials were especially disturbed. They sought to placate U.S. officials overtly, while subverting the U.S. drive for hegemony covertly. A secret Mexican agent operated in Nicaragua and Costa Rica to prevent support for U.S. conduct and policies in Panama. Porfirian officials assumed that any isthmian disorder might provoke a U.S. military response and thus jeopardize foreign investment in their nation's development.[35]

In the mid-nineteenth century, China, Japan, and the Pacific islands also shared interest in an isthmian canal and participated in New World development. The isthmian transit went two ways. People, products, and capital could flow west to east. Chinese labor built the Panamanian and part of the U.S. transcontinental railroads. Pacific basin laborers worked on isthmian plantations, on ship crews, and on projects along the west coast of the New World. By the late nineteenth century, the Japanese competed for transit, raw materials, and market opportunities in the Pacific basin, and they immigrated into the region. U.S. (especially Californian) and Hawaiian officials bitterly opposed the immigration of thousands of Japanese. Japanese officials meanwhile contemplated a role in a canal at Panama, in controlling Hawaii, and in building port and warehouse facilities in Mexico. All three matters provoked determined U.S. opposition.[36]

Liberalism promised material progress to the circum-Caribbean states as the result of railroads, harbors, mines, plantations, manufacturing, and urban development. Liberals or positivists, followers of French philosopher Aguste Comte's position that order, security, and progress best guided society, were especially prominent in Mexico, Guatemala, Brazil, and Chile in the late nineteenth century. Positivism persuaded caudillos or leaders to support growth and progress. However, it would not prove easy for domestic elites to retain control of the changing economic, social, and political direction of these transforming societies. Some foreigners clearly made great fortunes, some domestic participants (compradors) became wealthy, but the middle class and urban and rural workers shared at best in marginal fashion. And they were frequently not the masters of their fate. This imbalance left an enduring and unhappy legacy.

With the outbreak of war in 1898, U.S. expansion goals became alarmingly evident in the Pacific as well as the Caribbean. Despite U.S. attention to matters in the Caribbean basin, achieving long-term goals in the Pacific had not been forgotten. Alaska and Midway, for example, were acquired in 1867 to support trade with Japan, Korea, and northern China—not for their value as new farming or mining territory. Even before the isthmus was pierced by a canal, the Pacific basin had an increasingly militant U.S. presence.

CHAPTER 3

The Great Powers in East Asia and the Pacific 1840s–1890s

Early western visitors to Asia embellished the impressive realities with exotic and fantasy images. Adventure, beauty, and wealth lured them into deeper involvement and a search for a fortune. A major role in Asia seemed essential for great power status. The British, German, French, Russian, and U.S. governments expanded aggressively in the Pacific basin between the 1840s and World War I. German leaders judged participation in the world economy essential for prestige, prosperity, and security—to be one of the "Three World Empires" destined to survive the lottery of power.[1]

From its birth, the United States had participated in the Pacific basin. After U.S. commercial contact with China began in the 1780s, the U.S. government sought to formalize relations, to facilitate commerce, and to enhance security for traders and sailors. Between the Monroe Doctrine (1823) and the [Theodore] Roosevelt Corollary (1905), expanding global interests altered the U.S. perspective on the Pacific. In the first eighty years after independence, the commercial and whaling fleets and missionaries had built a strong presence on the west coast of the North American continent, on several Pacific islands, and in East Asia. Oceania and China grew as markets for the U.S. fur and lumber industries. But the Pacific basin was far from the east coast. It needed to be brought nearer with the technology of clipper ships and steam vessels and isthmian transit routes. By the mid-nineteenth century, ever more U.S. intellectuals, military leaders, and geopoliticians asserted rights and privileges for merchants, missionaries, sailors, diplomats, and travelers in the Pacific basin.[2]

Beginning about 1840, U.S. diplomacy labored to link the circum-Caribbean to the Pacific. The search for additional Pacific outlets underscored

U.S. desires for empire on the Pacific. Public and artistic activity incorporated a significant U.S.-Pacific relationship. While Herman Melville and James Fenimore Cooper characterized seafaring and whaling men, Walt Whitman envisioned empire in the Pacific. In 1860, Whitman's poem "The New Empire" captured the centrality of the sea at the heart of liberal expansion:

> I chant the world on my Western Seas; . . .
> I chant the new empire, grander than any before—as in a vision
>   it comes to me;
> I chant America, the Mistress—I chant a greater supremacy;
> I chant, projected, a thousand blooming cities; yet, in time, on those
>   groups of sea-islands;
> I chant commerce opening, the sleep of ages having done its work—
>   races, reborn, refresh'd. . . .[3]

The sectional crisis, however, threatened to destroy the U.S. march toward material and ideal objectives. The federal victory in the Civil War ended the internal threat to slice off the factors of production (southern land and black and white labor forces) and market area, a threat that would have limited the size, wealth, growth, and security of the United States.[4]

Of course, the United States was not alone in pursuing Columbus's vision. The European powers also strove to reach South and East Asia more efficiently. The Pacific islands only attracted much metropole attention in the second half of the eighteenth century as more European and U.S. vessels entered the Pacific from the east. Generally, only the materially successful nations could pursue Columbus's objective with urgency. Commerce instigated increased activity. German historian Werner Sombart observed the difference between securing and taking advantage of opportunities: "Earlier the state led the economy, now the economy leads the state."[5]

The North Atlantic states and Japan, following European growth, development, and material accumulation models, sought to connect the population and resources of the Pacific basin with those of the North Atlantic region. These states schemed to acquire rights to a canal route and naval stations in the Caribbean, Oceania, and along the coasts of the New World and Asia. In the late nineteenth century, multiple ports or small colonies were considered essential because steamship technology made numerous coaling stations essential.

In the huge expanse of the Pacific basin, Japan and China played important if vastly different roles. Japan's long history of isolation left it no acute record of conflict or memories of cultural bias and degradation in its contact with North Atlantic merchants or officials. It modernized and participated actively in the development of the Pacific basin, while China struggled to respond to foreign intrusions and civil disorder.

Historically, China's size and central location in Asia had stimulated the western imagination. Since the sixteenth century, Russia from the north and Britain, Portugal, Holland, Spain, and France from the west and south had pressured relentlessly to enter China's interior. Western intrusions grew slowly and steadily until the early nineteenth century. Although modest in number, the foreign intruders marked Chinese civilization.

Opium and what some called the opium of the masses—religion—defined the sharply rising tension between the west and China in the nineteenth century. Western merchants purchased tea, silk, porcelain, and jade, but the Chinese would accept few western trade items in exchange. Western merchants had to pay their unfavorable trade balances in gold and silver. To stem the drain of precious metals, the western governments and merchants insisted that the Chinese government accept opium—with a high value by weight and readily available in Asia—in partial payment for Chinese goods. The British, the chief traders in China and able to acquire large quantities of opium in India, insisted upon the opium trade to redress a persistent unfavorable balance of payments. The termination of the East India Company's monopoly trade privileges with China in 1834 increased the political pressure in England for action to assure that Guangzhou (Canton) was open to the eager, new, aggressive British traders and that they could trade in opium. U.S. merchants had already entered the opium trade in the 1790s.[6]

The western insistence upon the opium trade triggered the first major conflict between the western powers and China, the Opium War of 1838–1842. This war greatly eroded China's effort to hold the west at bay. Peace came in several treaties—at Nanjing (Nanking) with the British in 1842, at Bogue (Portuguese port of Boca del Tigre) with the British in 1843 (this pact incorporated the first extraterritoriality concession in China), at Wangxia (Wanghia) with the United States in 1844, and at Huangpu (Whampoa) with the French in 1844. These treaties defined special rights for westerners and allowed western warships to venture up China's rivers to protect missionaries. More importantly, these treaties essentially exempted foreign merchants and missionaries from Chinese law and authority. Naturally, Chinese officials resisted such an interpretation of extraterritoriality, but western diplomats commonly compelled acceptance of their version. Western diplomats, missionaries, and naval officials trickled into China before the first opium crisis and streamed in after. In post–Opium War China, the "alien dogs" (pit bulls)—missionaries, diplomats, merchants, adventurers, and soldiers—bit into China and marked the relations between the east and west for the next century.[7]

After the First Opium War, trade grew steadily. Historian Jonathan Spence argued that "the new foreign presence in China coincided with—and doubt-less contributed to—new waves of domestic violence." Meanwhile, western merchants and officials and Chinese government agents argued over the interpretation of the treaties. After the Crimean War of 1854, France and Britain renewed their attack against Chinese resistance to the 1842–1843 treaties. The Second Opium War (1856–1858) enforced the European version of the first agreements and extracted important new concessions from China. The Tianjin (Tientsin) Pact of 1858 included the most-favored-nation clause, many-sided extraterritoriality, consular courts, legalized opium importation, more ports open to trade, unhindered trader activity, and compulsory religious free-dom in China. China had to open a foreign bureau, drop the term "barbarian" in documents, allow missionaries inland, and permit foreign diplomats to reside in Beijing (Peking). Chinese officials continued to resist western intrusions, but gunboats and treaties commonly resolved disputes, and in that order. Decades of significant conflict with Muslims located in the west of China had weakened Chinese ability to resist western intrusions.[8] The west forced extensive transfor-mation of Chinese political, economic, and social life.

Since the British, Dutch, Portuguese, Spanish, Russians, and French had established trading houses and other connections in Asia, the U.S. govern-ment demanded equal treatment and sought enhanced opportunities for its merchants and missionaries. In 1845, the U.S. representative in Guangzhou (Canton) was elevated from consul to commissioner; in 1857 the agent be-came an envoy extraordinary and minister with residence in Beijing. In 1866, U.S. Minister to China Anson Burlingame proposed distancing the U.S. gov-ernment from some diplomatic excesses. He provided partial return of Chi-nese sovereignty in some treaty ports, granted the Chinese government the right to consulates in U.S. ports, and agreed to reciprocal freedom of religion. The U.S. government also conceded reciprocal most-favored-nation rights except in naturalization cases. Burlingame believed a healthy, long-term rela-tionship required more equitable treatment. His improvements faded after he left office, however.[9]

Opportunities for trade or missionary activity in East Asia improved. In the 1860s and 1870s, U.S. steamship companies and U.S. steamships domi-nated China's inland waterways. Washington offered the Pacific Mail Steam-ship Company (PMSS) a subsidy of $500,000 for twelve round trips a year if it started service by 1 January 1867. So on that date the first regular transpacific passenger, mail, and freight steam vessels left San Francisco for Hong Kong and Kanagawa (Yokohama). By the mid-1870s, Pacific Mail extended service to New Zealand and Australia. Soon the Occidental and Oriental Steamship Company—with wealthy major shareholders Leland Stanford, Collis P. Huntington, Charles Crocker, and Mark Hopkins—competed with Pacific Mail.[10] The Opium Wars and U.S. steamship technology opened new commercial ties and missionary opportunities.

Less than two decades after the Opium Wars, China's diplomatic relations with the world, its internal order and sentiments toward foreigners, and its commercial ties to the globe were dramatically altered. The U.S. and European governments demanded a Chinese diplomatic presence in the United States and Europe. The new western diplomatic power and trade increased the burden on Chinese society. The Opium War settlements disrupted China's domestic economy because the victors forced western trade on China and supervised customs duties. These trade and customs policies tore down China's protective tariff and devastated its handicraft and textile industries and other small businesses. The introduction of mass-produced articles destroyed the livelihood of many Chinese. Unemployment and underemployment rose and small businesses failed. Famine and starvation increased. The reduced consumer income shrunk the market for all other products and services. In the wake of economic disorder, banditry, vagrancy, and troublemaking increased. In the generation after the First Opium War, China experienced four major rebellions and scores of local disturbances that were inspired in part by foreign influences. Some traditional Chinese leaders hastily adopted aspects of western military technology and international law that undermined the very values they endeavored to preserve. The western victories in the Opium Wars complicated Chinese culture and politics.[11]

As the government weakened in the post-Taibei (Taiping) years (1861–1895), foreign capital expanded notably in China. In many operations, Chinese merchants, Chinese networks, and compradors played significant roles, yet with few exceptions the ultimate control rested with foreign firms. The foreigners insisted upon rules that further hamstrung the Chinese economy.[12]

China suffered a stream of foreign encroachment from the First Opium War until the Sino-Japanese War of 1895. Then came a flood. After the Second Opium War, the Qing (Ch'ing) pursued a modest reform program of accommodation to western forms. As early as 1864, Li Hongzhang, China's most prominent leader in the late nineteenth century, recognized the urgent need for reform and for western technology to help China survive.[13]

With a disrupted economy and significantly reduced customs revenue, the Chinese government faced a trade deficit, a budget deficit, and rising unemployment. It had little success levying taxes to cover the deficits, in part because foreign-controlled customs revenue was excluded. One symbol of progress in western eyes, the railroad, wrecked havoc with the traditional communications systems. The bargemen, cartmen, innkeepers, and small tradesmen engaged in traditional transportation suffered massive unemployment. These professions sank toward oblivion. The historian Immanuel Hsu concluded: "By the end of the 19th century, the country was beset with bankruptcy of village industries, decline of domestic commerce, rising unemployment, and a general hardship of livelihood."[14] Many Chinese officials blamed foreign penetration for the increasing banditry and the numerous secret societies that challenged authorities. Other Chinese officials and most foreign merchants and officials hoped more formalized ties between China and the west would rectify the disorder.

Belatedly, the Chinese government accepted the need to deal formally with foreign governments. In 1877, the Chinese named their first resident minister abroad in London. Soon other Chinese diplomats and students went overseas. The Qing built western arms manufactures and established schools to teach foreign languages. Despite considerable expenditure on foreign technology, the partially westernized Chinese army was defeated in two brief wars — by the French in 1885 and by Japan in 1895. The Chinese court and society struggled to understand these events. Among the explanations for the weakness were: the debilitating effect of concessions to western states, uncertainty about the value of Confucian and traditional thought, internal division, and the superiority of western ideas. Reform was discredited. For China's traditional leaders, the large expenditures in western military technology and the challenge to old ways had produced two defeats. China's inability to resist modern weapons sped up the foreign penetration. Yet, strangely, China's governing elite decided that the defeats proved the virtue of the old ways, not of the victorious western military technology.[15]

Western technology was prying open Chinese, Japanese, Southeast Asian, and Oceanian societies. In addition to the United States, China, and Japan, four European powers — Great Britain, France, Germany, and Russia — sought to exert preeminence over large areas of Asia and Oceania. Several other European powers — the Netherlands, Belgium, Spain, Portugal, and Italy — expected to assert authority over limited areas in Asia and Oceania.

The story of Germany (particularly of Hansa cities Hamburg, Bremen, and Lübeck, but also Prussia) revealed the rapid development of economic and political interest in the Pacific basin. By 1816, Hansa merchants imported tea directly from China. In the 1820s and 1830s, the Johann Cesar Godeffroy house out of Hamburg traded actively on the west coasts of South and North America. Soon Hansa and other German merchants, often sailing from Valparaiso, Chile, traded in the South Pacific and Philippines. When the British government, increasingly committed to free trade, terminated its monopoly of Chinese coastal trade in 1849, Hansa vessels quickly dominated the market. About 1850, Godeffroy sent its first trading vessel to the South Pacific. By 1857, its branch in Apia, Samoa, gathered copra—dried coconut meat that supplied oil for soap and candles—and conducted general trade. This firm transformed the economic history of the Pacific islands when it decided to build coconut plantations—that is, to own the trees and to hire labor rather than to rely upon native harvests. Copra plantations introduced corporate capitalism, sustainable production, labor-management relations, and worldwide distribution of copra oil. Germans soon ran plantations on the northeast coast of New Guinea and islands in the South Pacific.[16] Life in the South Pacific altered dramatically after the 1850s.

The opening of Japan and the Second Opium War elevated the interest of Prussian officials and German merchants in Asia. Prussia followed the Hansa states into the region because it needed them to support its domestic Customs Union (Zollverein) and its goal of a "kleindeutsch" solution in Germany (unification without Austria)—in opposition to the "grossdeutsch" version of unification under Austrian leadership. Austria, directing its ship *Novarra* on a world naval expedition in 1858, sought maritime leadership in the German question versus Prussia. Prussia responded. Its East Asia expedition of 1859–1861 incorporated half of Prussia's small navy. Similar to the U.S. Exploring Expedition, Prussian exploratory service in the Pacific made careers. Of the sixty-four officers and cadets on the four ships, twenty-three became admirals or generals, and two served as secretary of the navy. In the 1860s, Prussia tried to acquire naval stations in East Asia and Costa Rica to win support from the trade-driven states of northern Germany and to undermine Austrian leadership.[17]

German commerce was important in Oceanian trade from the 1850s to 1914. By 1860, German traders controlled about 70 percent of the foreign trade in the South Seas. This trade accounted for less than one percent of German trade, but the South Seas share of German trade grew. German investment reached 400 million marks at most. Competition among the great powers complicated Hawaiian and Samoan affairs. After 1850, German imports to Hawaii surpassed those of Great Britain. Prussia negotiated for special privileges in Hawaii just before unification in 1871, but the Franco-Prussian War, subsequent German domestic problems, and apparent U.S. willingness to offer Hawaii reciprocity killed the agreement. Once the Prussian treaty disappeared, the U.S.-Hawaiian reciprocity agreement died. In 1875, German merchants complained about Washington's plans to wrap Hawaii into a U.S. most-favored-nation treaty. German plans included other islands as well. In 1876 Germany negotiated use of Tonga's Vava'u harbor as a coaling station in exchange for recognition of Tongan nationhood.[18] Hawaii and various South and Central Pacific islands continued to hold commercial interest to Germany.

German activity in the Pacific islands grew more determined in the 1870s and 1880s, and Hansa traders crept north into the Central Pacific. Historian Hans-Ulrich Wehler noted the competition: "The rising English-U.S. rivalry in the Pacific, which clearly increased after the beginning of the 1870s, quickly grew into an international competition as first the German Empire, then France again appeared on the stage in service of their merchants. . . . German interests clearly stood out . . . in the Malaya peninsula and in Micronesia, Melanesia, and Polynesia. And it drew the first governmental supporting activity in its trail."[19] German politician Friedrich Fabri and others considered "overpopulation, overproduction, and surplus capital" the cause of the German economic and social crises. These weaknesses required German overseas expansion to alleviate disorder.[20]

As the Germans developed trade centers, plantations, and naval coaling stations in the Pacific basin, German leaders looked for additional unclaimed territories in the South Seas (and Africa) that the German empire could claim. Southeast Asia and the German colony of New Guinea were important for raw materials and as trading centers for Germany's South Pacific and East Asian trade. German merchants, however, encountered problems in the 1870s and 1880s with Spain's tariff laws and customs officials in the Philippines and Central Pacific. An 1877 agreement prevented Spain from levying tolls where it had no officials. To block German merchants, in 1879 the Spanish declared their Philippine customs effective in the Caroline Islands. Then, in August 1885, an ambitious captain raised a German flag on Yap, already claimed by Spain. The Spanish government protested. Through papal mediation, Germany got settlement rights, free trade, and a naval station in the Carolines, but Spain retained sovereignty. Still, by the 1880s Germans controlled about 80 percent of all foreign trade in the Carolines and Marianas. The desire for trade with the Philippines smoldered.[21]

German traders and planters had particular interest in Samoa and the Marshalls. The Marshall Islands were annexed in October 1885, after the largest German trading firms claimed such a policy would be particularly proper. German and U.S. competition in Samoa accelerated. German merchants wanted copra plantations, and U.S. officials wanted to formally annex the deepwater harbor at Pago Pago (the U.S. government had acquired the right to build a naval station there in 1878). On 14 June 1889, the British, Americans, and Germans avoided war by fashioning a tripartite protectorate over Samoa. Annexation was attractive because the copra price remained high despite an international economic crisis.[22] The Marshalls and Samoa remained areas of multiple foreign interests into the late nineteenth century. German merchants expanded relentlessly in the South and Central Pacific islands from the 1860s to the 1890s.

The Franco-Prussian War of 1870–1871 offered an opportunity to transform French and German relations in Asia, but the changes turned out to be modest. France remained active in the Pacific and especially in Southeast Asia, and Germany increased its activity after 1871. Thus Franco-German tension was transported to the Pacific basin. French interests expected Ferdinand de Lesseps's Panama canal to bring advantages to French activities in the Caribbean, the South Pacific, and Southeast Asia. For example, the French government asserted national interests in a proposed railroad from Tonkin to China's Yunnan province. Resulting French-Sino tension erupted into conflict, and the French drove the Chinese army from Tonkin in 1885. This French victory persuaded the European powers that China was ripe for railroads and development projects. More intense French activity in Southeast Asia and Panama reflected, perhaps, the need to find raw materials within the French colonies to replace those lost with the transfer of Alsace-Lorraine to Germany. Historian Jacques Binoche-Guedra concluded: "The primary function of colonies within the French economy seems to have been to sustain the fragile or declining industrial sectors."[23] Such a policy worked best if France controlled support points, communications stations, and a great power position in the world.

Among the Anglo-Saxon powers in the Pacific in the late nineteenth century, the United States, Australia, and New Zealand were expansive, while Great Britain exercised restraint. Australian officials considered the attempts of foreign powers to acquire South Pacific islands a means to transfer European conflicts and ambitions into the South Pacific. The British did view the islands as pawns to bargain with for more vital territorial or diplomatic matters. Australian nationalism exhibited equivalents to Manifest Destiny and the Monroe Doctrine for the South Pacific. To shield their homelands, Australia and New Zealand pressured the British to annex Fiji and New Guinea. One Australian historian distinguished the U.S. version from "Australian spread-eagleism [which] did not in any significant degree reflect an aggressive and self-righteous democratic morality." Australian annexationism was defensive; they intended to keep other foreign powers at a distance.[24] Of course, the Monroe Doctrine had a similar objective for the United States in the western hemisphere.

U.S. interest in East Asia and the Pacific was demonstrated through its conduct toward Hawaii, Japan, and Korea, and the acquisitions of Alaska, Midway, and part of Samoa. American consular officials, naval officers, and entrepreneurs also intervened and used, or threatened to use, force frequently in Southeast Asia during the nineteenth century. U.S. policy followed the British and French in Asia initially, but after mid-century America exercised initiative. Washington brought the treaty port system—the western imperialist product of the two Opium Wars—to Siam (1855), Japan (1858), and Korea (1882). With enormous populations and abundant resources, Oceania and Asia had a high risk/reward profile for those seeking spectacular material rewards.[25]

Hawaii, geographically isolated from any continent or island group, held special attraction for any power seeking to build a Pacific basin presence. Beginning in the late 1840s, Hawaiian foreign trade shifted steadily to the U.S. west coast, but Hawaii continued to serve the Pacific basin as a central point for migration, trade, communication, and whaling.[26] Hawaii and other islands in Oceania remained attractive to adventurers, self-servers, the curious, and the greedy.

Hawaii's potential for commerce or colonization appealed to the Asian states also. Chinese immigrants had formed a modest part of Hawaii's population since the mid-nineteenth century, about 10 percent in 1878 and 22 percent in 1884. In the mid-1880s, Japanese immigrants also arrived in large numbers. Japanese leaders expected the resettling of Japan's surplus population to be a source of strength and potential wealth. By 1890, Japanese made up almost 14 percent of the island's population. The Chinese and Japanese immigrant shares of Hawaii's population were:

Hawaii	1878	1884	1890
Total population	58,000	80,500	89,990
Number and % Chinese	5,916 (10.2 %)	17,937 (22.3%)	15,301 (17.0%)
Number and % Japanese	—	116 (0.1%)	12,360 (13.7%)

Hawaiian leaders feared mounting Japanese immigration and trade, and Tokyo's insistence upon the rights of Japan's nationals in Hawaii.[27]

Asian and Oceanian participation in the development of the Pacific basin is often overlooked. Chinese labor built the Panama, U.S.–Central Pacific, and several west coast railroads in Latin America. Chinese and Pacific islanders worked in mines and on coffee and other agricultural plantations in Mexico, Guatemala, Nicaragua, and Costa Rica. The Chinese came mostly as coolie labor, but the Japanese arrived as farmers, merchants, or craftsmen. Many U.S. citizens and officials viewed this Chinese and Japanese expansion eastward as a grave threat to U.S. interests.

A variety of interests moved North Americans westward. Merchants, seamen, and diplomats were not the only North Americans active in the islands and mainland of the Pacific basin. Expanded contact with inhabited islands awoke the interest of religious bodies. Whaling brought missionaries to tend the souls of the sailors and the indigenous. The historian Ralph Kuykendall observed that starting in 1819: "The American missionaries were quietly but certainly getting a foothold in [Hawaii]." Perhaps the most enduring western-indigenous contact in the Pacific islands was not religion, however, but between white men and indigenous women.[28]

Among the foreign influences in Oceania and Asia, Christian missionary activity was perhaps the most pernicious. In Oceania, missionaries from all countries filled larger roles than merely spreading the gospel. They taught, healed, preached, advocated ethical conduct, and encouraged sincerity. The principal Protestant agencies were the London Missionary Society and the American Board of Commissioners for Foreign Missions. The missions sought to penetrate local society with elements of western civilization and to expand formal control, while the indigenous peoples tried to play the missions against each other to extract the best result. Missionaries also became intermediaries between companies and islanders: "Swindlers and saints alike depended on island power-holders." Assimilated cultural values and economic power, nevertheless, limited the role of missionaries. When Christianity and commerce clashed, God's agents often redefined His wishes to accommodate sound business practices.[29]

The special role for French missionary activity—represented through a wide variety of religious orders—influenced French policy in East Asia and the Pacific islands. The French missionaries were active in Indo-China, China, New Caledonia, Tahiti, Tonga, and New Guinea. Both British and French religious people struggled in the New Caledonias until Rear Admiral Auguste Febvrier-Despointes raised a French flag and annexed the islands on 24 September 1853. Despite this action, a French priest did not arrive until 1883. Tahiti's English pastors had that island's first French missionaries expelled, but finally, in August 1838, Admiral Abel Dupetit-Thouars compelled Tahitian queen Pomare IV to accept French Catholic missionaries and to respect the rights of French subjects. In June 1880, the French annexed Tahiti. Tonga, under missionary domination, had a large percentage of professed Christians by the turn of the century. The French Catholics who founded missions on New Guinea in 1847 labored about three decades before Protestant missionaries arrived.[30] French use of nationalism and religion to bolster its position in the Pacific basin encountered other great powers in opposition.

The German latecomers quickly assumed a major role in Pacific affairs, at first through merchant entrepreneurs and then the German navy. Germans placed a low value on missionary activity, so foreign missionaries often served in German influence areas. In 1858 the English-language Boston Mission established a station in the Marshalls, where German missionaries only visited. An agent of the Stapenhorst and Hoffschläger firm arrived in 1863 to trade. The Germans worked with the Boston Mission as partners in the Marshalls because no German missionaries were found to replace them. The German businessmen reluctantly accepted the Americans, despite their poor ability to teach the natives German, for the missionaries opposed alcohol and encouraged work and modest, moral conduct. Still, the Boston Mission presence in a German trading area produced tension in cultural, political, and economic spheres.[31]

Missionaries commonly served as moral authorities and tamers of disgruntled laborers. One scholar relished the irony of ascetic, puritanical Boston missionaries striving to convert "extroverted, lusty islanders of the Carolines and Gilberts" to a this-worldly behavior pattern of asceticism, pacifism, and preparation for the next world. For decades the London Missionary Society had produced English-speaking workers for the German colony in Samoa. German missionaries only arrived in 1879. Despite the strain between British and American missionaries and German officials in Samoa, a reciprocal relationship developed. The missionaries relied upon the government for law and order, and the government relied upon the missionaries for education, socialization, westernization, and some German language training. In search of a reliable and productive labor force for Samoa, Germans first banned alcohol, then allowed beer sales after 1898 because the German Tsingtao brewery on the Shandong peninsula needed markets. The German government did not allow its desire for a managed labor force to prevent the parts of its empire from cooperating. The colony in Shandong was more important than the colony at Samoa, so the need for a docile Samoan labor force had to adjust to Shandong's development.[32]

Roman Catholic missionaries had limited access to China for several centuries, and the first Protestant missionaries arrived in China in 1829. Overall, however, Christianity appeared socially disruptive and divisive to the Chinese. In historian Immanuel Hsu's judgment, "Christianity, as a 'heterodox' faith in China, became a basic cause and focus for anti-foreignism." Hsu has reminded us: "Imbued with the teaching of Confucianism, Taoism, and Buddhism, the Chinese resented the invasion of Christianity under the protection of gunboats." Missionaries were hated because they relied upon intervention to protect them, and they constantly sought special advantages. Foreign interference in Chinese social, cultural, and economic activity and disparagement of things Chinese stepped up in the late 1850s and again in the 1890s.[33]

Historian Joseph Esherick described the mounting tension as western missionaries disrupted Chinese society. The missionaries, sheltered by diplomats and naval forces, moved freely about China but won few converts. They commonly attracted the criminal, the disgruntled, and the marginal and weak members of communities because the missions offered them food, shelter, and, most importantly, some protection from local officials. The Chinese called the converts men who "eat by religion" since they lived off church wealth. Many converts accepted money from the church, bullied their fellow countrymen, and then used missionary intervention to avoid punishment for their conduct. In Hsu's critical view: "The public demonstration by the missionaries of their protective power, influence, and wealth attracted the weak and the opportunistic to the church but repelled the strong and the proud."[34] This pattern generated disgust toward many missionaries and their followers, and ultimately retribution.

Missionary work's progress was exceedingly slow in China. Generally, Christian missionaries were quite successful in Japan until the 1880s. At the same time, they became more numerous and disruptive for China. In Japan the converts remained nationalists, but the widespread reaction against reform and westernization isolated the converts in China. The missionaries presumed that they were liberating Asians from degenerate and decadent cultures. A Philippine historian described the altered perception of missionaries and their supporters from the "imperialism of righteousness" to the "righteousness of imperialism" around the turn of the century.[35]

Nineteenth-century American and British missionary work was closely linked to domestic social reform, but the slums of Pittsburgh and Manchester differed from Chinese villages and Pacific islands. U.S. missionary activity was given new urgency about 1890 when the Student Volunteers for Foreign Missions channeled youth toward missions. During the late nineteenth and early twentieth centuries, American churches under progressive influence became increasingly interested in "the social gospel" (addressing social conditions of urban workers in order to get them back to church) reform of politics, poverty, slums, and injustices. U.S. missionaries under this influence addressed secular topics as well as salvation. Much of the new missionary fervor was directed toward a Chinese society in crisis. Progressive Chinese wanted radical reform, but reactionaries and nationalists vented their wrath by attacking foreigners, especially missionaries. Earlier missionaries had gained the trust of the Chinese through their personality and scientific capability. From the mid- to late nineteenth century, these new missionaries entered and functioned behind the protection of gunboats.[36]

Missionary activity was a recurring source of tension not only between westerners and Chinese, but among the western governments supporting missionaries. The Treaty of Tianjin compelled China to permit Chinese to convert to Christianity. Initially Portuguese officials, then French ones, monitored western missionaries and issued internal religious passports to all missionaries in China. The French struggled to retain control of missionary passes. In 1889, however, the German government insisted on registering German missionaries in its consular books. In 1890, the German Empire, in a social imperialist step, assumed protection of the Catholic church in Shandong to demonstrate to the German Catholic states the government's interest in their affairs.[37] The great powers even competed over missionary activity.

Missionaries themselves often obscured the impact of the missionary activity by writing glowing reports home to promote their work. Few people in the United States understood how little the philanthropic missionary efforts were related to Chinese aspirations, or how they burdened U.S. diplomatic relations. In the late 1870s, U.S. Minister in China George Seward complained that U.S. diplomatic and consular agents were occupied chiefly with responding to incidents with missionary roots, and thus the U.S. government became the chief defender for propagating the Christian faith.[38] Missionary activity drew upon the spirit of foreigners rather than any needs in Chinese society.

Western missionaries, military men, and diplomats markedly influenced the east-west relationship, and they created openings for technology, culture, and business. The western powers tried to shove China into a western mold. One historian summarized the burden of foreign imperialism upon late-nineteenth-century China: "Victorious in a series of wars, the Western powers had imposed their presence on China and . . . invest[ed] heavily in the country, especially in mines, modern communications, and heavy industry. The impact of foreign imperialism was profound, intensifying tensions already generated by the self-strengthening movement." In the treaty cities, compradors—

Chinese merchants who served as intermediaries between foreign importers and Chinese retailers—conducted foreign business. Foreigners were seldom seen in Chinese cities, and when seen, they were regarded as exotic or menacing. Even those Chinese involved in diplomacy—considered a contaminating contact with foreigners—were often disparaged and humiliated upon their return.[39]

Before 1890 Chinese influence crumbled in the southern and northern border regions. In the south, the British and the French were the chief foreign actors. In the Chefoo Convention of 1876, the British obtained more open ports on the Yangzi and the right to reside in Yunnan province. The French and Chinese clash in 1884–1885 ended Chinese suzerainty in northern Vietnam, and in 1887 the British eliminated Chinese influence in Burma. That same year, Portugal received the permanent concession of Macao, formerly a leased territory. In the north, Russia, Germany, Japan, and Britain demanded more rights. Russia expanded into Mongolia and Turkestan. Germany eyed the Shandong peninsula. The British valued Weihaiwei. Japanese influence grew in Korea.[40] The metropoles were eroding Chinese authority.

In Japan, authority was modernized and centralized under the Meiji reform. When gunboat diplomacy had entered Japan in the 1850s and 1860s, foreign culture and conduct challenged domestic culture and conduct. The Meiji leaders responded to western imperialism by building a strong government and expanding. Historian Marius Jansen concluded that "Japan's imperial expansion began before its industrial growth." Direct resistance to the west seemed futile and dangerous; an option was to emulate western techniques. Japan used state power to gain material advantage from less-developed peoples. Japanese religious groups, like the principal western religions, were unlikely to oppose expansion. Shinto, which became the state religion in the 1880s, described the extension of Japan's perfect governance to neighbors as an act of generosity. Western imperialism had a large, ironic role in Japanese modernization because only radical reform promised defense against the danger imperialism posed. Most Japanese welcomed expansion and accepted the costs involved to achieve greatness.[41]

The "most distinctive feature of Japanese imperialism," according to one prominent historian, "is that it originated within the structure of informal empire which the West established"—the treaty port system in Japan and China. The bulk of the Japanese empire was compact and close to the metropole. Only the South Pacific islands were distant and dispersed. Japanese training cruises first visited the South Pacific in 1875. In 1884, the Japanese government immediately disavowed two officials who raised the Japanese flag over atolls in the Ralik chain. In the late 1880s, a Japanese trading mission visited the South

Pacific. Japanese attitudes toward colonial governance envisioned an Asian empire of common cultural heritage, racial kinship, and strategic consider-ations.[42] The South Pacific stretched original Japanese expansion goals.

Western expansion was closing the options for Japanese expansion in Asia. An 1887 memo by Foreign Minister Inoue Kaoru concluded: "We have to establish a new, European-style empire on the edge of Asia." In *Imperialism: The Spectre of the Twentieth Century*, written a year before the British intel-lectual John Hobson wrote his classical study of imperialism, Kotoku Shusui called imperialism amoral and found Japanese imperialism militaristic and jingoistic, the least admirable characteristics of selfish man. Still, most Japa-nese leaders accepted social Darwinism as the basis for Japanese expansion and the idea that both democratic and autocratic governments expanded. As a once-passive spectator to western expansion in Asia, Japan pursued the idea of reforming itself and its neighbors to gain protection against the west.[43]

The drama of Japanese expansion took form in the late nineteenth cen-tury in Korea. After decades of dispute over the control of Korea, China and Japan went to war in late July 1894. The Japanese military surprised observers with its fighting capabilities. The Chinese forces, meanwhile, proved unfit for modern warfare. Corruption and tradition had kept the Chinese army and navy from modernizing. The Chinese army lacked adequate medical, com-munications, and logistics services. The navy had been granted 36 million taels for modernization, but Empress Dowager Cixi took the funds for her pleasure. The navy fought one day and then no more. The war ended quickly and Japan leveled harsh demands.[44]

With a Japanese victory assured, the European powers each looked for their share of the pie. On 30 March 1895, the Russian government had warned Japan not to disturb the status quo in Liaodong (Liaotung), where Russian interests were expanding. The Dual Alliance bound France to Russia. The German government welcomed Russian engagement in Asia rather than in Central and Southeast Europe, where Russian Pan-Slavic policies threatened Germany's Hapsburg ally, the Austro-Hungarian empire. Japan ignored the Russian warning. On 23 April 1895, six days after the Sino-Japanese War ended, the Triple Intervention—Russia, France, and Germany—warned Tokyo that Japanese possession of the Liaodong peninsula would menace Beijing, mock the independence of Korea, and threaten peace in the Far East. Japan reluc-tantly returned Liaodong in exchange for an additional 50 million taels of indemnity.[45] Many Japanese resented what they considered public humilia-tion and the loss of advantages obtained with blood and treasure.

China had more fortune in peace than in war. Japanese leaders assigned the Russian government much of the blame for the loss of Liaodong, but the Chinese saw the Russians as heroes. Russia replaced China as Japan's problem in Korea. After helping China resist Japanese demands, Russia requested permission to build an arm of the Trans-Siberian railroad across Manchuria to Vladivostok in order to defend China. The Chinese emissary to the coronation of Nicholas II in 1896, Li Hongzhang, granted the railroad right-of-way, and the Chinese and Russian governments signed a fifteen-year alliance in response to Japan's rising status. Li believed that he had obtained twenty years of peace for China. Instead, only three years later, rebellion and foreign invasion disrupted the peace.[46]

The financial burden of the Sino-Japanese War and the corruption of Chinese and foreign officials and bankers placed China under the thumb of foreign moneylenders. Before 1894, China seldom borrowed, and when it did, it repaid the loans quickly. To finance the war against Japan, China borrowed £5 million from the British and Germans, secured by customs taxes. The Shimonoseki Treaty added £23 million to China's burden. The original financial plan for China relied upon Sir Robert Hart, the honest, longtime head of the Imperial Maritime Customs. Western banks and speculators, attracted by the prospect of fees and discounts, persuaded their governments to demand an inclusive, but corrupt, loan. In 1895, 1896, and 1898, western banks and speculators completed three large loans of almost £48 million. The combination of debt repayment and the burden of corruption (large chunks of the vast loans disappeared into the banks and private accounts) siphoned off the internal capital and played a large part in wrecking the Chinese economy.[47] Western bankers and diplomats promised bigger, better, and more. They succeeded in the area of corruption.

After the Sino-Japanese War, Japan replaced China as the leading state of East Asia, and it contested with the western powers for imperial leadership in East Asia and Oceania. In 1895 Japan secured control of Taiwan in the south and greater privileges in Korea in the north. Japanese acquisitions paved the way to challenge Russia and China for control of the Manchuria–northern China mainland and to contest with the west for domination of Southeast and East Asia.[48] U.S. leaders worried that the territorial claims and financial arrangements indicated the beginning of a division of China.

U.S. merchants, whalers, missionaries, and naval personnel established ties with Hawaii, Samoa, and other islands in Oceania in the search for secure whaling and commercial stations and to find trade goods for use in the China trade. They added bêche-de-mer, shells, sandalwood, and other Oceania products to the furs and timber from the northwest coast of North America for trade in the Pacific basin. By the late nineteenth century, the search for harbors serving the Pacific basin grew increasingly more important as the U.S. production capacity, rising support for an isthmian canal, and the development of the west coast encouraged merchants, manufacturers, and shipping firms to search for new opportunities. Pearl Harbor, Pago Pago (Samoa), and Manila were viewed as the best harbors in Oceania in the 1840s and remained targets for expansionists in the 1890s. Occasionally, U.S. officials contemplated naval bases in the Far East.[49]

U.S. agents and entrepreneurs encountered considerable competition from German, British, and French merchants and officials. By the 1880s and 1890s, Japanese migrants, merchants, and shipping firms were also searching throughout the whole Pacific basin for opportunities for migration, raw materials, commercial activity, and investments. These five powers plus Russia, Italy, the Netherlands, and Portugal were competing in China for commercial, raw material extraction, financial, and investment opportunities. Some geopoliticians, military leaders, and entrepreneurs considered the Suez Canal and the Indian Ocean the chief route to the Pacific, but more envisioned an economic network that stretched from Europe through the Caribbean to the Pacific basin. Columbus's dream had been renewed.

The Europeans, Americans, and Japanese all sought to expand their involvement in, and extraction of value from, Asia and Oceania. The various powers used different methods. Japan's agents asserted Asian brotherhood. The Europeans drew upon Christian missionary and commercial arguments. The U.S. officials, missionaries, and entrepreneurs tried to assert religion, commercial needs, security needs, and ideas like duty, fairness, and mission. At the end of the nineteenth century, U.S. leaders asserted a "special relationship" with China and Asia, a manifest destiny, which supposedly summoned the United States to Asia.

CHAPTER 4

U.S. Domestic Developments and Social Imperialism 1850s–1890s

Two developments marked the U.S. political economy during the late nineteenth century. The steady incorporation of the west and the rapid growth of a technologically and industrially based economy shaped modern America. These urban, industrial centers demanded ever more labor, so immigrants (and domestic migrants) helped form an urban society. Although slavery was eliminated in the south, the nation remained racist toward blacks and Hispanics and added powerful ethnic prejudices toward the new Catholic, Orthodox, and Jewish immigrants from southern and eastern Europe (and Asians). The continuous tension within late-nineteenth-century U.S. society encouraged expansion as a response to the recurring domestic problems of recession, social discontent, labor wars, widespread poverty, and political corruption.

During the Civil War, the Republican government had adopted many liberal, free-market changes to facilitate economic growth. These changes replaced older mercantilistic forms. With much of the population shifting from rural to urban areas, wealth and power were concentrated in a few, largely urban dwellers, while the bulk of the U.S. population lagged behind. The tensions in U.S. society erupted into mounting violence, crime, and disorder. Increasingly, the leaders of the U.S. political economy presumed that social imperialism would alleviate domestic disorder and facilitate even more rapid accumulation for the few. The secession crisis and the Civil War signaled the changing of the guard, or in this case the creation and distribution of wealth and power.

In the 1840s and 1850s, demographic and material growth in the north threatened the southern way of life economically (a liberal economic order) and politically (a liberal social and political order). Some southerners sought to ameliorate domestic tensions through the social imperialism response of filibustering, or military adventuring. Many southern leaders suspected that slavery would be rejected in the newly opened land in the west, so they urged either separation or expansion to the south — Mexico, the Caribbean islands (especially Cuba), or Central America. The Civil War resolved the struggle over whether slavery would extend into the west. After the conflict, the Gulf-Caribbean remained a target, but new types of expansionists — railroad magnates, agrarian businessmen, canal enthusiasts, merchant capitalists — demanded easier access to the fabled wealth of the Gulf-Caribbean and Asia.

Parts of U.S. society considered social imperialism the proper tool to pursue U.S. objectives in the Gulf-Caribbean area. Social imperialism defined a link between metropole and periphery in which the preservation of well-being and security in the metropole rested on its ability to ameliorate domestic social woes through ties to the periphery. Obviously migration and labor supply, cheap food and raw materials, factors of scale, and markets for production, capital, and technology impacted social relations in the political economy. For example, one could control disorder from low wages and unemployment with cheap food and raw materials because these factors lowered the cost of living for the poorly paid workers without wage increases. Commonly in the last half of the nineteenth century, intellectual or political leaders argued that the alleviation of domestic problems needed foreign activity.[1]

The highly respected scientist and onetime Confederate naval officer Matthew Fontaine Maury prescribed a course of empire that Columbus knew and southern leaders should have heeded. Maury envisioned transit to the Pacific as vital: "I regard the Pacific railroad and a commercial thoroughfare across the Isthmus as . . . parts of the great whole which . . . is to effect a revolution in the course of trade. . . . Those two works . . . are not only necessary fully to develop the immense resources of the Mississippi valley . . . but . . . their completion would place the United States on the summit level of commerce." The isthmus region was, in his view, the "barrier that separates us from the markets of six hundred millions of people — three fourths of the population of the earth. . . . and this country is placed midway between Europe and Asia; this [circum-Caribbean region] becomes the centre of the world and the focus of the world's commerce."[2] Maury's geopolitics touched visionaries and money-grubbers alike across the United States.

Liberal ideology and technological innovations offered new ways to realize Maury's prophesy. This perspective illuminates why the Gulf-Caribbean attracted such intense international competition in the Civil War. The Civil

War and Reconstruction era separates much of the New World from much of the Old in the international conflict between liberalism and conservatism. Liberalism, expressed in the works of Adam Smith and John Stuart Mill, emphasized the need for liberty in an open, accessible economic, social, and political order. This meant a free labor system (hence the end of slavery). Liberalism taught that well-being, individualism, and progress came out of the marketplace. Liberals also wanted to reduce the role of government, and generally they accepted urban, secular, and materialistic lifestyles. The pre–Civil War era conservatives cherished aristocratic values and were religiously oriented, patriarchical, and suspicious of common people. They tended to value rural life and land, rather than the merchant and industrial goals of the liberals.[3] Technology favored the liberals because it facilitated material progress. Material growth and development in the United States in the mid-nineteenth century were tied to abundant land, a steady labor stream (slave labor and immigrants), the technological revolution, and the gradual shift of national ideology and common wisdom from mercantilism to liberalism.

In the years before the Civil War, "King Cotton" assumptions rested on the belief that Europe needed southern cotton, when all it really needed were fibers for textile production. European textile mills and consumers around the world located alternative sources of cotton, switched to alternative fibers, or developed alternative consumption patterns to mitigate the cotton shortage. The south had rebelled to assert its independence in the mistaken view that independent political authority would alter dramatically its economic relationship to the world. Its economic dependence upon Great Britain (and Europe) hampered its self-sufficiency and self-governance. To achieve real independence, the southerners needed to distance themselves from Britain and develop independent production, finance, and distribution facilities and thereby accumulate wealth and transform their economy into a semi-periphery one.[4] Alternative products or altered consumption patterns undermined the influence of peripheral states upon the world economy. In this sense, cotton (much of its production capital and all of the processing and distribution were controlled outside the South) was the equivalent of bananas (all of its capital and distribution were controlled outside the banana-producing countries).

The north, restrained in its growth to metropole status because it lacked capital, had to take advantage of domestic accumulation. It could exploit the south and nearby semi-periphery areas. Given the hold of the metropoles on the processes of accumulation and their advantages in technology, a transformation from semi-periphery to metropole would be difficult.[5] Of course, North

American entrepreneurs intended to control the material value produced in the circum-Caribbean.

In the twentieth century, however, most historians have slighted the story of southern interest in the Caribbean—other than filibustering—and focused upon Confederate relations with Europe. Even Confederate activity in the Caribbean is interpreted mostly in regard to the region's role as intermediary in trade with Europe. Certainly, the diplomatic recognition, munitions, war materials, and financial wealth of Europe attracted Confederate attention. The Confederacy, however, appointed about half of its foreign agents to posts in the isthmian-Caribbean area. Confederate leaders did view the circum-Caribbean as useful for exchanging cotton for European manufactures, but also for buccaneering and other attacks upon northern interests. The war nudged territorial expansionism off center stage. The West Indian islands and Mexico served as way stations for blockade runners, as rest stops for Confederate travelers, and as communications bases for agents operating in the circum-Caribbean. The isthmian transit routes conveyed gold from California to the east. For many Confederate leaders, the lure of treasure ships was as strong as in the days of Sir Francis Drake and the buccaneers.[6]

Some northern leaders recognized the need to fit the United States into a world economy, including Lincoln's secretary of state, William H. Seward, who, as a senator, had outlined such objectives since the 1840s and 1850s. He spoke out strongly for territorial and commercial expansion. He expected the United States to serve as an intermediary between the civilizations of the east and west, which would "mingle . . . on our own free soil, and a new and more perfect civilization will arise to bless the earth, under the sway of our own cherished and beneficent democratic institutions."[7] Latin America might follow the proper road. In 1860, Seward saw amid the rebellions of the Latin American republics "the preparatory stage for their reorganization in free, equal and self-governing members of the United States."[8] Seward wanted the United States "to command the empire of the seas, which alone is real empire," and this would advance the U.S. position in the "commerce of the world, which is the empire of the world." In the Senate, he explained the ties of industry to commerce and empire: "Put your domain under cultivation and your ten thousand wheels of manufacture in motion. The nation that draws most materials and provisions from the earth, and fabricates the most, and sells the most of production and fabrics to foreign nations, must be, and will be, the great power of the earth."[9]

Since 1607, North Americans had proclaimed expansion—not the status quo, contraction, or division—as their destiny. Although most liberals thought of domestic development, commercial expansion, and opposition to territorial acquisition, Seward accepted the need to acquire territory to support trade expansion. Seward and other expansionists proposed rail, steam, and telegraph communications to link the U.S. economy with Latin America, the Pacific islands, and Asia. The Republican government, following liberal free-market economics, wanted to expand, not contract, the nation's market area. First it had to stop secession, the separation of land, labor, and capital from the national market, and then it had to protect areas for future expansion and accumulation—such as the circum-Caribbean—from European encroachment. Liberalism's growth-or-decay duality suggested that secession threatened the nation's well-being, progress, and independence. Secession implied a difficult future for the north and the possibility of a decaying social order.[10]

During the Lincoln administration, radicals and moderates on one hand and conservatives on the other differed over how best to prevent division of the nation and resist foreign efforts to limit future expansion. While Lincoln's administration intended to persuade France to withdraw from Mexico, some radical and moderate Republicans urged more confrontational action. Some radicals used President Andrew Johnson's unwillingness to compel French withdrawal to support their position in favor of impeachment. A growing interventionist sentiment in the United States intertwined a major but controversial foreign relations problem with serious domestic disagreements.[11]

In the 1860s, U.S. liberals implemented a national development program that included a national currency, a national banking system, a protective tariff, mining education, and aid for communications, transportation, immigration, and agriculture. Beginning in the 1870s, the political economy spurted into a period of rapid growth, punctuated with grave crises that were characterized by widespread social unrest, violence, misery, and political corruption. One persistent economic issue of late-nineteenth-century politics, the tariff, commonly generated wealth for the few at the expense of the many. The severe maldistribution of wealth burdened economic stability. When a variety of domestic steps failed to halt the recurring depressions, cheaper raw materials and foodstuffs and expanding foreign markets were touted as panaceas to reduce unemployment and thus lessen social strife.[12]

Most textbooks for U.S. history or U.S. foreign relations have devoted little space to the period from 1865 to 1898. It has been presented as a time when the U.S. government was concerned mainly with Reconstruction and the development of the west, or as a period in which confused U.S. leaders were unable to agree upon the proper course to pursue internationally. Scholars need to consider alternatives. Domestic politics shaped by a long economic depression worked to promote a program of expansion. Columbus's quest to reach the wealth of Asia shared a primary purpose with the liberal programs of the 1860s: both incorporated the idea of "material progress." U.S. leaders moved toward imperial policies as soon as they recognized the inability of the domestic economy to run near capacity if restricted to distribution within the home market.

The late-nineteenth-century world's fairs served to display great power technology and to help sell its products and racial view of the world. The fairs advertised the abundance and marvel of great power material culture and its capacity to transform the life of the dominant nations. The U.S. and British world's fairs underscored the Anglo-Saxon preeminence among the peoples of the world. They elevated productionism to a religion, in the view of some students. One claimed: "World exhibitions are the sites of pilgrimages to the commodity fetish," while another called the fairs the "Missa Solemnis of capitalist culture." Cultural scholars have described these late-nineteenth-century world's fairs as "ritualistic displays of goods and power." The world's fairs displayed the power, material abundance, and innovative technology of the Anglo-Saxon and western societies and also their pretended racial and cultural superiority over the periphery.[13]

Within two decades of the 1873 depression, most leaders recognized the need to pursue social imperialism. For example, James G. Blaine had long advocated Henry Clay's American System in its New World dimensions. He modified it in the crises of the late nineteenth century to include Hawaii, Puerto Rico, Cuba, and any area deemed essential to make the U.S. commercial empire in Latin America or Asia work. He favored formal U.S. control of the harbor of Pago Pago during the 1884 conference on Samoa. By 1889–1890, his mode of operation altered; he supported revolutions, diplomatic coercion, and perhaps military intervention in selective cases. For example, in the 1870s, Blaine had opposed direct action in Hawaii. By 1890 he was willing to accept military or other forms of coercion to settle the Hawaiian matters.[14] His American System incorporated much of the Pacific basin, a viewpoint consistent with that of modern Americans.

The U.S. economy went through three spikes of panic—1873 to 1878, 1882 to 1885, and 1893 to 1898—during the long world economic disturbance from 1873 to 1898. These crises played havoc on the lives of all Americans. Industrialists, investors, and workers suffered together, if not equally. Even the unemployed, the marginalized, and the outcasts suffered because the thin mesh of social aid that held them above water weakened and frayed in these unpredictable economic times. In the 1890s, manufacturers, politicians, shipping firms, and merchants sought to alleviate widespread domestic turmoil through selective expansion to facilitate trade and investment.[15]

U.S. intellectuals, economists, and some business people explored "over-production" or "glut" explanations that assigned surplus production with the responsibility for factory closures, layoffs, and social suffering. So-called over-production was in fact underconsumption, since millions of U.S. residents lacked adequate food, clothing, shelter, education, and medical care. The inability to distribute adequate food, shelter, and health care even to many full-time workers revealed ethical and moral bankruptcy. Unable to establish domestic policies to distribute well-being fairly or to alleviate the disorder, U.S. political leaders moved slowly toward social imperialism — reacting to domestic social problems through international activity. Consider the domestic efforts to improve railroads, ports, and rivers so that wheat would find larger markets in Europe, Latin America, and Asia, while there was widespread hunger and malnutrition in U.S. factory and mining centers. Presumably, exporting to stimulate domestic economic activity that created jobs would ameliorate domestic social problems. Cheaper and quicker communications would increase exports. The U.S. government wanted more trade, investment options, cheaper raw materials, security of communications, and even opportunities for businessmen, laborers, and capital to seek short-term engagement and profit. To obtain these, the United States and the western industrializing states — whose leaders faced similar situations — became increasingly competitive and acquisitive.[16]

From the late nineteenth to the early twentieth centuries, the United States was transforming itself from a semi-periphery state into a metropole state. Its social imperialist policies exploited the southern and western regions and the transit, market, and investment opportunities of the Central American–Caribbean region. Social imperialism masked the problems, the burdens, and the injustices of a metropole's political economy. In phrases that epitomized the consequences of this policy, the U.S. political economy needed "to export the social problem" and "to export the unemployment." Policy makers openly discussed the expected benefits of social imperialism for the domestic U.S. economy; only rarely, however, did they consider the consequences for the host societies — the peripheral and semi-peripheral states.[17]

One common critique used against social imperialism and open door imperialism — open, equal access to an economy (but given the military, diplomatic, and economic disparity among nations, an open door does not produce a fair field) — complains that trade with Latin America or Asia made up only a very small part of the U.S. Gross National Product (GNP). This argument is defective. The U.S. government used specific (counting items) and ad valorum (value determined by weight) tariffs, so importers maximized undercounting, underweighing, and undervaluing to minimize their duties. Thus two common responses: first, imports were undervalued, and second, they often represented scarce, necessary raw materials for major industries such as the steel industry, hence their specific dollar value does not measure their importance to the economy. Besides these points, another needs to be made. Since holding companies and early multinational corporations were significant players in the turn-of-the-century expansion, analysis of trade needs to consider price transferring. This practice is a regular post–World War II phenomenon, but it has been a common device since the nineteenth century.

Price transferring allowed manipulations through apparent sales in order to maximize gain and to avoid social responsibility. For example, the bananas, coffee, minerals, sugar, cotton, and other products from U.S. firms in the circum-Caribbean frequently entered U.S. ports by price transferring, not market transactions. The firms controlling the distribution of these products managed the volume or listed prices to minimize taxes and fees, and to mask the value of the products leaving the country of origin. Some countries taxed exports or determined the tax value of a firm from its economic activity. Cheap products reduced export taxes and lowered the tax evaluations of the firms. Through schemes like price transferring, the banana-producing countries received very little revenue from United Fruit, even though those countries supplied all the fruit in this immensely profitable world banana trade.

For the U.S. situation, minimizing the number or weight of an item was easier to do when the product was not sold in a marketplace, but transferred within a group of interrelated businesses. The low export prices, sometimes administratively set, seconded arguments about the low value of the firms operating on the isthmus. For example, stems of hundreds of bananas entered the United States with a value of a few cents and then were resold in wholesale and retail markets for perhaps 10, 20, or 50 times the invoice price. Price transferring diminished importation figures and undervalued the role of trade in the Gross National Product. Thus, import figures need to be multiplied by some factor to present a "realistic" view of the role of importation in the Gross National Product. That figure would become clear through study of nineteenth-century price transfers and other forms of duty evasion or value manipulation.

Collective bodies of capitalists (domestic holding companies and multinational corporations) under cover of liberal, free-market rhetoric spearheaded the drive to enter foreign areas. The ideology praised individualism and free-market values, but the agencies of market penetration and accumulation were collectivized, bureaucratic, planning organizations — holding companies and multinational corporations that used schemes like price transferring. U.S. businessmen and politicians looked first to Latin America for markets because that region had long been expected to share an economic future with the northern neighbors. But U.S. officials rarely studied the Latin American economic situation or consulted with Latin American leaders because the U.S. vision expressed in the Monroe Doctrine, Manifest Destiny, Pan-Americanism, and the open door aimed to resolve U.S. domestic problems, not to meet Latin American needs.[18]

Pan-Americanism, initiated in the 1880s, exposed fundamental differences between the U.S. and Latin American visions. While U.S. officials proposed programs to assure U.S. commercial expansion, the Latin American delegates struggled unsuccessfully to include political, social, and cultural affairs and investment on the agenda of Pan-American meetings. Selling U.S. "overproduction" meant keeping domestic employment and production high while increasing the unemployment and subsequent social and political problems in areas that accepted the exports. This was "exporting the unemployment." Some U.S. leaders recognized this. Because the peripheral states had fewer financial or political resources to control social unrest, a few of these U.S. leaders warned prophetically that pursuing the Pan-American commercial program and the open door policy would involve the United States in wars and revolutions around the world.[19] The more the U.S. leaders saw export of goods or capital and import of cheap food and raw materials as the solution to the domestic disorder, the less they could tolerate revolt, revolution, domestic disorder, or war among the peripheral societies.

The United States was not the only metropole state that tried to enlarge its marketplace by expanding into other regions. From 1873 to 1898, the shock waves of the world economic crisis persuaded political, business, and military leaders in numerous metropole and semi-periphery nations to expand through colonialism and informal imperialism. For several generations, this time period was called the Age of Imperialism. U.S. businessmen and government officials sometimes mouthed free-trade rhetoric, but they did not welcome foreign competition in the Caribbean–Central American region and tolerated it reluctantly in those parts of Oceania and East Asia considered vital to U.S. security and economic prosperity.[20]

Metropole firms commonly controlled the land, labor, capital, and distribution systems that drove the political economies in peripheral societies. By the mid-nineteenth century, transnational firms had large shares of world shipping, transoceanic telegraph cables, maritime services, and marketing operations. No region in Latin America, Oceania, or Asia was exempt from their reach. In the late nineteenth and early twentieth centuries, multinational corporations or metropole states supervised much of the world economy.

The fulfillment of Columbus's dream, entrepreneurial profits, and metropole security required a canal at Tehuantepec, Nicaragua, the Darien region, or between Colón and Panama City. Railroads were poor substitutes. Regardless of which route was promoted, the core idea was an isthmian canal under U.S. control. In December 1897, six months before the U.S. warship *Oregon*—a vessel in the Pacific ordered urgently around Cape Horn to protect the southern U.S. coastline—fastened attention on the naval-military justification for a canal, the National Board of Trade observed: "The growing commerce of the United States with the west coast of South America, the islands of the Pacific and Asia, as well as with Alaska and our own Pacific States, . . . [and] the development of China with its four hundred million people would seem to demand . . . the construction of the Nicaraguan Canal by the United States Government."[21] The St. Louis Merchant Exchange heartily endorsed the National Board of Trade's view. In 1897, after decades of debate about the merits of various sites, and stimulated by de Lesseps's failure, the U.S. government named Admiral John G. Walker to head a commission to select the site for a U.S. interoceanic canal. In 1901, the Walker Commission recommended Nicaragua because American companies already held canal rights there and the French interests were asking $109 million for the failed Panama venture.[22] The voices calling for a canal often pointed to Asia.

The metropole states and the multinational corporations established comprador relations with individuals and groups in the periphery. The compradors, principal local agents on the periphery, had two chief functions. They facilitated the entrance of foreign corporations and political influence, and they managed the domestic order in the peripheral society because disorder reduced business opportunities and increased the likelihood of foreign involvement on the isthmus. Compradors normally operated within the private sector. When they entered the public sphere, they became collaborators. Occasionally, in search of power, wealth, and prestige, local leaders entered directly into collaboration.

Collaborators in the circum-Caribbean stifled the disorder that arose from nationalist disgust over the loss of sovereignty and from worker protest against imperial exploitation. Often disorder was most efficiently and quickly removed by political repression, but repression often generated violent resistance, and the ensuing spectacle alienated metropole supporters of democratic and human rights. When this occurred, metropole leaders—under siege in their own political castles—sought rescue in the quick restoration of order, at times through military action (internal friendly military revolts, comprador coups, or intervention) to remove former collaborators. Disorder on the periphery posed a threat to the home. One American social imperialist response to the world economic crisis involved a war to acquire naval bases and a subsequent canal route. The naval bases and canal would facilitate exports and thus preserve or expand the domestic job market. It is not surprising that the War of 1898 "consolidated United States maritime power in the Pacific."[23]

U.S. domestic activity was mixed with expansion, the adoption of European liberalism, affirmation of a U.S. mission, and the adoption of materialism as the nation's measure of success. The sectionalism and Civil War period helped to direct several problems toward new courses. U.S. society continued to voice idealism, and the populace assumed that the nation's direction was liberty and freedom, but in actuality the nation moved on an economic, social, and political set of ideas that responded to material objectives and lauded material accumulation. The idealism was a parallel path, generally cosmetic and nonessential in reality, but not in the world of imagination. By the end of the nineteenth century, U.S. politics were most easily organized around wealth and materialism. Those accumulating wealth in the economy struggled to transform the political process to a more materialistically responsive system. Pursuing natural competition, into war if necessary, elevated masculine characteristics, such as military action against Native Americans, the Spanish, Filipinos, Chinese, Panamanians, Nicaraguans, Haitians, Dominicans, and Mexicans over the course of several decades, and confirmed late-nineteenth-century images of masculinity and natural competition.[24] But laissez-faire and social Darwinism both valued competition and conflict in a male power structure.

The changes needed to move from rural, small-town agricultural communities to an urban, industrial society challenged U.S. citizens to "search for order" (or disorder, whichever created opportunities to acquire wealth and power) and to examine old beliefs and common wisdom. Relationships and values—the anchors in social activity and shared history and custom—underwent significant alterations. In the realm of political economy, the appeal to a liberal order won many converts, but others sought explanations in socialism, populism, utopianism, religion, and religious revivalism, to mention a few of the more widely adopted explanations. These views all had influence upon U.S. social imperialism. The religious aspect was evident in the revival of terms like destiny, duty, mission, and burden to explain U.S. actions. U.S. missionary activity increased markedly in Asia; this activity can be viewed as an effort to export the need to convert and to increase the flock, especially in the face of science's and Darwinism's challenges to religious belief. President William McKinley's claim that he knelt in prayer at various points in deciding to fight Spain and to acquire the Philippines catered to these sentiments. So would America's sending five thousand U.S. troops against the Boxers in China in 1900 to ensure that the U.S. missionaries and Columbus's dream of exploiting Asia would not die.

CHAPTER 5

JT6

Three Crises

The 1893 Depression, China, and Cuba

Three overlapping developments shook U.S. society in the 1890s. U.S. leaders pondered the need for military responses to the world economic crisis of 1873–1898 (especially difficult in the United States from 1893 to 1897), to the preliminary division of China (1894–1898), and to the revolts in Spain's Cuban and Philippine colonies. They worried about the constant need for military force to restore order in domestic factories, cities, and railroad lines (as examples, the Homestead strike of 1892, the Haymarket massacre of 1884, and the Pullman strike of 1894). The reliance upon state or federal military to maintain domestic order undermined the idea of democratic government and allowed the image of men on horseback coming to power—in other words, that U.S. society might begin to appear like Latin American revolutionary societies. Some leaders urged social imperial policies to alleviate the domestic discontent, to preserve democratic institutions, and to ameliorate international and domestic turmoil. Various leaders recognized the dangers arising from the conflux of these three crises.

The 1890s were catastrophic for Spain, the United States, and China. The severe U.S. depression in 1893 had direct repercussions in Spanish Cuba, where economic hardship reinvigorated a militant independence movement. As Spain struggled with its own domestic civil tensions, revolts arose in the Philippines and Cuba. Both areas attracted U.S. attention because the disorder lay along the primary route for tying the North Atlantic to East Asia. U.S. leaders seized the opportunity to expel Spain from its Caribbean and Asian colonies and to co-opt leadership in the ongoing search for a better, less costly route to the wealth of Asia. There, the assault upon China's sovereignty and territorial integrity after the Sino-Japanese War (1894–1895)—when the great powers seized parts of defeated China—added urgency for U.S. policymakers.[1]

Walter LaFeber, a prominent U.S. diplomatic historian, epitomized 1898 with a cryptic chapter title in *The American Age*: "Two Crises, One War." LaFeber noted that: "During the early 1898 run-up to the war with Spain, [President William] McKinley closely associated the crises in the Caribbean and Asian theaters. As revolution threatened Cuba, so European imperialism endangered China. The U.S. business community tried to keep Asia in the forefront of the nation's debate."[2] The descriptive power of LaFeber's chapter title improves if altered to become "Three Crises [1893, Cuba, and China], Three Wars [1898, Philippines, and Boxers]." The War of 1898 and its aftermath tie the domestic, circum-Caribbean, and Pacific basin problems to the progressives' search for order and opportunity from the 1890s to 1921.

While European powers had contemplated more direct activity in China since the time of Marco Polo, the catalyst for action in 1898 came from the Japanese and Europeans grasping for Chinese territory between 1894 and 1897. By the early 1890s, the Japanese government had created the institutions of modernization—a treasury, administrative order, and the rudiments of constitutional democracy. It mobilized the nation's resources to become an industrial and imperial power. Japan, which was modernizing, ended the Sino-Japanese War with a favorable treaty at Shimonoseki that extracted an immense war indemnity equivalent to 4.5 times the 1893 Japanese government budget. This sum paid Japan's war expenses, strengthened its military, and financed industrial expansion without overseas loans.[3]

The Meiji made getting rid of the "treaties of shame"—the unequal treaties which opened Japan to the west—an overriding objective. By the 1890s, Japan was strong enough to end the treaty port and unequal treaty system. The Sino-Japanese War then dramatically altered Japan's role in Asia and the world. Japanese expansion on the mainland followed primitive capitalist accumulation, not finance capitalism. One historian noted that "Japanese imperialism becomes the illegitimate child of Western capitalism, with international rivalry as midwife." He considered that Japanese "imperialist ambition was a logical response to awareness of living in an imperialist world." Japan, eager for status and economic and military prestige, pondered the danger of western division of China without its participation. Between 1878 and 1914, the western powers increased their share of the globe's surface from 67 percent to 85 percent.[4] Still, Japanese financial and territorial demands on Chinese sovereignty and territorial integrity disturbed U.S. policy makers, but the U.S. government could not stem the division of China into protectorates and spheres of influence without resorting to force. The alternatives were diplomatic activity and appeals to that elusive world opinion. In only twenty-five years, Japan turned from threatened to threatener.

Gaps in China's Great Wall—a wall symbolic of foreign exclusion—became ever wider after the 1895 defeat by Japan. Britain had been the principal foreign influence on the Qing (Ch'ing) regime, and the British banks had entered first with loans. Russia pursued "peaceful penetration" to gain advantage from China's defeat, while German officials aimed to locate and acquire naval and coaling stations to support its challenge to Britain and France in East Asia. Germany was second to Britain in trade with China, but it had no Hong Kong for commerce, finance, coaling, repairs, and security. Britain and France competed in South China—the French advanced north from Indochina and Thailand, while the British spread north from India and Burma. The French sought influence in Guangdong (Kwangtung), Guangxi (Kwangsi), and Yunnan provinces and a harbor off the South China coast. These incursions plus railroad and mining concessions wrung from China's officials increased resentment among the Chinese.[5]

Competitive imperialism drove the great powers, attracted by the mounting signs of profound Chinese weakness in the 1890s, into hectic actions to ensure that they got their share. The Chinese at Qu-Fu, Confucius's birthplace, deeply resented German bishop Johann Baptist Anzer's insistence upon building a major Christian center in that town. The German priest wanted to exploit the reputation of that site for the Christian religion. German emperor (Kaiser) William II was not content with Germany's situation in East Asia because every other great power had a naval base. In preparation for a greater role, Germany had seized the Solomon Islands and part of New Guinea. But in 1895, China rejected a German request for a naval base. In 1896, Admiral Alfred von Tirpitz traveled to China and personally selected Qing-Dao (Tsingtao) on the Shandong peninsula as the site for a German naval station. The Kaiser warmly agreed. The German foreign ministry, impatiently awaiting an excuse to occupy the place, explained: "In the last couple of years, there had been several incidents which would have justified action, for example, in the conduct towards our missionaries." The Kaiser informed the admiral in East Asia that "as soon as the time arrives, occupy the site without delay." The Kaiser, who had proposed the seizure of Formosa in 1894, used the killing of two missionaries on November 1897 to strike for his long-desired naval station. He telegraphed Foreign Minister Bernhard von Bülow: "The Chinese had finally given us the 'reason and an incident.' . . . I decided immediately to seize the moment." William II personally asked Nicholas II if Russia would object to Germany acquiring Qing-Dao. Nicholas, in an awkward spot, gave a vague assent to avoid saying no. He did not want his cousin William II to seize Qing-Dao, yet he did not wish to be the only ruler saying no.[6]

The Kaiser ordered the fleet to Qing-Dao to take possession of the bay, "and when necessary finally to show the Chinese with the most brutal callousness, that they should not take the Kaiser lightly and it is a bad mistake to have him as an enemy."[7] Two weeks later, three German ships entered Qing-Dao Bay. Over seven hundred armed men went ashore. The Chinese troops withdrew surprised. The Russian government, claiming primary rights in Qing-Dao, warned it might send ships. The German government held firm. A week later, the Russian government dropped its opposition to the Qing-Dao annexation and prepared to occupy Port Arthur. On 6 December 1897, Bülow spoke of Germany's "place in the sun." Tirpitz welcomed Germany's role in opening China to world trade. On 15 December 1897, William II sent his brother, troops, and ships to Qing-Dao with instructions: "Should anyone undertake to offend us or to want to injure us in our clear right, then oppose them with armoured fist!"[8] The Chinese government appealed to the great powers for aid to resist the German assault, but Russia and France backed Germany while the British and United States said little or nothing.[9]

In March 1898, Germany obtained a ninety-nine-year lease to Qing-Dao and the right to build two railroads in Shandong. The German lease included 150,000 square kilometers of territory, railroad and mining concessions, and 33 million Chinese. Qing-Dao, "the Empire's Hongkong," a 560-square kilometer harbor, was placed in the navy department. The Germans planned a trade center, a program of development and agricultural activity, a modern water system, and the most modern harbor in Asia. They concentrated on this site and these costly projects because they lacked power in East Asia for additional expansion. The possession of Qing-Dao and the surrounding area, heavy with Confucian history, increased the Chinese hatred of foreigners.[10]

Some newspapers in Germany repeated an insightful, if flippant, commentary on the murdered German missionaries: "When these demands are met, the two missionaries will have done well to allow their massacre. Seldom have two human lives brought the Fatherland so many advantages. Other European nations have lost more than two missionaries in China, but we are not aware that their martyrdom was used so openly to gain railroads and coaling stations." Neither the Kaiser nor Bishop Anzer, both ardent expansionists and overjoyed with the military intervention, apparently displayed any significant public dismay at the death of the two German missionaries.[11]

The other ambitious powers responded to German expansion within weeks. In December 1897, Russia obtained a twenty-five-year lease on Port Arthur and Dalian (Darien, Dalny, or Lüda) on the Liaodong peninsula under the pretext of protecting China from the Germans, and a railroad concession from the two ports to Yingkou (Yingkow) and the Yalu River. Russia appropriated the Liaodong peninsula for 30 million taels (after the Triple Intervention had made China pay 50 million two years earlier to deny Japanese acquisition of Liaodong). The British leased Weihaiwei (on the Shandong peninsula) for twenty-five years—a "cartographic consolation"—and Kowloon near Hong Kong for ninety-nine years. The Chinese government also promised the British not to alienate the Yangzi valley to any other power. Soon other spheres of influence were parceled: the British took Changjiang, Russia took Manchuria. A Franco-Belgian syndicate and the Russo-Chinese Bank secured the Beijing-to-Hankou (Hankow) railroad that brought Russian influence to the Yangzi.[12] Russia's reputation among the Chinese, elevated after the 1895 peace, was severely weakened. The struggle over the Chinese loans was complicated with mining and railroad concessions; Britain reinforced its control of the Imperial Maritime Customs Administration. Some historians have judged that "the attempt to move inland fueled a reaction to foreign intrusion which culminated in the Boxer Rising."[13]

Japan was livid after Russia seized Port Arthur and Germany occupied much of the Shandong peninsula. In 1895, the Triple Intervention—Russia, Germany, and France—had demanded Japan return these areas to preserve Chinese integrity. As insufficient consolation, Japan obtained a sphere of influence in Fujian (Fukien) province, opposite Taiwan. France leased Guangdong Bay for ninety-nine years, obtained a sphere of influence in the Guangdong-Guangxi-Yunnan provinces, and gained the right to build a railroad into China from Annam. The U.S. government barely participated in the concession frenzy, although the U.S. Navy wanted a base at Shanxi (Sanmen) Bay. The U.S. and Belgian governments obtained railroad concessions. The Empress Dowager Cixi rejected Italy's demand for a sphere of influence and the lease of a naval base in Zhijiang (Chekiang) province.[14] Some saw these steps to compel concessions as indicative of China's future. Many in the United States wished to alter that future.

In early 1898, U.S. Minister to China Charles Denby "wired excitedly" to the State Department that Germany and Russia lusted to partition China. Denby believed: "Partition would tend to destroy our markets. The Pacific Ocean is destined to bear on its bosom a larger commerce than the Atlantic," and in noncolonized Asia "we are destined to find our best customers."[15] The view that the Pacific offered greater commercial prospects for the U.S. future than the Atlantic was not new to those discussing overproduction, nor was it new that Germany, Japan, and Russia were keen competitors for that trade. Western leaders since Columbus had often insisted on the immense potential value of the Pacific basin.

The populations of the metropoles and periphery states distrusted, mis-understood, and criticized each other's cultures and goals. The periphery states commonly had to deal with major intrusions of foreigners, foreign ideologies, and foreign institutions. Anti-missionary activity in China was matched by anti-Chinese outrages in the United States (and other parts of the world, in-cluding Guatemala and Costa Rica). In the west, vigilantes commonly at-tacked Chinese immigrants and laws restrained Chinese immigration.[16] The Chinese, however, were not allowed to stop the immigration of foreign mis-sionaries or businessmen into their own country. The repercussions for the November 1897 attack upon two German priests showed the price of vigi-lante action in China: the Chinese were compelled to open up ever larger areas to foreign intrusion.

Chinese society struggled to respond to the increasing foreign intrusions. Secret associations with a long history of critique of Chinese society partici-pated actively in the complaints against foreigners. The conflict between those arguing to preserve tradition and those arguing for reform helped paralyze the Chinese government. Proposals to reform China's military, industry, and edu-cation received no clear response, but the Empress Dowager Cixi favored tradition. There was no clear agreement on the sources of Chinese weakness, an urgent consideration after the war with Japan. There was no consensus whether China borrowed too little or too much from foreigners. Clearly, Ja-pan had retained much tradition, yet it was powerful.[17]

In the 1890s, China was wracked with socio-economic and political dis-order. Corruption and discontent increased after the Sino-Japanese War. To revitalize China's military, the Chinese forces in the north were placed under a Manchu favorite who was ordered to train the army in the most modern methods so it could resist western demands. A separate "100 Days of Reform" attempted to modernize China in the sense of European education and guid-ing outlook, and to remove or reduce traditional institutions.

The Beijing government was weak and getting weaker. Almost every inch of strategic and resource-rich China had been claimed, spoken for, or secretly coveted. In the hard times of the late nineteenth century, more Chinese con-verted to Christianity, but the number still remained tiny. From 1890 to 1900, Christian converts grew by about 50 percent, from 537,000 to 850,000. Still, only 0.2 percent of the total population had converted, and many of these had converted for the material benefits and protection. The Boxers and other spirit or martial arts societies opposed Christianity because it was foreign, unfriendly to Chinese customs, aggressive, and protected undesirable and criminal Chi-nese. Not surprisingly, the Boxers began their rebellion on the Shandong pen-

Fig. 1. "Le Gâteau Chinois" ("The Chinese Cake"). The United States (in the form of Teddy Roosevelt), Japan, and the European powers divide China, Manchuria and Korea. From left to right, William II, French President Émile Loubet, Nicholas II, the Mikado, Roseveldt [*sic*], and Edward VII of England. (Courtesy of Dr. Georg Mondwurf, Bremerhaven, Germany)

insula against the Germans who had seized the birthplace of Confucius, one of the most revered spots in China.[18]

The western states intended to seize territory, advantages, or privileges in China. Chinese scholars and cartoonists often used the melon image (the French preferred a cake) to represent the cutting up of a whole, including the western urge to carve up China. For the modern, fast-food world, pizza is a more fitting image, in part because western leaders sliced up a flat projection on a map or a naval chart rather than the globe (figs. 1 and 2). Historian Paul Varg described U.S. policy as aiming "to open China to western trade and cultural influences and to do so regardless of Chinese feelings." He discounted the "myth about mutual friendship and Chinese goodwill toward the United States."[19] In the 1890s, the U.S. public and officials mentioned Cuba more than China, but they had long eyed opportunities in Asia. U.S. society, when it looked to the Caribbean, commonly imagined access to isthmian transit, a route to the Pacific, and the security needs to protect that route. Everyone wanted a slice of China.

Fig. 2. "Gâteau des Rois et des Empereurs" ("The Cake of Kings and Emperors"), *Le petit journal.* Queen Victoria and Emperor William II glare at each other over the Shandong peninsula, and both Czar Alexander II and the Japanese emperor stare at Port Arthur. French Marie is intrigued, while the Chinese official is alarmed and signals halt to the division. (With permission of Société NATHAN, Paris, France)

In the late nineteenth century, the European powers measured the military and economic potential of various regions. The leaders of the industrializing nations were commonly motivated and driven to hasty action as the result of what Paul Kennedy in *The Rise and Fall of the Great Powers* refers to as the "theory of the Three [or Four] World Empires." This common belief held that "only the three (or, in some accounts, four) largest and most powerful nation-states would remain independent." Kennedy noted that "Admiral Alfred von Tirpitz urged Kaiser Wilhelm, to build a big navy, so that it [Germany] would be one of the 'four World Powers: Russia, England, America and Germany.'" In Kennedy's interpretation, "the established powers, Britain, France, and Austria-Hungary," acted to maintain their international status while the new powers, the United States, Germany, Russia, Italy, and Japan, tried to "break through to what Berlin termed a 'world-political freedom' before it was too late."[20]

This view of world politics encouraged the expansion of great and near-great powers in Africa, Asia, Oceania, and even Latin America (where the Monroe Doctrine staked out a priority position for the United States). U.S. well-being and power were defined in terms of ties to Latin America and Asia. The Germans and Japanese were considered special threats to the U.S. position in the Caribbean and Asia, and Russia posed a major challenge in Asia. Japan imitated its middle-class-oriented North Atlantic competitors, but its expansion was overwhelmingly military in governance.

Regardless of any "justification" for German or Japanese expansive conduct, U.S. officials commonly judged these two as especially dangerous to U.S. well-being and security. Japanese actions in Korea, Formosa (Taiwan), and China and the threat to the Philippines disturbed U.S. expansionists and the military. Japanese activity elsewhere in the Pacific basin, in Hawaii and California, on the Central American isthmus, and in Mexico provoked U.S. security concerns (and racial fears). The growing number of German land-owners, merchants, and entrepreneurs in Mexico, Haiti, Venezuela, Brazil, Costa Rica, Nicaragua, and Guatemala had alarmed some U.S. observers for decades. Likewise, Germany's economic and political power in the circum-Caribbean region and its conduct in Nicaragua, Haiti, the Philippines, Cuba, China, and Samoa unsettled U.S. public figures and officials.[21]

Before the turn of the century, Theodore Roosevelt and other U.S. expansionists acknowledged the value of Asia for the U.S. future. In the spring of 1897, Assistant Secretary of the Navy Roosevelt wanted U.S. control of Hawaii and a Nicaraguan canal "at once" because Japan was set to get two new battleships from England. Roosevelt assumed that once Hawaii was "in our hands most of the danger of friction with Japan would disappear."[22] The *New York Journal of Commerce* in December 1897 asserted that free access to China was the solution to overproduction surpluses. The missionary Josiah Strong, the New Englander Brooks Adams, and others fed the popular and governmental presumption of Asia's value for U.S. well-being and security.[23]

By the 1890s, the British and Germans had ceased to threaten Hawaii, but Japan surfaced as a major problem. Once the U.S. government allowed planters and agents to overthrow the Hawaiian queen, its interests in Hawaii were tied not only to immoral conduct, but to responsibility for subsequent events. U.S. planters, naval officers, and diplomatic agents sought protection, expansion, and a naval base to protect the west coast of North America and commerce with East and South Asia. A minor crisis erupted when Hawaiian officials refused to allow Japanese immigrants to debark in March 1897. The U.S. government energetically defended Hawaiian authority in this case. It notified the Japanese government that it would not tolerate compulsory pressure in response to the Hawaiian refusal. When Japan appeared to consider landing troops, Secretary of State John Sherman prepared to declare the islands a protectorate. Japan found no support from European powers to block U.S. interference in Hawaiian-Japanese affairs.[24]

Many German officials disliked U.S. society because it seemed too democratic and undisciplined. The German military had a low opinion of the U.S. military and felt humiliated by U.S. resistance to German objectives in Samoa. When war broke out between Spain and the United States, German leaders hoped a combined European representation in Washington would shape matters in Spain's favor. However, Great Britain's opposition blocked European collective action. In Asia, the German government wished to acquire the Philippines in order to challenge British commerce more effectively. The German merchants in the southern Philippines and in the Central and South Pacific asserted a better claim to the islands than the United States. While the Kaiser condemned U.S. annexations in 1898, he was not averse to securing some of Spain's Pacific possessions. The Kaiser's complaint—similar to the U.S. disparagement of European expansion—condemned who won the prize, but not that there was a prize-awarding contest.[25]

In addition to clashes in Samoa, the Philippines, China, the Congo, and over the sale of U.S. pork in Germany, U.S. and German societies competed for access to the canal, naval and coaling stations, investment, commerce, and political influences in the circum-Caribbean, where the key to a successful exploitation of Pacific basin opportunities lay. Prior to World War I, there were more German investments, settlers, and firms in Central America than there were from the United States. The nature of imperial competition and the peculiar U.S. sense of insecurity (it acted as if it posed no threat to any power when it expanded its investment and market activity, but all other powers threatened it if they did) unsettled the U.S. government in Central America, where it considered German interests aggressive and threatening.[26] But every expansive power sought the prestige of a worldwide chain of support for its navy, merchants, settlers, and missionaries.

Each ambitious North Atlantic state and Japan envisioned a chain of coaling, cable, and naval stations, along with a canal to advance its world competitive position. German officials envisioned naval and cable stations from the homeland to St. Thomas in the Danish Virgin Islands, across an isthmian canal site, to the Galápagos and Samoa, and finally to Qing-Dao, China. Branches would run to Africa, Mexico, South America, and New Guinea. There was always an argument to justify the goal. The German naval attaché in Washington, D.C., for example, argued that German dignity and its commercial and strategic objectives required a secure naval station in the West Indies. The empire did not have to dominate Middle America, he noted, but its legitimate aspirations demanded a strong point near any canal.[27] Securing communications to exploit the Pacific basin explained many German actions at Manila Bay and in Samoa, Hawaii, the Sulu Archipelago, the Carolines, Qing-Dao, Nicaragua, Venezuela, Haiti, and the Virgin Islands.

Historian Hans-Peter Ullmann summarized German expansion at the turn of the century: "Then next there was the 'governmental imperialism' of the Emperor, the imperial administration, and the principal bureaucrats." *Weltpolitik* (an integrated world policy) encompassed power policies, nationalism, and a naval building policy that, Ullmann observed, "served inner political goals." He continued: "The majority of industrialists, merchants, and bankers foresaw no advantage from a formal imperialism, and the tiny economic value of the German colonies confirmed their judgement. . . . Nevertheless, many entrepreneurs believed that they could no longer meet the competition in the world markets only with commercial means, but they needed to secure for themselves the power of the state."[28] "Governmental imperialism," which pursued status, prestige, and a fair field for German entrepreneurs in the world market, elicited a broader base of support.

The French government was routinely less confrontational than the German. Nevertheless, it desired to halt U.S. expansionism that threatened to overrun French entrepreneurs in Asia and Latin America. French participation in the world economy received a boost in 1895 with the formation of the Union Coloniale Française, a group of influential businessmen, financiers, and politicians lobbying for support for ventures in the colonies. The Union Coloniale Française generated interest in foreign areas and world economic ties. French entrepreneurs and military interests were more evident in North and West Africa, Southeast Asia, and the Middle East, but they also sought opportunities in China and the circum-Caribbean. In the Caribbean basin, however, a French consular agent feared that the European diplomats and businesses were seduced to believe that they could acquire wealth where informal U.S. protectorates were in place.[29]

A French canal at Panama promised to rejuvenate France's geopolitical and economic importance. The Universal Interoceanic Canal Company's bankruptcy in the late 1880s, however, had spooked French capitalists away from isthmian projects. In the 1890s, French investors formed the New Panama Canal Company in an effort to save French pride, reputation, and as many francs as circumstances would allow. French officials quietly supported the Panama project and opposed the U.S.-backed Nicaraguan route. But the deeper the late-nineteenth-century economic crisis became, the more determined U.S. businessmen were to build a canal.[30]

Domestic problems from the depression of 1893 and the competition in China and the circum-Caribbean (revolts in Cuba, Panama, and Nicaragua) threatened a prosperous, secure world. In 1898, the U.S. government used force to extend its control in the Gulf-Caribbean and to assure premier access to the Pacific basin. A well-known historian of U.S. expansion, Thomas McCormick, cogently rejecting the oft-cited "explanations" for U.S. intervention in Cuba, argued: "America's insular acquisitions of 1898 were not products of 'large policy' imperialism. Hawaii, Wake, Guam, and the Philippines were not taken principally for their own economic worth, or for their fulfillment of Manifest Destiny, or for their venting of the 'psychic crisis.' They were obtained, instead, largely in an eclectic effort to construct a system of coaling, cable, and naval stations for an integrated trade route which could help realize America's overriding ambition in the Pacific—the penetration and ultimate domination of the fabled China market."[31] The great powers competed to support their expanding political economies, not to build humanitarian, missionary, or free democratic societies.

Many journalists, intellectuals, and U.S. government officials accused Spain of suppressing the freedom and self-government of the Cuban people. They also alleged that the Spanish troops treated the general population and the captured Cuban insurgents with great cruelty. The Spanish were held responsible for widespread hunger and suffering, and, of course, the blowing up of the USS *Maine* in Havana harbor in February 1898. The U.S. press led the public to interpret Spanish conduct in Cuba as an affront to U.S. values, ideals, and expectations for the future. In addition, Spain's activity hindered U.S. recovery from the depression of 1893 and undercut U.S. efforts to stabilize the Caribbean area in conjunction with the construction of an isthmian canal.

U.S. political and military leaders were determined to secure the Caribbean-isthmian route to the Pacific basin, where half the world's population lived, and to prevent Cuba from becoming prey for a rival European metropole (fig. 3). Most informed U.S. inhabitants knew of the Cuban revolt; few dreamed of the remote Philippines. Leaders with geopolitical outlooks thought of the Pacific. At a banquet of the Middlesex Club in Boston on 27 April 1898, expansionist Senator Albert Beveridge of Indiana insisted: "We are a conquering race, and . . . we must obey our blood and occupy new markets, and, if necessary, new lands. . . . the trade of the world must and shall be ours. . . . Our

Fig. 3. "Uncle Sam to the European Powers," *Boston Globe.* The U.S. press envisions the U.S. role as halting great power expansion. (With permission of Louis A. Pérez Jr.)

Knocking at the door.—*Chicago Tribune.*

Fig. 4. "Knocking at the Door," *Chicago Tribune.* Before the war of 1898, dirty and hungry waifs (Cuba, the Philippines, and Puerto Rico) seek U.S. assistance for advancement. (With permission of Louis A. Pérez Jr.)

institutions will follow our flag on the wings of our commerce" (fig. 4). He expected an Anglo-Saxon "division of the world's markets so that the result may be just." He welcomed Anglo-Saxon authority, "if it means such an English-speaking people's league of God for the permanent peace of this war-worn world." And he knew: "The Philippines are logically our first target."[32] Here, Beveridge advocated social Darwinism, liberalism, and expansionism into the Pacific basin to satisfy U.S. material and spiritual needs, a full diet of social imperialism.

The conduct of the War of 1898 revealed the objectives of U.S. leadership. Senator William P. Frye of Maine, later appointed one of five peace commissioners, knew the goal was to secure canal access and an entrepôt harbor in East Asia—what some contemporaries called an "American Hong Kong": "The fear I have about this war is that peace will be declared before we can get full occupation of the Philippines and Porto [*sic*] Rico."[33] The Pacific theater was key. The United States acquired what it needed there before it even sent troops to Cuba and Puerto Rico. War was declared on 21 April 1898, and the first battle occurred in Manila on 30 April; then Guam and Wake Island were taken, and only after 20 June did the U.S. Army land in Cuba. The island was conquered within a month, and Puerto Rico fell about a week later. Frye's fear was groundless; the administration knew its goals.

If the McKinley administration had shown signs of forgetting the expansionists' objectives in the Pacific basin, Massachusetts senator Henry Cabot Lodge and Rough Rider Colonel Theodore Roosevelt were prepared to remind him. Roosevelt urged Lodge: "You must get Manila and Hawaii; you must prevent any talk of peace until we get Porto [*sic*] Rico and the Philippines as well as secure the independence of Cuba." While Puerto Rico had modest value for securing a U.S. canal, it could prove dangerous in other hands. And it was a Spanish possession, thus fair game in a war over Cuba (fig. 5). According to Lodge, even Secretary of State William Day, who was not known as an imperialist, saw "there [was] of course no question about Porto [*sic*] Rico . . . the only question for us to consider is how much we should do in the Philippines." Lodge considered "the Hawaiian business as practically settled." The priority of Asia in a war to pacify Cuba attracted humorists. The gap between rhetoric and reality prompted a contemporary newspaper writer, not gender sensitive, to ask: "Why is Uncle Sam like a lady throwing a stone? Because it aimed at Cuba and hit the Philippines."[34] A miss of about eleven thousand miles.

U.S. policy aimed to control both Cuba and the Philippines. It imprinted its own views of race, class, and religion upon both countries. U.S. officials wanted to eliminate the Spanish authorities without transferring power to indigenous authorities (fig. 6), but rebel success threatened U.S. expectations. The Cuban autonomists joined the separatists' movement when they discovered that Spain could not accomplish reform or repression. By the spring of 1898, the rebels were capturing midsized towns and threatening the large cities. The prominent and productive historian of Cuba Louis Pérez Jr. concluded: "Within two years of Weyler's appointment, elites had abandoned all hopes of salvation from Spain." Conservative planters, facing a popular na-

From the St. Louis Globe-Democrat.

Fig. 5. "Uncle Sam and Liberty Enjoy Their Good Deed," *St. Louis Globe-Democrat.* After the war of 1898, charming, neat, yet commonly dressed lovely maidens (Cuba, the Philippines, and Puerto Rico) enjoy the benefits of U.S. intervention and assistance. (With permission of Louis A. Pérez Jr.)

tionalist Cuban victory, turned to the United States for salvation. In Pérez's view, "the U.S. leadership realized that Cuba was lost to Spain and might be lost to the United States also, but the intervention changed everything, as it was meant to." "So," he concluded, "the Cuban war for national liberation was transfigured into the 'Spanish-American War,' nomenclature that denied Cuban participation and . . . served to legitimize the U.S. claim over Cuba as a spoil of victory."[35] And conflict with Spain justified conquest of Spanish possessions near China.

The war in Cuba was much less taxing upon the U.S. armed forces and its political leadership than the fighting in the Philippines. (The armed resistance to U.S. interference in Cuban life occurred sixty-some years after the war with Spain in 1898.) While much of the early fighting in this war took

Ha! ha! "It didn't hurt a bit," Spain says.—*Los Angeles Times.*

Fig. 6. "Ha! Ha!" *Los Angeles Times.* Uncle Sam, the dentist, extracts the teeth (needed for sustenance, in this case the major centers of Spain's empire), the sources of Spain's consumption of imperial wealth. Painless? (With permission of Louis A. Pérez Jr.)

"SHELLING" THE ENEMY.

UNCLE SAM—"This one's tougher than the others, but it'll crack all right."

—*Judy, London.*

Fig. 7. "Shelling the Enemy," *Judy*, London. The U.S. military cracked the Spanish nuts (fortified towns) one by one. The Santiago campaign cost more than two hundred dead, while Mantanzas and Manila had much fewer casualties. (With permission of Louis A. Pérez Jr.)

place in the Pacific, the U.S. Navy did patrol Cuban waters. In late June 1898, U.S. land forces went ashore east of Santiago de Cuba (fig. 7). Cuban insurgents had cleared the beaches, so the U.S. forces landed without incident. Within three weeks of the landing Spanish naval units in Santiago de Cuba had been sunk in a flight attempt, and then the land forces surrendered. The alienation of the Cuban insurgents began as soon as they were no longer needed. The dark-skinned insurgent General Calixto García and his troops were denied entrance to Santiago de Cuba. Bacteria and mosquitoes more than artillery and infantry had produced heavy losses on all sides in Cuba. Less than four hundred U.S. military personnel died in battle, while five thousand died of disease and illness. The fighting in 1898 cost $250,000,000.[36] The costs were higher in blood and money in East Asia.

Once the fighting was over, McKinley appointed Whitelaw Reid, expansionist and editor-owner of the *New York Tribune*, to the team of negotiators to make peace on the right terms. Naturally, the Pacific basin was the key. In his diary, Reid explained: "If to [Hawaii] we now added the Philippines, it would be possible for American energy to . . . ultimately convert the Pacific Ocean into an American lake, making it far more our own than the Atlantic is now Great Britain's. Such a possession would . . . stimulate shipbuilding industry and commerce, and . . . add immensely to the national prosperity." He avoided applying the right of conquest because his vision rejected any U.S. acquisition through conquest.[37]

The U.S. vision of itself as a Pacific power originated in the colonial and early national periods. The U.S. Exploring Expedition of 1838 had described three great island harbors in the Pacific outside of Japan—Pago Pago (in Samoa), Manila, and Pearl Harbor. The vision fathered reality. The U.S. government acquired a naval base in Pago Pago from an 1878 agreement with Great Britain and Germany. Congress endorsed the annexation of Hawaii during the war. And the Paris Peace Commission negotiated to place Manila in U.S. hands. By the end of 1898, the U.S. government had acquired the three great Oceania harbors.

The desire for U.S. commercial expansion was not just the domain of imperialists. Senator George Hoar of Massachusetts was a determined anti-imperialist, but he saw the need for the U.S. political economy to share in the wealth of Asia. In early 1898, Hoar had urged McKinley to choose peaceful means rather than war to settle the Cuban situation. Hoar's anti-imperialism, however, made an exception with regard to Hawaii because it was essential "in order to help us get our share of China." Hoar, to justify his view, drew a line on a flat map from the Aleutians Islands to the southern tip of Chile. This line demonstrated that Hawaii was, indeed, geographically within the American continent and thus protected by the Monroe Doctrine. But ex-president Grover Cleveland was "ashamed of the whole affair [Hawaiian annexation]." One of the quirks of human nature is innocent honesty. The anti-imperialists also wanted a few possessions. If the U.S. anti-imperialists of the 1890s had persuaded the U.S. government only to acquire the possessions that one or more of the anti-imperialist leaders saw as necessary for a prosperous and secure United States, the U.S. empire would have looked as it did when the "expansionists" ruled from the White House and Capitol Hill.[38]

Since U.S. society considered involvement in Asia and the Caribbean region as necessary for national well-being and security, the U.S. government established extraterritoriality and protectorates from Cuba to China. It limited sovereignty and independence in nations located along that axis and thus firmed up its control of transit and security points along the route to fabled Asian wealth. It stymied Danish plans to transfer the Virgin Islands to Germany, German efforts to obtain all or part of the Galápagos Islands from Ecuador, Mexican plans to lease land in Magdalena Bay (in La Paz, Baja California) to a Japanese firm, and Costa Rican prospects to sell the Cocos Islands (the island group closest to the Pacific side of a Panama canal). When Secretary of State Elihu Root learned that Costa Rica contemplated the sale of the Cocos Islands, he repeated U.S. unwillingness to purchase them, yet cautioned that the U.S. government would view "occupation of the Cocos Islands by any European power . . . [as] a menace to the United States." Root's gratuitous statement reduced the value of the Cocos to zero. After 1903, Costa Rican officials also feared that Costa Rica's persisting border dispute with Panama would suffer from formal U.S. protection of Panama.[39] The U.S. government closely monitored all sites near the canal, to which it assigned security value.

The United States had little contact with the Philippines before 1898; modest trade in the early nineteenth century weakened in subsequent decades. The Suez Canal—an engineering and technological achievement—first brought the Philippines closer to Europe; then commercial submarine telegraph cables strengthened the ties. But still, Spanish efforts to extract maximum value in a distant, tenuous relationship made their rule onerous. The indigenous Filipinos suffered from the great cruelty of Spanish friars (who extorted land and labor) and their local allies. Torture was common and only wealthy Filipinos could flee the cruelty. Before 1872, Filipinos had revolted thirty-four times against Spanish rule. In 1897, after a year's resistance, several Philippine nationalist leaders, including Emilio Aguinaldo, had negotiated a deal to reform local government and to end the violence. The arrangement required some rebel leaders to accept exile. But Spanish authorities failed to fulfill the agreement. The U.S. government, after declaring war on Spain, transported Aguinaldo back to the Philippines to renew the fight against the Spanish. The insurgents quickly controlled the islands—except for Manila, a few ports, and the Muslim areas. Moorfield Storey observed that "when the American troops reached the Islands in 1898, there was no anarchy and the Filipinos were governing themselves." The U.S. troops landed without opposition because Filipino forces controlled the area.[40]

A Philippine state, however, was not considered viable by Washington officials, given the intense imperial competition in East Asia. The U.S. government believed that Japan or Germany would seize the islands, and if Germany acted first, the British would consider that action a threat to its East Asia position. In any event, the U.S. economy needed a warehouse and distribution center for Asian and western Pacific trade. German historian Klaus Hildebrand noted that in the international sphere everyone combined with everyone against everyone in East Asia, Africa, and Latin America. And racism played a part. The final surrender of Manila was staged to save face for the defeated Spanish and for the transfer of control to a white western power rather than a brown-skinned indigenous people. Inexplicably, some historians treated the acquisition of the Philippines as accidentally happening. But more blood was shed in the Filipino resistance to American conquest than in three hundred years of Spanish oppression, and ten times as much blood and treasure as during the War of 1898. After the War of 1898, the United States no longer viewed Spain and England as principal rivals in China and the Pacific, but looked at Russia, Germany, and Japan with greater distrust.[41]

Scholars James C. Thomson Jr., Peter W. Stanley, and John Curtis Perry have denied that U.S. expansion was "wholly—or even primarily—economic in motivation." Many entrepreneurs did seek relief from overproduction, but "the promotion of foreign trade and investment was not, in itself, the essence of the expansionism of this era." The U.S. government emerged as "one of the key forces in the international balance of power. . . . The United States government itself was the expansive force." In fact, the U.S. government switched formally to promotion rather than protection of U.S. economic interests abroad during the depression of 1873 in response to the alleged glut of overproduction. U.S. expansionists sought not only "a measure of relief from overproduction, but social discipline and a restoration of national purpose." Aggressive promotion of U.S. interests became a duty of the U.S. Navy also after the War of 1898.[42] Thomson, Stanley, and Perry are partly correct. The U.S. government emerged as an international player, but to promote and protect U.S. investment and commerce in order to alleviate the social disorder resulting from the glut. Balancing power was, at best, a strategy to achieve that goal.

The State Department certainly disagreed with the conclusions of Thomson, Stanley, and Perry. In April 1898, the State Department informed its officials that "every year we shall be confronted with an increasing surplus of manufactured goods for sale in foreign markets if American operatives and artisans are to be kept employed the year around. The enlargement of foreign consumption of the products of our mills and workshops has, therefore, become a serious problem of statesmanship as well as of commerce."[43] Why risk lives, prestige, and honor abroad unless there was something to win? The U.S. government has seldom pursued idealism, and never for long. When necessary, it quickly supported brutal, authoritarian regimes that would create the order and stability required for U.S. entrepreneurial and financial access to their political economies. The goals were not religion or culture, since the U.S. government seldom pursued with persistent determination social or religious freedom in societies that were open to U.S. trade and investment. The most reliable measure of U.S. intervention has been access for various direct and indirect U.S. economic interests to stable, ordered governments, and the expectation that access would boost U.S. well-being and security.

Spain resisted the erosion of its political influence and economic and cultural ties in the New World. Its loss of fifty thousand fighting men and the large financial costs had catastrophic impact upon its government. The "generation of 1898," Spanish intellectuals who had objected to the lack of political and social reform before 1898, represented a spiritual protest. After the defeat, humiliation, and loss of Spain's colonial remnants, protest in Spain grew more fervent. One step to counter U.S.-led Pan-Americanism involved "hispanismo," a revival of Hispanic and Latin cultural ties. Spain held an Hispano-American conference in Madrid in 1901. The Central American republics proudly participated, but showed little serious interest in the concrete plans of the Madrid conference.[44] Don Quijote, flamenco, and *los toros* were no match for the House of Morgan, United Fruit, and the U.S. Marines. Still, Spain had lost Manila and San Juan Hill, but it had no intention of surrendering economically or culturally to Calibán.

Columbus and the U.S. government invested considerable time and energy in the Caribbean, but both ultimately eyed Asia. The British, German, Dutch, French, and Japanese also recognized that the Caribbean and the isthmus were vital midpoints between the wealth, consumption needs, technology, and productive energy of the North Atlantic states and the teeming masses of Asia. One chief consequence of promoting U.S. economic and political interests has been constant involvement in conflict around the world. While western activity in Asia created trade, investment, raw materials, cultural exchange, and Christian missionary activity, the balance sheet goes further.

CHAPTER 6

☖

The War of 1898
in the Pacific Basin

From the sixteenth to the eighteenth centuries, European powers did not produce enough to conduct more than modest trade. But in the late nineteenth century, the highly productive, resource-consuming industrialized powers needed industrial and consumable raw materials, labor, markets for overproduction, investment opportunities, and a stake in the future of selected external areas of resources. The conflux of the three crises of the 1890s posed strategic, economic, and cultural problems for all great powers. For Germany, lagging Great Britain in industrialization and empire building, the crises of the 1890s presented an opportunity to gain colonies, status, and access to resources while weakening Great Britain (fig. 8).

To secure and develop these factors of growth for the United States, the national political economy shaped U.S. policy in the Asian stage of the War of 1898. While the press and public in the United States spoke of Cuba, the ambitions and competitiveness of the major powers found new direction and urgency in the Pacific basin. Economic, social, and political turmoil touched the great powers and the periphery states, but the goal remained to secure a North Atlantic–Pacific connection. The 1898 version of Columbus's dream required isthmian transit, naval stations along the access routes in the Caribbean and across the Pacific, and a distribution base in East Asia. The U.S. government used patriotic fervor to acquire bases in both the Caribbean and Oceania (fig. 9). The War of 1898 propelled American participation in the Pacific beyond the U.S. west coast, Hawaii, and Samoa.

The war expended much more blood and treasure in the Pacific basin than in the Caribbean region. And it produced a variety of territorial acquisitions. On 25 May 1898, the naval commander of troops leaving San Francisco

Fig. 8. "John Bull." A German postcard image of the situation in China. John Bull (Great Britain) had controlled China for decades. In the 1890s, the great powers were subdividing Britain's China. (With permission of Michael Bolln, www.altepostkarten.de)

for Manila unsealed presidential orders that instructed him to seize Guam. On 20 June, after the USS *Charleston* fired a dozen shots over the fort at San Luis d'Apra (the chief port on Guam), several Spanish officers apologized for their inability to return the salute because of lack of munitions. The U.S. captain informed them that he had not fired a salute; rather the two countries were at war. Because their underwater cable was inoperable, the fort had not been notified of the hostilities. In January 1899, a U.S. naval officer formally annexed Wake Island, claimed by Lieutenant Charles Wilkes sixty years earlier.[1]

Former president of the American Historical Association Henry Adams, historian Foster Rhea Dulles, and satirist Peter Finley Dunne are among the more interesting analysts of U.S. expansion. Adams knew that Puerto Rico would be taken, but he had not wished for the Philippines. Acquisition of the Philippines, Adams noted, meant that "in London, the balance of power in the East came alone into discussion."[2]

Acquisition of the Philippines raised new questions of empire and colonialism. Filipinos were civilized and showed no desire for American rule. In Foster Rhea Dulles's view: "It became increasingly clear as 1898 gave way to

Fig. 9. "Off to War Parade, Denver." The trans-Mississippi west eagerly joined the war to liberate Cuba. Flags of the Cuban revolutionary government and the United States flutter over the parade. Many western units were sent to the Philippines, however. (With permission of the Western History/Genealogy Department, Denver Public Library)

1899 that [Filipino leader Emilio] Aguinaldo was ready to fight for his liberties, and that his followers were fully as determined to defy the power of the United States as they were that of Spain." Dulles thought "the Filipinos were not interested in his [McKinley's] conception of duty, humanity, civilization. They were interested in the independence of their country and . . . they could expect no aid from the American President."[3]

The Irish barkeeper Mr. Dooley, the spokesman in Peter Finley Dunne's widely read humor column, understood the meaning of the Philippine acquisition and subsequent war. Dooley said:

Whin we plant what Hogan calls th' starry banner iv Freedom in th'e Ph'lippeenes . . . we'll larn thim a lesson. . . . We say to thim: "Naygurs," we say, "poor, dissolute uncovered wretches," say we, "whin th' crool hand iv Spain forged man'cles f'r ye'er limbs, as Hogan says, who was it crossed th' say an' sthruck off th' come-alongs? We did, by dad, we did. An' now, yr miserable, childish-minded apes, we propose f'r to larn ye th' uses iv liberty. In ivry city in this unfair land we will erect schoolhouses an' packin' houses an' houses iv correction, an' we'll larn ye our language, because 'tis aiseir to larn ye ours thin to larn ousilves ye'ers, an' we'll give ye clothes if ye pay f'r thim, an' if ye don't ye can go without, an' whin yr're hungry ye can go to th' morgue—we mane th's resth'rant—an' ate a good square meal iv army beef. . . . an' whin ye've become edycated an' have all th' blessin's iv civilization that we don't want, that'll count ye wan."

Dunne was also hard on the moralistic and humanistic arguments advanced to support U.S. expansion by war. He had Dooley comment: "Take up th' white man's burden an' hand it to th' coons." Dooley noted the crass reality behind the alleged humanitarianism: "Hands acrost th' sea an' into some wan's pocket."[4]

Some major political figures, including House Speaker Thomas Reed and Senator George Hoar, saw racism and anti-democratic conduct guiding U.S. relations with the Filipinos. After peace in the War of 1898, Hoar observed, the U.S. government and military "crushed the Republic that the Philippine people had set up for themselves, deprived them of their independence, and established there, by American power, a Government in which the people have no part, against their will." In fact, many Filipino municipalities had instituted self-government after the Spanish willingly or unwillingly departed.[5]

In the 1890s, U.S. society debated immigration restriction. Speaker Reed distrusted the 1898 version of U.S. idealism: "Now we are going to take in eight million barbarians and semi-barbarians, and we are paying twenty million dollars to get them."[6] Reacting to the U.S. payment for the Philippines, he remarked acidly, "We have bought ten million Malays at $2.00 a head unpicked," and added in a most prescient comment, "nobody knows what it will cost to pick them." Picking them was dangerous and costly. On 4 February 1899 fighting broke out between Filipinos and U.S. troops.[7] The fighting endured for decades.

Dunne and Dooley recognized the difference between a benefactor of civilization and a bandit. Dooley described the potential fates for Emilio Aguinaldo around 1899. Claiming that Aguinaldo mistakenly thought "th' bom [boom] was still on in th' hero business," Dooley recognized that Aguinaldo sought to make "th' Ph'lippeens indepindint on us f'r support. . . .

If he'd [laid down his arms] come in, ye'd be hearin' that James Haitch Aggynaldoo'd been appointed foorth-class postmasther at Hootchey-Kootchey; but now th' nex ye know iv him 'll be on th' blotther at th' polis station."[8]

Speaker Reed shared Dunne's satirical humor over U.S. conduct in the Philippines. Aguinaldo was captured in March 1901. Reed, in mock surprise, asked his partner: "What, are you working today? I should think you would be celebrating. I see by the papers that the American Army has captured the infant son of Aguinaldo and at last accounts was in hot pursuit of the mother."[9] Then the conflict seemed to wind down.

The war was costly, and forces on both sides committed atrocities; the inhumanity reflected the intensity. By the summer of 1901, things seemed nearly over in the northern islands. But at Balangiga on Samar Island, a U.S. detachment was overrun and seventy-four U.S. soldiers killed. Major General Adna R. Chaffee determined to end the conflict in the northern islands. He sent one brigade to southern Luzon and a second to Samar Island.[10]

At Balangiga, most U.S. soldiers had died in the fort or trying to cross the bay to Leyte. U.S. troops in Leyte quickly crossed the bay to find a ghastly sight of dead and mutilated U.S. soldiers. Ignoring the pleas of several old women, the U.S. commander ordered the 250 Filipino dead cremated, not buried. A search of the jungle produced twenty Filipinos, who were then massacred. Apparently, the Army believed that the Spanish general Valeriano "Butcher" Weyler's cruel policy in Cuba had been correct. Brigadier General Jacob H. "Howling Wilderness" Smith, in command on Samar, ordered the 250,000 inhabitants into concentration camps, with a kill-on-sight order for those not in the camps. General Smith ordered, "I want no prisoners. I wish you to kill and burn; the more you kill and burn the better you will please me. I want all persons killed who are capable of bearing arms in actual hostilities against the United States." He specified all males over ten to be killed. In response to a confirming question: "Persons ten years and older are those designated as being capable of bearing arms?" Smith replied, "Yes." He wanted the whole island made into "a howling wilderness." Smith unwisely put his orders in writing. Guided by Smith's orders, a field officer called a summary court-martial when he learned that there was a plot against the Marines. The officer wrote: "It became necessary to expend eleven prisoners."[11] Later, Smith was court-martialed and retired.

In southern Luzon, Brigadier General J. Franklin Bell operated concentration camps without adequate food, sanitation, or medical supplies. When the U.S. press and Congress heard about operations in Samar, Luzon, and other locations, a public relations nightmare erupted for the U.S. military.

Fig. 10. "Hospital in the Philippines." High illness and casualty rates during the long U.S. military activity in the Philippines (from 1898 until at least 1913) required many large medical facilities. (Courtesy of the National Museum of Health and Medicine, Armed Forces Institute of Pathology, Washington, D.C. [SAW 74])

Many in the U.S. Congress and public apparently believed "Butcher" Weyler had been wrong. The harsh operations had been deadly for many Filipinos, but the U.S. generals suffered only short-term disadvantages. The tarnished reputation of most U.S. commanders recovered miraculously. Each of the three ranking generals from the Luzon-Samar campaign eventually became the ranking general of the U.S. Army.[12]

The Philippine insurrection, unlike the invasion of Cuba, was no minor affair. By mid-1900, two-thirds of the U.S. Army was engaged in the Philippines. The cost of the war from 1899 until 1902 was high: 4,234 dead, 2,818 wounded, and thousands succumbed to diseases contracted in the islands (fig. 10). The immediate monetary cost through 1902 was $600 million, or about the equivalent of $30 billion in year 2002 currency. Many millions more were spent in benefits and pensions. The U.S. Army fought 2,811 engagements to "civilize" the Filipinos. And these costs in blood and treasure do not include the years subsequent to the self-declared "end" to the conflict in 1902, because at that time much of the blood and some of the monetary cost were transferred to the Philippine authorities.[13]

The Philippine Insurrection (or Filipino War) officially lasted until July 1902, but regional and guerrilla fighting continued incessantly. After 1902, U.S. casualties declined as the fighting became more sporadic and a larger share of combat was shifted to Philippine forces. One historian argued that the Philippine revolt was the United States' "first major step into Asia as a world power." That view overlooks the acquisition of Alaska, Hawaii, Samoa, Guam, Wake, and Midway and extensive extraterritorial rights in China. The chief resistance to U.S. authority in the Philippines came from Muslims in Moroland (the Muslim-inhabited islands in the south), Mindanao, Samar, Jolo, and the Sulu Archipelago, near the Sulu Sea. Historian Stanley Karnow concluded: "Moro dissidents continued to struggle against the infidels for years, and their heirs are striving to this day to establish an autonomous state."[14]

The Muslim Filipinos had never recognized Spanish rule. Naturally, they refused to allow Spain, which never controlled them, to transfer anything to the Americans. Before 1898, under a modus vivendi, the Spanish had controlled a few garrisoned towns during the day and nothing much at night. The Spanish did not interfere in the Muslims' religion, customs, or the management of their affairs. The first U.S. military commanders worked out similar agreements, except they curbed the slave traffic and certain "barbaric" practices. U.S. officials planned and implemented public works, communications projects, schools, hospitals, and sanitation programs. Despite what they considered accommodation, U.S. forces spent much energy fighting Moro groups in the first few years of U.S. military governance. This limited interference lasted until the American self-proclaimed "victory" in 1902. The arrogant goal to "develop, civilize, [and] educate" Moroland meant enduring conflicts with the Muslims.[15]

After the "victory" in 1902, Americans disparaged the Moros and their culture and became less accommodating. Generals Samuel S. Sumner and Leonard Wood and Captain John J. Pershing described the Moros as "savages." U.S. officials sought to collect taxes and redistribute land. The Moros resented paying taxes to a foreign, "infidel" government and being required to parcel out to newcomers land held for generations by Moros. U.S. plantation owners, Chinese merchants, and Christian Filipino settlers dominated the agricultural and commercial activity. U.S. education meant to "Christianize," yet the U.S. military did not hesitate to slaughter the opposition. Matters got worse. U.S. military units were re-engaged in campaigns in the Muslim islands by 1905. Persistent small skirmishes became full pacification campaigns.

Some engagements killed hundreds of people—mostly Moros, who normally carried inferior weapons. The fighting around Lake Lanao and on the island of Jolo was fierce; the two larger battles, Bud Daho (1906) and Bud Bagsak (1913), both occurred on Jolo. Bud Bagsak, with several hundred dead Moros, was the last major engagement between the Moros and U.S. forces, as the U.S. military administration of the region ended later that year. Each island or region of an island had its own "end" date, but often skirmishes continued for decades. (The kidnappings, killings, extortion, and "terrorism" in the southern Philippines in the past three or four decades have occurred mostly in the Moroland areas.) Later, Filipino Christians governed. After 1916, Christian Filipinos exercised growing responsibility until near total authority passed into Filipino hands in 1920. Whoever governed, Moro resistance always met with a vastly superior use of force—the U.S. Army, the Philippine Scouts, and then the Philippine Constabulary.[16]

Despite U.S. disclaimers, the U.S. and Spanish governments followed similar policies in Moroland. Both sought to exploit the natural resources of Mindanao and the Sulu region and to redirect the lucrative Moro trade from Southeast Asia to the Philippine market. Both had missionary objectives to change the values of the Muslims, as perhaps the only way to Christianize them. And both relied on force to convert the inhabitants to Christianity and to change their way of life. Yet different methods were available to imperial powers. The Dutch and British commonly ruled their colonies indirectly through native sultans or rulers; the Americans opted for the Spanish method of force and destruction of the opposition. Like the Spanish, the Americans considered the Moros savages and had little respect for their religion or culture. Disparagement and condemnation were essential to justify the brutality. While the Dutch and British wanted peace and profit, the Americans presumed that Americanized culture and religion had to accompany profits.[17]

U.S. conduct in the Philippines was contrary to the rhetoric justifying it. Senator Albert Beveridge asked the rhetorical question: "Would not the people of the Philippines prefer the just, humane, civilizing government of this Republic to the savage, bloody rule of pillage and extortion from which we have rescued them?" He did not expect nor accept the hard, honest reply that the "humane, civilizing" U.S. military reportedly killed more Filipinos in three years than the barbaric, authoritarian Spanish had in three and a half centuries. From 1897 to 1901, the McKinley administration emphasized its humane, Christian, and democratic mission, yet it launched two wars (the War of 1898 and the Filipino War), engaged in a third on foreign territory (the Boxer Rebellion), and produced a half million dead for humanity and Christianity. And the two states founded from this conflict (Cuba and the Philippines) experienced no democracy and occasionally inhumane treatment for generations.[18]

Admiral Alfred Thayer Mahan, the leading U.S. naval strategist, saw danger in an incomplete transformation of Asia's diverse peoples. He considered a semi-westernized east more dangerous than a non-westernized east. China posed a future threat in Mahan's view. It was "inert," but it could initiate "a wave of barbaric invasion." Mahan supported local interests and naval officials who wanted Hawaii annexed to become an outpost of U.S. civilization and a check upon future Chinese aggression.[19]

Mark Twain initially supported both the Spanish-American and the Filipino-American conflicts, but he was living in Europe, where the Boer War (the British conflict with the largely Dutch settlers in South Africa) and the Boxer Rebellion received more attention than the U.S. conflicts. U.S. and British officials in conflict with the Filipinos and Boers often commiserated with each other. The British and U.S. governments shared a mutual determination to suppress insurrection by aggressive inferiors.[20] And Twain accepted McKinley's claim that there would be no U.S. conquest of Cuba.

Liberating Cuba appeared a noble cause. But after reading the Treaty of Paris, Twain recognized that 1898 was not a noble war of elevated purpose. The U.S. government freed Cuba as a smoke screen, annexing other areas. Twain turned against a U.S. policy of acquisitions and protectorates. He reluctantly acknowledged that "we have gone there to conquer, not to redeem." He detested the treaty's protection of the "friars" claims—unjust and improper land grabs by Catholic orders in the Philippines. Twain became a vice president of the Anti-Imperialist League. He planned to write about the "water cure" (forcing large amounts of water into prisoners to compel them to talk) and the Captain Cornelius Brownell case, which concerned an officer who used the water cure. However, his sense of justice and emotions crippled his wit and satire. He condemned the "Christian butchers" and the senators who defended the U.S. soldier-criminals.[21]

The U.S. role in the Philippines drew comparisons with Spanish and British colonial misrule. In 1898, McKinley had said that the Spanish *reconcentrado* policy "was not civilized warfare. . . . It was extermination. The only peace it could beget was that of the wilderness and the grave." For many critics, U.S. conduct in the Philippines ran contrary to the Declaration of Independence and reaffirmed the condemned Spanish atrocities in Cuba. One observer complained: "At the first . . . test we throw the [U.S.] doctrine [of liberty] away and adopt the Spanish doctrine [force, torture, concentration camps, and authoritarian rule]."[22] The U.S. government first condemned Spanish repressive techniques as barbaric, and then adopted them.

Henry Adams wrote his brother Brooks Adams: "I hold our Philippine excursion to be a false start. . . . It is a mere repetition of the errors of Spain and England." He preferred directing the national energy to the North Pacific — Japan, Korea, and Russia. Judge Moorfield Storey and Filipinan Marcial Lichauco quoted Abraham Lincoln: "No man is good enough to govern another without that other's consent." And Lincoln had rejected slave owner arguments that "the inferior race are to be treated with as much allowance as they are capable of enjoying," considering those to be "arguments that kings have made for the enslaving of the people in all ages of the world." The Women's Christian Temperance Union and other social purity organizations sympathized with the Cuban and Philippine insurgents' desire for self-government, and they were highly critical of U.S. conduct, which they viewed as greedy, aggressive, and unjust in many instances.[23] The critics rejected the racism, inhumanity, and abusive geopolitics of U.S. action in the Philippines.

Some opponents of U.S. expansion asked hard, cynical questions of U.S. policy goals. Steel magnate Andrew Carnegie, a Scotsman who had long hated British imperialism, asked: "Has the influence of the superior race upon the inferior ever proved beneficial to either?" He expected military occupation of the Philippines to "antagonize the Filipinos and corrupt America's youth." The U.S. soldiers had a more desperate need of missionaries than the natives.[24]

Contemporaries and historians have ventured strange observations on the Filipino revolt. According to one observer, President McKinley ordered a "mission of . . . benevolent assimilation." Henry Cabot Lodge, blind to events, dishonest in judgement, or self-deluded, denied any "act of oppression against the Filipinos by any American soldiers or by the American forces of any kind in the Philippine Islands." In Beveridge's strange image, the Philippines became "the Gibraltar of the Pacific" and the protector of the U.S. west coast. Historian John Dobson argued that the "Philippine annexation was an artifact of the war and the way it was fought."[25] That view slights a century of ever deeper and more varied U.S. activity in the Pacific basin. Historian Gerald Linderman sketched a more realistic image: "The War of 1898 was not an accident . . . Americans, and no one else, must be masters of the cross-roads of the Pacific."[26] The acquisition of the Philippines was related to one hundred years of U.S. activity in the Pacific and four centuries of quest by North Atlantic maritime powers for Asian trade.

The inhabitants of the Philippines were not benevolently assimilated, nor casual artifacts, nor primitive protectors of the United States. Educator and philosopher John Dewey and General Wesley Merritt described the Filipinos as intelligent and disciplined. Admiral George Dewey considered them capable of self-government. In 1898 the Filipinos had turned over thousands of Spanish prisoners to the U.S. military. But wealthy Filipinos clamored for U.S. rule because they distrusted democracy and the rule of middle- and lower-class Filipinos. In its quest for order and opportunity, the U.S. government confirmed its racism and class biases. It turned to officials of the defeated Spanish colonial empire to form new governments in Cuba and the Philippines while rejecting members of the allied Cuban and Philippine insurgent forces. In both cases, defeated Spanish troops and officials were allowed to remain in Manila, Santiago de Cuba, and Havana, but the Cuban and Filipino insurgent allies, including the commanders and political leaders, were denied entrance to these cities. In Cuba, the formal surrender terms prohibited the Cuban insurgents from entering Santiago de Cuba and Havana. The racism and cynical opportunism evident in U.S. choices of white Spanish officers over brown Cuban and Philippine insurgents were not lost on the native leaders. Class and race carried more weight with U.S. leaders than democracy or self-government.[27] One unexpected legacy of U.S. intervention in the Philippines was the birth and growth of political cartoons. A U.S.-controlled mass media eventually gave way to a freer media, but in the intervening years, U.S. public education reduced the anti-American sentiment.[28]

Leaders of the mid-nineteenth-century anti-slavery, liberal crusade were often ethnocentric, even racist. In the late 1890s, the U.S. government acquired at least ten million people of mixed races. In German-American leader and former cabinet member Carl Schurz's view, "all of them [were] animated with the instincts, impulses and passions bred by the tropical sun."[29] In October 1899, Schurz, speaking on "The Policy of Imperialism" in Chicago, decided that 1899 was worse for the country than 1861 because "the attempt of 1861 was to divide the country. That of 1899 is to destroy its fundamental principles and noblest ideals." Schurz proposed as the proper "watchword of *true* patriotism: 'Our country—when right to be kept right; when wrong to be put right.'"[30] He worried that the policies needed to suppress inferior races might erode fundamental U.S. values.

Henry Watterson, editor of the *Louisville Courier-Journal*, saw a key element of social imperialism in the War of 1898. U.S. society would exchange domestic for foreign disorder: "We escape the menace and peril of socialism and agrarianism, as England has escaped them, by a policy of colonialism and conquest. . . . we exchange domestic dangers for foreign dangers. . . . We risk Caesarism, certainly, but even Caesarism is preferable to anarchism."[31] Social imperialism risked foreign conflict to alleviate domestic disorder and authoritarianism to stifle domestic discontent from a failed policy.

Inventive use of language obscured U.S. conduct. Captain Mahan adopted a form of modern-speak or political-speak to address U.S. imperialism. He preferred "outward impulses" to "imperialism," "liberate" as a code for "occupy," and "pacify" for "conquer." Many others in the press or government used similar language. The U.S. military introduced the Filipinos to modern war—burning, looting, the scorched-earth, rape, pillage, and the water torture. These troops took few prisoners and kept few records. To carry out a "near-genocidal policy," U.S. troops had to dehumanize the opponents with language and images—the enemy were "niggers," "googoos," "Kodiak ladrones," or "gooks." The human psyche required subhumans for extermination. General Jacob ("Hell Roaring Jake" or "Howling Wilderness") Smith, who encouraged combat savagery, was court-martialed and "admonished." Incredibly, it appears that his real error was not savagery, but reducing his orders to writing.[32] By 1901, the U.S. military used concentration camps, curfews, and kill-and-burn policies to "civilize" the Filipinos.

U.S. action in the Gulf-Caribbean and Pacific basins had responded to the depression of the 1890s. After the War of 1898, the U.S. economy experienced a boost in Asian and Caribbean trade. The importation of cheap raw materials and food reduced the price of manufactured goods and helped control wage pressures by reducing the cost of living. In one year, U.S. imports from Asia rose $40 million and exports rose $6 million; in the Caribbean, U.S. imports rose $14 million and exports rose $15 million. Still, Schurz found the arguments for new markets "ludicrously barbarous": "Why must we own the countries with which we wish to trade?"[33]

Germany, also an industrializing, expansive, status- and security-seeking power with world aspirations, often pursued objectives that mirrored U.S. government policy and entrepreneurial activity. The German government's wish list for empire was long: a naval station at the Canary or Cape Verde Islands, adjustments to the borders of German African colonies, and naval stations around the world, including the Sulu Archipelago, Mindanao, the Carolines, and Samoa. In September 1898, as the U.S. government planned to annex parts of Spain's colonies, according to one German historian, "German imperialists immediately sensed the possibility to benefit from the Spanish defeat" and declared German's rights to Samoa, the Philippines, and Central Pacific islands. Germany wanted the Philippines, but it extracted a secret agreement from Spain not to cede the Carolines to the United States. Then, after the U.S.-Spanish peace agreement, Spain ceded the Carolines, Palau, and the

Marianas in February 1899 to Germany for 17 million marks [ca. $5.5 million]. The German officials were after copra, also called "Micronesian gold," and trade.[34]

German colonies, like those of most other imperial and colonial powers, were supposed to contribute to national pride and reputation, to strategic security as a great and dynamic world power, to certain economic benefits in the present or future, and to some sense of a civilizing mission. The Pacific colonies were not what was expected; they were an economic burden on the government and some German firms. Individuals and individual firms — Godeffroy (until it failed in 1884), Deutsche Handels- und Plantagen Gesellschaft, and Jaluit GmbH — were enormously profitable in Micronesia: the Marshalls, Carolines, Gilberts, Marianas, and Mauru. After 1900, German mining (especially phosphates) became important. The value of Samoa and Qing-Dao increased after 1898. In October 1899, Tirpitz wrote Bülow: "Possession of the Samoa islands would assume greater strategic meaning for the German fleet . . . on the trade route from Qing-Dao over the German South Sea's possessions to South America . . . the significance of German control of the Samoa islands would increase, since the Panama Canal will indicate new routes for world commerce, and thus a new strategic military route will arise." The 1899 British-German treaty and a German-U.S. treaty arranged the division of Samoa. In this competitive era, German policy sparked conflict, while the British settled disputes with the United States and Japan.[35] German leaders also assumed a canal at Panama would elevate the value of the Pacific basin.

Some U.S. historians have misrepresented U.S. expansion, thus giving too much significance to the 1898 era. Historian Richard Welch enthusiastically, if inaccurately, observed: "Although the history of American expansion is as old as the nation, only with 1898 did we seek to establish extra-hemispheric colonies [ignoring Wake Island, Samoa, fifty guano islands, and earlier efforts to acquire Hawaii] and only with 1899 did we seek to impose by force of arms American sovereignty over millions of ethnic aliens [ignoring force used to acquire territory and ethnic aliens in the Indian wars, the Texas war, and the Mexican War]." Thomson, Stanley, and Perry agreed: "The real importance of the Philippines to the United States has been moral and exemplary, rather than strategic and economic." They declared it the only place outside the western hemisphere that the U.S. government ruled an imperial possession, and thus they overlooked Hawaii, Samoa, Guam, Midway, Wake, and the guano islands.[36]

Contemporary Asian society offers an alternative explanation to the fate of the Philippines. There was material and moral support for the Philippine insurgents. A shipload of weapons and ammunition from the Japanese Imperial armory headed for Emilio Aguinaldo foundered off the Chinese coast in late July 1899. Many essays published in China between 1899 and 1903 described the Filipinos as "pioneers of yellow race" in a global struggle against the "white race." In June 1902, a Hindu scholar deplored the U.S. conduct in the Philippines in a long article in the *Japan Times*: "The whole world sank with despondency at the sight of Republican America behaving like a cruel, tyrannical and rapacious Empire in the Philippines and particularly to the broken-hearted people of Asia who are beginning to lose all confidence in the humanity of the white races."[37] The military force and racism of the 1890s had marked much U.S. (and western) conduct in Asia and Oceania since the 1780s.

The U.S. government and entrepreneurs responded to the three crises with a set of expansionist policies that incorporated cheap labor, business opportunities, abundant raw materials, inexpensive food products, and military force at home and abroad. They secured management of strategic and commercial maritime stations and, after deciding Nicaragua was clearly a second choice for an isthmian canal, obtained control over perhaps the world's most valuable commercial transit point—the Panama Canal. To obtain and utilize these varied yet related developments, the U.S. government engaged in three conflicts—one in the Caribbean, one in Oceania, and one in Asia. The U.S. version of Columbus's route to the wealth of China extended its security interests to include management of the Caribbean basin waters and the isthmian land transit—Panama (after 1903), Nicaragua (1912–1932), Santo Domingo (1916–1924), and Haiti (1915–1934), and many parts of Oceania. The crises of the 1890s provoked conduct that was more harbinger than solution to international relations in both the Caribbean and Pacific basins.

CHAPTER 7

The Legacy of the Crises of the 1890s

⌐ As the new route from the North Atlantic to Asia was set, many areas vital for the transit were immersed in turmoil. U.S. self-interest fed, then repressed, revolutions in Santo Domingo, Haiti, Cuba, Nicaragua, Panama, Hawaii, and the Philippines. Washington officials have steadfastly maintained that these areas "benefited" from U.S. military occupation or protectorate status. The validity of this assertion needs testing. Mexico, Honduras, and China experienced internal disorder and brief U.S. intervention (in China, with a host of other Asian and European powers). The War of 1898 was not just a glitch in the histories of Spain, Cuba, the Philippines, China, and the United States, but part of their domestic developments and their response to the economic crisis of the 1890s. The significant task undertaken—fulfilling Columbus's dreams of a reliable route to the vast wealth of East Asia—incorporated perpetual disorder, conflict, security issues, cultural dominance, and a quest to control raw materials, investment opportunities, and distribution. Positive, but also negative, aspects of competition and conflict were integral to a laissez-faire liberal order.

The U.S. conquests in Asia and the Caribbean prompted fresh policies to implement U.S. objectives. The open door notes expressed U.S. wishes for a new relationship with Asia, just as the revived Pan-Americanism (the Mexico City meeting in 1901) did for the New World. Secretary of State John Hay, architect of the open door policy, characterized U.S. activity in the 1890s as part of "a cosmic tendency." He recognized the utility of the Philippines for Asian trade.[1] Scholars commonly note the transforming mark of the War of 1898 upon the Caribbean region, but less often the impact of 1898 upon Oceania and Asia. The U.S. government expected to alleviate its internal socio-economic disorder and the Cuban and Chinese crises by interacting with Asian societies, a goal that required an interoceanic canal.

The complex nature of liberal imperialism was reflected in U.S. politics. The fate of the Philippines and of imperialism was less an issue than it appeared in the 1900 election campaign between President William McKinley and Democratic and Populist candidate William Jennings Bryan. Bryan, an opponent of imperialism, had urged Democratic legislators to accept annexation in 1898 and then make the acquisition the basis of the presidential election. McKinley pleaded ignorance of various critiques of annexation. As Hoar noted, "Bryan sinned through cynicism while McKinley merely erred through ignorance."[2] The choice for U.S. society in the 1900 election was sin or error.

U.S. acquisitions during and soon after the War of 1898—Guantánamo Bay in Cuba, Puerto Rico, the Panamanian canal zone, the Virgin Islands, Hawaii, Samoa, Guam, Wake Island, and the Philippines—challenged other great power aspirations in the Caribbean and Pacific basins. Germany, with little empire, but forced to compete for power and prestige with the established empires, had difficulty adjusting. The intensifying worldwide U.S.-German competition stimulated the German government to draft operational war plans in the late 1890s which were reviewed and revised periodically. German plans assumed that the United States—a likely opponent—was most vulnerable in the Caribbean and isthmian region. German naval officials planned to seize the poorly fortified U.S. Caribbean bases and to use them to attack U.S. trade centers.[3] Between 1902 and 1905, however, German naval planning subordinated the Caribbean area to Anglo-Saxon competition in Europe, Africa, and East Asia.

When U.S. officials made clear in 1899 their desire to acquire and fortify the French canal concession at Panama, the British reluctantly surrendered their rights under the Clayton-Bulwer Treaty of 1850 and demanded instead demilitarized transit. After the U.S. Senate rejected a 1900 [John] Hay–[Julian] Pauncefote draft treaty that did not allow U.S. militarization of the canal zone, the revised Hay-Pauncefote Treaty of 1901 was a one-sided concession to the U.S. government. France's New Panama Canal Company was not so accommodating. It demanded an exorbitant price, so Admiral John G. Walker's Interoceanic Canal Commission recommended a canal in Nicaragua in 1901. Since a Nicaragua canal would have removed any value for the Panama concession, the French company wisely reduced its price 60 percent and sold its rights to the U.S. government in 1903.[4]

Many Mexican leaders considered U.S. action in Spanish Cuba disturbing, but U.S. subversion of Colombian sovereignty in 1903 to make a client state out of Panama was a most dangerous precedent. Mexico urged other Latin American governments to withhold recognition of the new Panamanian state. Mexico's President Porfirio Díaz and Foreign Minister Ignacio Mariscal considered the U.S. government a threat to the independence of every Latin American state. The United States had covertly aided a revolutionary movement against a friendly government solely and selfishly to obtain a secure and favorable canal treaty (compare with Che Guevara and the Cuban government, sixty years later, aiding revolutionary movements to create governments and conditions favorable to its security in the Caribbean).[5]

Conquest of the isthmus was not merely a set of political and military maneuvers. Technology and health sciences had developed adequately by the 1890s and early twentieth century to complete a canal at acceptable costs. Construction had to deal with large ship size, deep draft, speed of transit, massive earth excavation, difficult lock construction, and major disease control projects. Ultimately, six huge double locks were constructed, 310 million cubic yards of earth removed, and yellow fever, malaria, typhoid, and other diseases brought under control. The result was a massive technological and scientific project that allowed the steamship, mass production, and rapid communications systems in operation by 1914 to function effectively.[6]

The U.S. canal project at Panama meant economic hardship for Nicaragua. Nicaraguans had long expected an interoceanic canal to produce great material improvement for them, but the U.S. acquisition of the Panama route cancelled any U.S. project in Nicaragua. Nicaraguan president José Santos Zelaya refused to accept the U.S. determination of his country's future. He sent a prominent Nicaraguan to Europe and Japan to solicit partners for a joint canal venture. U.S. officials considered Zelaya's canal negotiations with European and Japanese interests near criminal. Colombia, forced to surrender Panama, was also—to say the least—displeased. The U.S. and Panamanian governments were concerned that one or more foreign nations might undertake a canal at Nicaragua or an alternative interoceanic transit at Colombia's Atrato River.[7] Governments from Mexico to Colombia distrusted a sole U.S. canal at Panama and U.S. rogue conduct throughout the Caribbean basin.

The gap between the U.S. and Mexican governments widened. Both used surrogates to pursue their objectives and to undermine each other's policies. Viewing Zelaya's scheming as a threat to its economic goals and security, the U.S. government expected Guatemalan president (and brutal dictator) Manuel Estrada Cabrera to remove the obstreperous Zelaya from office. Mexican officials meanwhile supported Zelaya in an effort to block Estrada Cabrera's attempts to dominate Central America. Mexican leaders believed that a Guatemalan-U.S. combination threatened instability on the isthmus and at Mexico's northern and southern borders simultaneously.[8]

As production, communications, and transportation technologies drew Asia and the North Atlantic closer, the independence and sovereignty of states along Columbus's route to Asia eroded slowly before 1898, and more noticeably thereafter. Until the War of 1898, the Walker Interoceanic Canal Commission, and U.S. acquisitions in Asia, U.S. diplomats had largely ignored El Salvador because it lacked a Caribbean coast. El Salvador paid a price for the U.S. decision to build the Panama Canal. U.S. military and commercial interests, reevaluating Salvadoran harbors, decided that Fonseca Bay, which lies between El Salvador, Honduras, and Nicaragua, offered the best harbor facility between Panama and San Diego. By 1905, the U.S. government had directly intervened in Salvadoran politics.[9] In the early twentieth century, U.S. interests expected to supervise the harbor areas on the Pacific side, such as Fonseca Bay; the Henry Cabot Lodge Corollary (1912, rejecting a Mexican offer to lease land to a Japanese firm at Magdalena Bay in La Paz, Baja California) to the Monroe Doctrine asserted this in a more formal manner.

The western powers exported Christianity—the community of Roman Catholicism or the individualism of Protestantism—along with the laissez-faire economic order, political ideology, capital, products, and services. The story of east-west contact often emphasizes military, diplomatic, or economic actions, so the role of missionaries is underestimated. Most Filipinos were Catholic Christians. Representatives from the American Bible Society and the British and Foreign Bible Society arrived in the Philippines shortly after the U.S. occupation of Manila in 1898. Soon other missionaries arrived: Methodist Episcopal, Presbyterian, Episcopalian, Baptist, United Brethren in Christ, Disciples of Christ, Congregationalist, Seventh-Day Adventist, Christian Science Society, and Mormon.[10] Most Protestant churches encouraged expansion to win converts from Catholicism.

Only the U.S. Army and conquest allowed Protestantism to become significant. Most Protestants viewed Catholicism, especially Spanish Catholicism, in historian Kenton Clymer's words, as "a corrupted form of faith." Protestants assigned the Catholics responsibility for the deficient culture in the Philippines. They pointed to the canteens and gambling spots to protest the transfer of power to Catholic Filipinos. Andrew Carnegie and many missionaries saw that commercial and missionary visions clashed in the Philippines. The drinking, smoking, and loose living of the commercial world—manifestations of a consumer society—contradicted the missionary's message of self-restraint and morality. Clymer noted: "Nationalistic resent-ments did sometimes erupt against American missionaries." U.S. missionaries were often paternalistic, yet they quickly trained Filipinos as pastors and church workers.[11]

U.S. missionary activity received more official support in the Philippines, but it had a longer history in China. The missionary activity in China was criticized sharply, but it stimulated interest in western merchandise. The mis-sionaries often called for protection. In the early 1890s, President Benjamin Harrison had encouraged missionaries to pursue an aggressive policy when he ordered gunboats for Chinese waters to protect them. The need for gun-boats underscored the rejection of the western missionaries. Repeated demands for compensation for injury or insult to missionaries and missions prompted U.S. diplomat Paul Reinsch's sarcasm in 1899: "Christian holy people in for-eign lands have never represented such a high material value." The Chinese ruling class hated foreigners, but especially those missionaries whose ideology threatened the basis of their authority.[12]

The foreign missionaries, in their ignorance, struggled to change what they viewed as flawed cultures. A more than doubling of U.S. missionaries in China coincided between 1890 and 1905 with U.S. expansion to link the North Atlantic with the Pacific basin. German historian Karl Rivinius noted that "the Boxer Uprising was directed against the missionaries, their work, and against the missionary sites and properties. Above all, at the turn of the cen-tury, an unrestrained hatred of foreigners grew stronger." Until the late nine-teenth century, most attacks were against French Catholics or British Protestants. During the Boxer incident, U.S. missionaries commonly called for retaliation and protested the early withdrawal of allied forces.[13]

In China, many exercise, martial arts, and self-defense societies prac-ticed what was called spirit boxing. Members of these societies were referred to as Boxers. In response to the severe economic hardships of the late nine-teenth century, the increased presence of western missionaries, the embar-rassments of the Sino-Japanese War, the disrespect of extraterritoriality, and the western concession-grabbing after 1895, some exercise associations pro-posed to expel foreign influence (fig. 11). The secret order Yi He Tuan (I-ho ch'uan), "Righteous and Harmonious Fists" or Boxers, changed in the late 1890s from anti-dynastic to anti-foreign and pro-dynasty. Most Chinese offi-cials and intellectuals viewed modernization as a cultural problem. Thus, the western missionaries and businessmen who acted aggressively, demanded more, and disparaged Chinese culture became targets for anti-western forces.[14] Conservative Chinese used anti-foreign rhetoric to condemn the

Fig. 11. "Chinesische Spottkarte. Chinese verjagt Europa" ("Chinese mockery card. China boots Europe Out"). Chinese equivalents of political cartoons were often circulated in a hand-sized format. Naturally, many Chinese expected Chinese troops to expel the Europeans in the Boxer crisis of 1899 and 1900. (Courtesy of www.deutsche-schutzgebiete.de)

reforms, and then the Boxer attacks upon foreigners and converts demonstrated the depths of anti-westernism.

The Boxers grew numerous and dedicated to removing foreign influence, but technologically they were far behind the western forces (fig. 12). The anti-imperialist and anti-foreigner views of many spirit boxing associations intensified. Since the Boxers rejected foreign influence, they shunned guns and preferred swords and lances. Placards, flyers, and popular expressions urged killing all foreigners to appease the gods. In late 1898, the Boxers, calling for an end to special privileges for Chinese Christian converts, attacked missionaries and killed some converts in the provinces of Jilin (Chihli) and Shandong, where the economy was depressed. The imperial government suppressed this rioting. The German missionaries in Shandong were especially aggressive and insensitive. In one scholar's view, the Boxer Rebellion became a "vivid symbol of everything [westerners] most detested and feared about China"—hostility to Christianity, resistance to modern technology, fiendish cruelty, xenophobia, and superstition.[15]

Fig. 12. "Chinese Boxer Troops." This photo might well show Chinese government troops, although it is labeled "Boxer Troops." The Chinese army used old models of modern weapons, while the Boxers commonly rejected such weapons and relied upon traditional ancient Chinese weapons. (Courtesy of John Guy, University of San Diego)

Anti-foreignism, present for generations, needed a spark to ignite. In the 1890s, China suffered a series of internal natural disasters—bad harvests, severe drought in northern China, floods, and pest plagues. The dumping of European and U.S. surplus textiles increased unemployment and misery. Other factors contributed to the disorder—imperial divisions, corruption, military defeats, and increasingly aggressive western commercial and missionary activity. The "white devil" was often blamed for problems, at times justly.[16]

Some ranking Chinese authorities, aware that the government might wish to use the Boxers, advised moderation in the suppression of the Yi He Tuan. When the Chinese government refused the Italian demand for a naval station at Shanxi (Sanmen) Bay in 1898, Italy backed down. Unfortunately, the Imperial Court assumed it could resist any power. In 1899, the Boxers were active again in Shandong and Jilin. In November 1899, the Chinese government ordered all Chinese authorities to resist all foreign aggression, but it had difficulty raising funds for the resistance because the customs revenues of many areas had already been assigned to western powers in 1897.[17]

Fig. 13. "War in China." The pig-tailed and large (population or land mass) Chinese male with western boxing gloves is behind the walls of Beijing (or China), resisting the German, French, British, Russian, and Japanese troops and their artillery. (Courtesy of www.deutsche-schutzgebiete.de)

In May 1900, the Boxers from Shandong moved toward Beijing. On June 13 they seized the city. The Chinese government joined the Boxers by declaring war on the western powers (fig. 13). On 21 June 1900, Chinese troops and Boxers defeated a western relief column. The Empress Dowager Cixi's (fig. 14) declaration of war stated: "The foreigners have been aggressive towards us, infringing upon our territorial integrity, trampled our people. . . . They oppress our people and blaspheme our gods. The common people suffer greatly at their hands, and each one of them is vengeful. Thus . . . the Boxers have been burning churches and killing Christians." The Boxers and the Chinese forces besieged Beijing's foreign compound, where 533 foreigners held off thousands of Boxers and government troops. In a small action, forty French and Italian troops—aided by a few westerners and several hundred poorly armed Chinese converts—defended Peit'ang (or the Northern) Cathedral (not far from the siege of the British legation compound), where about thirty-five hundred people sought refuge from thousands of Boxers and Chinese troops. About fifty defenders and four hundred refugees were killed. These sieges and the murder of the German minister to China boosted the anti-westernism.[18]

On 4 August 1900, a force of twenty thousand men, mostly from Japan, but also from Russia, Britain, the United States, and France, left Tianjin. On 14 August the relief column raised the siege and sacked the city. One historian estimated that during the Yi He Tuan activity the Boxers killed about two

Fig. 14. "Entrance of Chinese Empress Dowager, Cixi." A German postcard depicting the powerful and conservative Empress Dowager Cixi, ultimately a supporter of the Boxer uprising, using traditional transportation and displaying her wealth and authority. (With the permission of Michael Bolln, www.altepostkarten.de)

hundred western missionaries and about twenty thousand Chinese converts. Peace was draconian. Unable to distinguish between Boxers and non-Boxers, the western and Japanese troops were brutal, thieving, raping, looting, and indiscriminate in their punishment of Chinese. Several missionaries led retaliatory raids after the relief army arrived. President Theodore Roosevelt and U.S. officials had little respect for the French and German roles in Beijing's relief. Roosevelt appreciated German support against British hegemonial policies in China, however.[19]

The main body of German troops only arrived in China as Beijing fell to the expeditionary forces. The German troops treated the Chinese with noteworthy brutality. The Kaiser wanted revenge: "Beijing must be completely leveled." After peace talks began, German field marshal Alfred von Waldersee, who commanded the foreign troops in China, ordered seventy-five punitive expeditions (of which forty-eight were purely German). The German troops terrorized and massacred civilians during the raids. The U.S. commander in China estimated that during the punitive expeditions fifty innocent Chinese (including women and children) were killed for each Boxer killed. In memoriam, at the end of World War I, the Chinese of Beijing publicly celebrated the defeat of Germany.[20]

The Kaiser planned to manipulate the defeat of the Boxers to strengthen Germany's European situation. He wanted the maximum indemnity and intended to use the funds to support the German naval building program. He also expected the settlement to create opportunities for German capital in railroads and mining. For Field Marshall Helmuth von Moltke, the reasons for the German activity were clear: "If we want to be entirely honest, it is greed which has motivated us to slice the large Chinese pie. We wanted to earn money, build railroads, establish mining operations, bring European culture, that is, in a word, to earn money." Greed and conflict proved unreliable predictors of economic success. Germans invested 200 million marks to make Qing-Dao a model German city and naval base, but Japan conquered the area during World War I.[21]

The indemnity agreement distributed over 450 million taels (in currency values of 1900, 1.4 billion marks, £67 million sterling, or $333 million) to the western powers. Russia received 29 percent; Germany 20 percent; France 16 percent; Britain 11 percent; Japan 8 percent; the United States 7 percent; Italy 6 percent; and Belgium 2 percent. With interest, China would pay 1 billion taels over thirty-nine-years ($740 million).[22]

By 1901, the Empress Dowager finally conceded the need for reform, but Chinese nationalists opposed a Manchu-led reform movement. The Chinese nationalists' leaders did try to prevent local attacks on foreigners, which served as pretexts for foreign interventions. They wanted to retrieve sovereignty for China, manage China's economic development, and keep the nation's resources out of foreign hands. They also wished to end Manchu rule. The Chinese nationalists considered both the Manchu and the foreigners to be outsiders. Dissent increased. New Chinese nationalism appeared in the publication of Zou Rong's *The Revolutionary Army* in 1903, and the anti-American boycott of 1905. Manchu governance of China seemed impossible. Widespread military mutiny prompted the Manchu to declare the dynasty at an end in 1912.[23]

The religious-cultural clash between east and west was tied to factors such as anti-foreignism and the internal economic and political problems in Asia. The religious turmoil in Shandong was a response to foreign abuse of local Confucianism and disparagement of Chinese culture. Western leaders were seldom capable of evaluating so different a society, and they valued little the advice of scholars of Asia. Theodore Roosevelt seriously misunderstood the impact of the missionaries: "The work of the missionary tends to avert revolutionary disturbance in China, and to lead her into a position for peace and righteousness." He continued: "Now is the time for the West to implant its ideals in the Orient."[24] There was no evidence, and still is none, that China became more peaceful as western ideas and institutions crept into that traditionalist society. The contrary seems more consistent with the evidence of three centuries of significant western contact in China.

Occasionally a westerner perceived the limits of cultural contact. Sarah Conger, wife of the U.S. minister to Beijing, resented the foreign intrusions upon Chinese society: "Poor China! Why cannot foreigners let her alone with her own? China has been wronged, and in her desperation she has striven as best she could to stop the inroads, and to blot out those already made. My sympathy is with China." Another western woman in China noted that there was no mention of a Boxer rape (an indication it was probably rare) in all the reports of Boxer atrocities.[25]

One specific social imperialist response adopted at the turn of the century was an open door policy announced by Secretary of State John Hay in 1899 and 1900 in two sets of notes. The British preferred open door trade, especially in areas where other nations had special influence. They maintained a sphere of influence, however, as insurance in the game of competitive imperialism. The British held more than 60 percent of the China trade in 1899. In March 1898 and again in January 1899, British Minister Julian Pauncefote asked the State Department about jointly sponsoring commercial opportunity in China. The U.S. government became more receptive after the acquisition of the Philippines because it could take better advantage of an open door.[26]

The first open door notes in 1899 were politically expedient for the moment and the dangers, but the idea and objective originated in old U.S. policy. These notes preserved open commercial access to China. U.S. officials wanted Asia, Africa, and the Middle East—those areas less closely integrated into the North Atlantic economic order—to remain open economically to all on equal terms. In September 1899, Secretary of State Hay circulated an open door note with three main points: within a sphere, other powers could have vested interests and the treaty ports were open to all; within a sphere, there was no discrimination against other nationals in regard to harbor duties or to railroad charges; and within a sphere, the Chinese treaty tariff prevailed and Chinese officials would govern the collection of that tariff. On 20 March 1900, Hay declared the first set of notes agreed upon, and in the fall of 1900, a second set preserved Chinese territorial and administrative unity. The open door notes declared principles, not a formal policy. Yet, western powers grasped less greedily for territory, spheres of influence, and privileges after the notes.[27] The pie cutting subsided. Power was difficult to balance in the uncertainty from the many land and sea forces in Asia after the Boxer uprising.

Historian John Dobson argued that "the American Open Door policy was primarily an effort to preserve free trade in all of China." In fact, there was much more to preserve: by 1900 there were six thousand miles of railroad concessions in China, and the Inland Waters Steam Navigation Act practically gave foreign countries sovereign power on the great Chinese waterways. The open door in China involved access, with a "fair field and no favor," in Hay's words, to investment and to extract raw material. It severely restricted Chinese sovereignty. The open door became standard U.S. policy in Africa, the Mediterranean, and the Near East.[28]

The open door reflected U.S. strategic and military interests. The Japanese gave it only modest attention. China took little interest. "It was an American policy," historian Akira Iriye, a specialist in U.S.–East Asian relations, observed, "intended to safeguard American interests, and there was no reason why the Chinese should feel interested." Despite the open door notes, some U.S. interests contemplated special privileges. On various occasions, the U.S. Navy sought Shanxi Bay, which lay north of Fuzhou (Foochow) on the Fujian coast, where Japan had special privileges; Japan opposed the idea, but so did some in the U.S. government. Yet, the simultaneous emergence of the United States and Japan as imperialist powers had great significance for Asia.[29]

The State Department under Hay did not believe a naval base was necessary for defense of the Philippines or for access to China. After 1898, Iriye found that the U.S. State Department "evinced no interest in actively promoting private business in China; it refused to intercede on behalf of the China Development Company when the Chinese awarded the Hankow-Beijing railroad concession to a Belgian syndicate, and it declined to act together with Britain to keep China from being carved into colonies and spheres of influence." Yet, U.S. action played a role in keeping China from becoming divided into restricted spheres, such as Indochina or Korea had. Wishes, desires, and expectations differ from will and execution. Hay intended to protect American interests without resorting to drastic measures or playing power politics. In Hay's view, even the security of the Philippines did not require forceful measures. The U.S. Navy's General Board thought otherwise. The suspicion of Japan's interest in the Philippines and Asia metamorphosed into distrust after the Russo-Japanese War. As early as 1906, the U.S. Navy's Orange Plan, aimed at Japan, was intended to defend the Philippines.[30] Defense of the Caribbean basin, however, involved immediate and, if necessary, large-scale U.S. naval activity.

Contemporaneous with the open door in China, Theodore Roosevelt announced a militaristic "big stick" policy for the Caribbean basin. Big stick diplomacy combined race ideology and naval policy. Historian Raimund Lammersdorf argued that Roosevelt's foreign policy was not based primarily upon economics, social imperialism, or power politics, but on racial ideology. Yet, Roosevelt's sense of historical dynamic kept him from social Darwinism. For Roosevelt race was not entirely biological; he interchanged the terms race, people, and nation.[31] The big stick was applied in the Caribbean basin numerous times as protection for U.S. strategic and interoceanic transit interests.

The U.S. government considered the isthmian canal so vital to its commercial world that it could not tolerate opposition. It moved to restrict further the territorial sovereignty of Latin American states. U.S. leaders expected subservience from local and foreign agents. The interoceanic transit increased the security and maritime roles of the circum-Caribbean. U.S. leaders wanted no foreign force used to collect debts in the New World, nor foreign control of key strategic points even by contractual arrangements. The (Theodore) Roosevelt Corollary restricted the financial independence of Latin American states. Before the Roosevelt Corollary, Henry Adams, Philippe Bunau-Varilla, and other contemporaries observed the obviousness of such a stance. It removed debt repayment as justification for foreign intervention. In the West Indies, Adams warned: "Sooner or later [the U.S. government will] have to police those islands, not against Europe, but for Europe, and America too." The U.S. government might have to take special steps to secure the circum-Caribbean area.[32]

The Lodge Corollary to the Monroe Doctrine expressed the U.S. government's intent to restrict the territorial sovereignty of New World countries. It expressed firm opposition to metropole competitors acquiring strategic locations. The Lodge Corollary killed a Japanese-Mexican project near the port of La Paz because the U.S. government particularly distrusted Japanese (and also German) objectives in the circum-Caribbean. The French and British were viewed as less determined opponents of U.S. policies.[33] In Latin America, the U.S. government and entrepreneurs expected, rather than an open door or "a fair field and no favor," the favored field they presumed was theirs under the Monroe Doctrine.

While a military response to pushy U.S. policies remained one option, German leaders differed about how best to respond to the Monroe Doctrine and U.S. hegemony in the New World. Few German officials and political economists presumed that German entrepreneurs could withdraw from Latin America and still deliver a high standard of living for Germany. The stakes were simply too high. Yet, the expansionist activities of German nationals challenged U.S. geopolitical interests on the isthmus.[34] German officials found no simple response to this complex situation.

German entrepreneurs recognized the competitive value of the isthmus in the world market. Albert Ballin, director of the Hamburg-America Passenger Company (HAPAG), claimed that a Panama canal would be a powerful weapon in U.S. hands. An associate reflected upon the "unhealthy consequences [which sole U.S. control over the canal] would have for German trade." Secretary of the Navy Admiral Alfred von Tirpitz asserted that Germany's "growing foreign interests" demanded a shortened route to the Pacific Ocean and "our occupation of foreign stations." He cautioned that "Germany's strategic position in the eastern areas of the Pacific Ocean . . . would be very tangibly weakened by a transfer of the future isthmian canal to sole North American control." The imperial government, Tirpitz warned, had to accept military risk in the Central American–Caribbean region "given the present and future significance of our varied economic relations to Latin America and the Pacific."[35] But German- and U.S.-perceived interests in the Caribbean and Asia clashed. After 1905, the burden of naval competition with Britain, increased tension with France, and events in North Africa pulled German military planning priorities away from confrontation in the Caribbean.

Americans were suspicious of German activities in the Caribbean and Pacific basins. The Monroe Doctrine rejected German (or any other European) political or colonial expansion into Latin America. U.S. writers acknowledged the powerful historical forces driving German expansion: population pressure, expansive domestic industries, and the need for guaranteed overseas markets. In the view of historian Richard Challener, Admiral George Dewey, the victorious naval commander at Manila Bay in 1898 and longtime president of the Navy's General Board, "never recovered from the acute case of Germanophobia he had acquired when Admiral Otto von Dieterichs sailed into Manila Bay in 1898." Dewey influenced the General Board toward suspicion of Germany and a rosy view of the British. In the early twentieth century, the General Board and the U.S. Black Plan hypothesized a German assault in the Caribbean as a likely strategy.[36]

The French government and businessmen also sorted through a mix of strategic, cultural, and economic factors to participate in a highly competitive world. By 1900, French influence on the isthmus included several military missions, cultural institutions, and financial circles that continued a major role in Central America. Many French politicians and businessmen expected a revived foreign trade to vitalize the nation's stagnant domestic production.

French leaders wove commercial revitalization into their civilizing mission. French officials divided on the desirability of competing or cooperating with the United States, but, in any event, their ambivalent opposition seldom did more than delay U.S. activity. And some French leaders speculated that U.S. goodwill might be useful in the ongoing struggle between France and its allies and Germany and its allies.[37]

From 1898 to 1917, the U.S. government acted to bind the North Atlantic area to the Pacific basin through purchases, conquests, and diplomatic agreements regarding naval stations, harbors, and canal routes. It resurrected Pan-Americanism, and it had heightened expectations of benefits from "social imperialism." The new external markets, investment opportunities, and plentiful raw material sources in the New World and Asia ameliorated the internal crisis in the United States for a few years during the early twentieth century. The U.S. role in Panama's successful "revolution" in 1903 and the consequent canal treaty diverted attention from U.S. domestic problems, made many critics feel proud, supplied jobs, and created a market for several key sectors of the economy—construction, technology, and heavy industry. The new image of U.S. relations with Latin America incorporated communications lines, tariff arrangements, and an increasing number of investors and bankers. A canal would facilitate access to the west coast of Latin America and the Pacific basin and build a link between the two U.S. coasts and the Mississippi Valley.[38]

The U.S. government bolstered its positions in the circum-Caribbean after the War of 1898. The circum-Caribbean region's resources and transit opportunities were enhanced by the immense resources of the Pacific basin. The Navy's General Board sought Caribbean naval stations because once the Panama Canal opened to traffic, "aggression on the part of individual foreign powers could be assumed." On 4 October 1902, soon after the decision to acquire the Panama Canal rights, the U.S. government created a Caribbean Division within the North Atlantic Station. The Caribbean Division expected to "protect" and to "advance" U.S. interests. This subtle shift in U.S. overseas policy objectives—to advance or promote (aggressive) as well as to protect (passive)—became State Department policy during the 1870s depression. The shift in language signaled a change from a reserved, conservative stance to an active, dynamic, and expansive conduct. About 1902, the Navy was enlisted in pursuit of this objective. The need to promote U.S. interests abroad drove many of the arguments for going to war over Cuba and for acquiring the insular possessions in the Caribbean and Pacific basins. During the early twentieth century, the Navy adopted the State Department's promotion of U.S. market expansion in the Caribbean and Pacific basins.[39] The circum-Caribbean especially became a region open for U.S. investors, fortune hunters, and speculators.

From the 1890s to the 1920s, societies in the circum-Caribbean were racked with a turmoil that recalled the filibusterers of the 1840s and 1850s. Private U.S. soldiers-of-fortune out of New Orleans and Mobile became the modern filibusterers and served a new generation of investors and entrepreneurs, the "banana men." Unlike earlier mercenaries who fought for political factions, these soldiers-of-fortune were hired guns in the service of class, regional politics, and foreign economic interests. They were primarily the weapons of private enterprises and secondarily agents of political struggle. In the late nineteenth and early twentieth centuries, more entrepreneurs and mercenaries entered Central America to acquire control over land, the native work force, some ports, and those rivers that connected the Atlantic coast with the interior. The early twentieth-century mercenaries and the mid-nineteenth-century filibusterers both sought to dominate the land, labor, and communications on the isthmus.[40] And the goals of these new filibusterers remained attuned to social imperialism. The banana men sought to transfer problems which seemed unsolvable within U.S. society—inadequate opportunities for capital, cheap labor, entrepreneurial skills, and adventures—into the surrounding areas and to profit from the sale of cheap foodstuff and raw materials to the U.S. political economy.

These entrepreneurs and their mercenaries ransacked the wealth of the isthmus for several decades until institutions of organized capitalism (multinational corporations) limited competition and enforced an ordered removal of the value in the circum-Caribbean economies. The region suffered major revolts, revolutions, or U.S. occupation—Cuba (1898–1902, 1906–1909, 1917–1920), Haiti (1915–1934), Santo Domingo (1916–1924), Panama (1899–1903), Nicaragua (1906–1932), and Mexico (1910–1920). The economic and military pillaging of the region caused human and material losses, uncertainty, and suffering.

Within two decades of 1898, the U.S. government had established an impressive U.S. presence in the Caribbean, the Pacific, and East Asia. In addition to the protectorate over Cuba (and a naval base at Guantánamo), the U.S. government acquired Puerto Rico and the Virgin Islands, plus a long-term lease on the Panama Canal zone. It occupied Haiti, Santo Domingo, and Nicaragua for long periods, and parts of Mexico and Honduras briefly to implement "civilizing missions." On the west side of the isthmus, it added Hawaii, Wake Island, Guam, the Philippines, and part of Samoa to its pre-1890s possessions of Alaska, Midway, about fifty guano islands, and extensive extraterritorial (sovereignty) rights in China. These steps were intended to defend the Caribbean and the Pacific water routes leading to the Panama Canal and the commercial routes in Oceania.[41]

The U.S. role in suppression of Cuban and Philippine darker-skinned nationalist forces posed problems for America's black soldiers and community. Some black Americans suspected that U.S. involvement abroad would divert attention from racial crises at home; others argued that domestic blacks would gain respect when compared with foreign people of color. After the Republican victory in 1900, however, most blacks accepted U.S. colonialism. But some black leaders remained cynical about any gains for domestic blacks or altered humanitarianism from U.S. whites. In 1902, Edward E. Cooper observed: "It seems that our white friends have a habit of expending their sympathy upon the black man who is farthest off."[42]

Historian Louis Pérez Jr. noted the historical distortions of the War of 1898, which were meant to "purify" white U.S. authority and "darken" native Cuban claims to victory: "The attempt to discredit [Cuban] independence was surpassed only by the effort to deprecate its advocates. Independence was as unworthy an ideal as its proponents were unfit to govern." General Leonard Wood denigrated the former allies whose military prowess cleared the beaches of Spanish troops at Santiago de Cuba and saved thousands of U.S. killed, wounded, and sick. He called the Cuban soldiers "ignorant masses," "unruly rabble," and "trouble makers." U.S. authorities sought to deny independentista leaders opportunity to mobilize Cuban nationalism. When local politics selected colored leaders in 1900, Wood regretted: "The [white] men whom I had hoped to see take the leadership have been forced into the background by the absolutely irresponsible and unreliable [dark-skinned] element." By late 1900, the U.S. administration faced the possibility of withdrawal without having settled the internal structure of hegemony. The U.S. leaders considered the Cubans' refusal to elect the "best men [whites]" proof of their incapacity for independence.[43]

By 1901, the U.S. government insisted that the Cuban constitution had to contain an unrestricted right of U.S. intervention. But no responsible native government could enter into a treaty which impaired Cuban freedom. Finally, the U.S. government obtained an agreement that validated all the acts of the U.S. military government. Still, Secretary of State Elihu Root judged the Cuban response harshly: "If they continue to exhibit ingratitude and entire lack of appreciation of the expenditure of blood and treasure of the United States to secure their freedom from Spain," U.S. public opinion will turn more unfavorable. Root was self-deluded; mostly Cuban blood and treasure had defeated the Spanish.[44] The distortions and self-deception of the U.S. role in the Philippines and China were similar.

The Philippine and Boxer rebellions against western rule were not isolated acts. From the time of Magellan to Captain James Cook, the Pacific island inhabitants had, at times, received the westerners with curiosity or friendliness, but such relations commonly turned to violent protests against western intrusions. Time brought more foreigners, with ever more demands upon Oceanian and Asian peoples. Periodically, the indigenous peoples replied with force, often against foreign possession and use of land. In 1878, the Melanesians initiated an important resistance of Oceanians against the French. They protested against European livestock entering their yam and taro fields and against European seizure of their lands. A second rebellion in 1917 protested French conscription of Melanesians for service in World War I. The Maori continuously resisted British rule in New Zealand. Neither did the Germans escape serious revolt. German interference in political customs led to major revolts in Samoa and Pohnpei. The United States and the Philippine governments endured unending Muslim resistance in Moroland up to the present.[45] Western intruders in the Pacific basin commonly encountered persistent resistance to their efforts to transform the indigenous societies.

Historian David Hanlon, a student of indigenous resistance, found that the colonizing nations justified their rule and the accompanying violence, domination, exploitation, and racism with "rituals of possession, denigrating descriptions of Micronesian societies, the usurpation of indigenous political authority, and the promotion of alien, disruptive systems of religion, education, and economy." In 1908, one wary, cynical observer remarked that the density of population in the Solomon Islands was "in inverse ratio to the degree of civilisation exhibited." But the Pacific basin's population played a different role for some western states. Metropolitan France had long battled a declining birthrate and stagnant population in comparison with other European great powers. Colonel Charles Mangin, a hero of French colonial conflicts, outlined the role of colored reserves for the French army in *La Force noire* (1911). The French government used the colonies as a source for reserve combatants. Colonial troops accounted for 6 percent (78,000) of the French dead in World War I; about 556,000 colonials served in the military, and 184,000 colonials were called to France as laborers. Historian Jean Martin labeled the French reliance upon conscripted colonials as "blood tribute."[46]

The world's fairs of the late nineteenth century confirmed Anglo-Saxon superiority and liberal materialism while increasingly glorifying empire and colonialism. In the United States, the world's fairs at Omaha (1898), Buffalo

(1901), and St. Louis (1904) stated the U.S. position in crescendo with regard to the Philippines. At Omaha in late 1898, just after the U.S. government acquired the Philippines as part of a Pacific basin empire, there was a small, rather inactive Philippine village. Three years later at Buffalo, there was a large "Philippine Village" in the center of the colonial exhibits. Finally, at St. Louis in 1904, after the Philippine insurgency had been declared over, the "Philippine Reservation" contained twelve hundred Filipinos and was placed in the center of the fair grounds. Fair goers were allowed to move through the Reservation and interact with the Filipinos. The U.S.-trained Philippine Scouts and Constabulary policed the Reservation to demonstrate that the U.S. government could uplift and civilize their little brown brothers. The central role of materialism was advanced in a racial manner with the use of chairs, sewing machines, and other western material items in the Philippine native houses and settings. Civilizing the natives meant adding western material production to their lifestyles. The materialism and law and order of the Reservation showed that the Filipinos had already benefited from U.S. technology and America's political system. The racial and moral superiority of the United States uplifted Filipinos.[47] Colonialism was an expression of U.S. moral and material strength. This encouraging imagery, unfortunately, reflected poorly upon Philippine reality.

Trade with the Pacific basin was altered between the 1890s and World War I. U.S. trade with Asia and Oceania was modest until the 1890s depression and the acquisition of the U.S. Pacific colonies, and then it became an increasingly significant part of U.S. commerce. From 1821 to 1896, the United States exported from 2 to 5 percent of its goods to Asia and Oceania. From 1897 to 1917, that exportation rose from 6 to 9 percent, and from 1919 until World War II, the U.S. exported between 11 and 21 percent of its products to Oceania and Asia. The United States obtained 5 to 15 percent of its imports from the Pacific basin during the years from 1821 to 1896. Those figures rose to between 15 and 20 percent in the years between 1896 and 1915. Then from 1916 until World War II, between 25 and 35 percent of U.S. imports came from Oceania and Asia.[48] The Pacific basin's share of U.S. trade grew about threefold between the mid-nineteenth and mid-twentieth centuries. U.S. Asian possessions and the completion of the Panama Canal stimulated U.S. commercial activity in the Pacific basin.

U.S. engineers began work on the canal in 1904, and it was completed, except for closures from subsequent disruptive landslides, in August 1914. Between 1904 and 1914, the U.S. government spent $352 million for construction. The human cost, including the French period in the 1880s, amounted to twenty-five thousand deaths. After World War I, the canal's use grew steadily until it bore ship traffic equal to that of the Suez Canal by 1930.

Around the turn of the century, some Chinese and other Asians saw more than just China as victims of imperialism. The term "Asia" surfaced from imperialism and attempts to subject the non-west to a western-dominated world system and to fit it into concepts of nationalism and regional formation. A different "Asia" discourse took place, seeking a radically politicized cultural regional concept. For many Asians, Japan's success in wars with China and Russia and its rampant industrial productivity made it the model for their own development. The year 1907 saw the formation of the Asian Solidarity Society (also called the Asiatic Humanitarian Brotherhood) in Japan out of Chinese intellectuals, Japanese socialists, and Indian, Filipino, and Vietnamese exiles, but the group was short-lived. The Chinese roots of the Asian Solidarity Society allowed a view of Asia that was not a component of global capitalism, a Japan-centric concept, or an adjunct to a state-dominated internationalism. Asia had meaning independent of the west.[49]

As a continuation of policy decisions made in the 1890s, the United States engaged in five twentieth-century Pacific conflicts: the Boxer Uprising (1898–1901), the Philippine insurrection (1899–c. 1920), the Pacific theater of World War II (1941–1945), Korea (1950–1953), and Vietnam (1950–1974), and intervened militarily many times throughout the Caribbean region. China and Cuba have had many of their best times when they managed to limit the intrusion of foreign interference in their domestic life (Cubans have suffered in the past decades because of continued U.S. interference). The North Atlantic intruders pursued a self-proclaimed mission to alter the religion and culture of the Asian societies. In the end, as historian Paul Varg, a student of U.S.-Chinese relations, has argued, China alone restored order and built strength in the country, but it had to fight the west so long that it has remained distrustful of western ideology and alleged humanitarianism.[50] He could have included Cuba in this observation.

Most Asian societies responded to the rapid rise in foreign missionaries, businessmen, and officials with suspicion, distrust, anger, and hatred. The Boxer Rebellion and the cruel, deadly Filipino War against U.S. occupation also represented Asian nationalist responses to encroaching foreign powers that attacked the culture, undermined local authority, and challenged the sovereignty of the Asian societies. The Chinese civil war of 1911, which adopted a more anti-foreign, anti-imperial character after 1919, was also in part a consequence of the War of 1898 and the Panama Canal, which facilitated foreign penetration of Asian societies.

Mao Zedong and Ho Chi-Minh did not create the tensions in Asia. The revolutions they headed merely expressed a common Asian reaction in a determined form to over three centuries of gradual western intrusion followed by several decades of rapid march toward the fulfillment of Christopher Columbus's (and Uncle Sam's) vision of penetration and extraction of value.

Notes

Introduction

1. Peter Novick, *That Noble Dream: The "Objectivity Question" and the American Historical Profession* (New York, 1988), 8–9.

2. Ernest R. May, *American Imperialism: A Speculative Essay* (New York, 1968), ix.

3. Louis A. Pérez Jr., *The War of 1898: The United States and Cuba in History and Historiography* (Chapel Hill, N.C., 1998); Thomas J. McCormick, *China Market: America's Quest for Informal Empire, 1893–1901* (Chicago, 1967); Foster Rhea Dulles, *America in the Pacific: A Century of Expansion*, 2d. ed. (New York, 1969); David F. Healy, *The United States in Cuba, 1898–1902: Generals, Politicians, and the Search for Policy* (Madison, Wis., 1963); Nell Irvin Painter, *Standing at Armageddon: The United States, 1877–1919* (New York, 1987); Whitelaw Reid, *Making Peace with Spain: The Diary of Whitelaw Reid (September–December 1898)* (Austin, Tex., 1965), 58, 82, 178; Walter LaFeber, *The American Search for Opportunity, 1865–1913*, vol. 2, *The Cambridge History of American Foreign Relations*, 4 vols. (New York, 1993), 103–82; Walther L. Bernecker, ed., *1898: su significado para Centroamérica y el Caribe* (Frankfurt, 1998), esp. 17–35, 61–75, and 113–29.

4. Norman A. Graebner, "The Year of Transition: 1898," in *An Uncertain Tradition: American Secretaries of State in the Twentieth Century*, ed. Norman A. Graebner (New York, 1961), 1.

5. Daniel R. Headrick, *The Tentacles of Progress: Technology Transfer in the Age of Imperialism, 1850–1940* (New York, 1988), 95–128; Daniel R. Headrick, *The Tools of Empire: Technology and European Imperialism in the Nineteenth Century* (New York, 1981), 157–64; Daniel R. Headrick, *The Invisible Weapon: Telecommunications and International Politics, 1851–1945* (New York, 1991), 50–72; Orville Schell and Joseph Esherick, *Modern China: The Making of a New Society from 1839 to the Present* (New York, 1972), 25–27, 34–35; David J. McCreery, *The*

Sweat of Their Brow: A History of Work in Latin America (Armonk, N.Y., 2000), 108; Timothy Parsons, *The British Imperial Century, 1815–1914: A World History Perspective* (Lanham, Md., 1999), 25–30; Alfred W. McCoy and Ed. C. de Jesús, eds., *Philippine Social History: Global Trade and Local Transformation* (Quezon City, Philippines, 1982), 453.

6. Headrick, *The Tentacles of Progress*, 18–48; Headrick, *The Tools of Empire*, 165–79; David M. Pletcher, *The Diplomacy of Trade and Investment: American Economic Expansion in the Hemisphere, 1865–1900* (Columbia, Mo., 1998), 41–42.

7. McCreery, *The Sweat of Their Brow*, 108; Parsons, *The British Imperial Century, 1815–1914*, 25–30.

8. Walter LaFeber, *The New Empire: An Interpretation of American Expansion, 1860–1898* (Ithaca, N.Y., 1963), 197–241, 403–17; Hans Rosenberg, *Grosse Depression und Bismarckzeit*, 2d ed. (Berlin, 1976); Hans-Ulrich Wehler, *Der Aufstieg des amerikanischen Imperialismus* (Göttingen, Germany, 1974), 7–73, 190–216, 242–76; Robert L. Beisner, *From the Old Diplomacy to the New, 1865–1900*, 2d ed. (Arlington Heights, Ill., 1986), 120–57; McCormick, *China Market*, 17–52, 177–95. William A. Williams, *America Confronts a Revolutionary World* (New York, 1976), and Robert Freeman Smith, *The United States and Revolutionary Nationalism in Mexico, 1916–1932* (Chicago, 1972), deserve rereading with regard to the 1890–1930 years. See also Thorstein Veblen, *The Theory of the Leisure Class* (reprint; Mineola, N.Y., 1994), for a non-Marxist argument about the "predatory" behavior of accumulation, materialism, and prestige. David M. Pletcher, *The Diplomacy of Involvement: American Economic Expansion across the Pacific, 1784–1900* (Columbia, Mo., 2001), offers an alternative view with regard to the aggressiveness of U.S. conduct.

9. In my view, the world system's theory of Fernand Braudel and Immanuel Wallerstein offers the most useful and insightful scholarship for understanding the modern world.

10. Walter LaFeber, *The American Age: United States Foreign Policy at Home and Abroad since 1750* (New York, 1989), 189; Lawrence S. Kaplan, *Entangling Alliances with None: American Foreign Policy in the Age of Jefferson* (Kent, Ohio, 1987); J.C.A. Stagg, *Mr. Madison's War* (Princeton, N.J., 1983), 501–17; Mary W.M. Hargraeves, *The Presidency of John Quincy Adams* (Lawrence, Kans., 1985); Norman A. Graebner, "John Quincy Adams and the Federalist Tradition," in *Tradition and Values: American Diplomacy, 1790–1865*, ed. Norman A. Graebner (Lanham, Md., 1985), 97–127; Robert V. Remini, *Andrew Jackson and the Course of American Empire, 1767–1821* (New York, 1977); Robert V. Remini, *Andrew Jackson and the Course of American Freedom, 1822–1832* (New York, 1981); Paul H. Bergeron, *The Presidency of James K. Polk* (Lawrence, Kans., 1987); David M. Pletcher, *The Diplomacy of Annexation: Texas, Oregon, and the Mexican War* (Columbia, Mo., 1973), 94–105; Kenneth E. Shewmaker, "Daniel Webster and American Conservatism," in *Tradition and Values: American Diplomacy, 1790–1865*, ed. Norman A. Graebner (Lanham, Md., 1985), 129–52; Ernest McPherson Lander Jr., *Reluctant Imperial-*

ists: Calhoun, the South Carolinians, and the Mexican War (Baton Rouge, La., 1980).

11. John Denis Haeger, *John Jacob Astor: Business and Finance in the Early Republic* (Detroit, Mich., 1991), 94–137; John H. Schroeder, *Shaping a Maritime Empire: The Commercial and Diplomatic Role of the American Navy, 1829–1861* (Westport, Conn., 1985), 3–56, 139–64; Norman A. Graebner, *Empire on the Pacific: A Study in American Continental Expansion* (1955; reprint, Santa Barbara, Calif., 1983), esp. 83–122, 217–28; John K. Fairbank, *China: The People's Middle Kingdom and the U.S.A.* (Cambridge, Mass., 1967); Akira Iriye, *Across the Pacific: An Inner History of American–East Asian Relations* (New York, 1967), 1–50; James Gerber, "Gold Rushes and the Trans-Pacific Wheat Trade: California and Australia, 1848–1857," in *Pacific Centuries: Pacific and Pacific Rim History since the Sixteenth Century*, ed. Dennis O. Flynn, Lionel Frost, and A.J.H. Lathan (London, 1999), 125–50.

12. Walter LaFeber, "That 'Splendid Little War' in Historical Perspective," *Texas Quarterly* 11 (1968): 89–98; McCormick, *China Market*, 107; LaFeber, *The American Search for Opportunity*, 144–45.

13. Walter LaFeber, *Michael Jordan and the New Global Capitalism* (New York, 1999), 22–23.

1. Exploration and New Territories, 1780s–1850s

1. Robert Aldrich, *The French Presence in the South Pacific, 1842–1940* (Honolulu, Hawaii, 1990), 17–24, 333; Jean Heffer, "Des Américains dans l'archipel. Sumatra, 1832: premier engagement américain en Asie du Sud-Est," *Archipel* (Paris) 40 (1990): 49–64.

2. David McCullough, *The Path Between the Seas: The Creation of the Panama Canal* (New York, 1977), 19–40; Miles DuVal, *Cadiz to Cathay: The Story of the Long Diplomatic Struggle for the Panama Canal* (Stanford, Calif., 1947); Helen Augur, *Passage to Glory: John Ledyard's America* (Garden City, N.Y., 1946), 120–27, 173–227.

3. William A. Williams, *The Roots of the Modern American Empire: A Study of the Growth and Shaping of Social Consciousness in a Marketplace Society* (New York, 1969), 4–231; Norman A. Graebner, *Empire on the Pacific: A Study in American Continental Expansion* (1955; reprint, Santa Barbara, Calif., 1983), 1–21; Charles Vevier, "American Continentalism: An Ideal of Expansion, 1845–1910," *American Historical Review* 65 (Jan. 1960): 314–27.

4. Foster Rhea Dulles, *America in the Pacific: A Century of Expansion* (Boston, 1932), 1–2.

5. Herman Melville, *Moby Dick or The Whale* (1851; reprint, New York, 1957), 477.

6. Ralph S. Kuykendall, *Hawaiian Kingdom, 1778–1893*, 3 vols. (Honolulu, Hawaii, 1966–1968): 1:304–7, 309.

7. Donald Denoon, ed., *The Cambridge History of the Pacific Islanders* (Cam-

bridge, Eng., 1997), 154; W. Patrick Strauss, *Americans in Polynesia, 1783–1842* (East Lansing, Mich., 1963), 1–18, 140–45; W. Patrick Strauss, "Pioneer American Diplomats in Polynesia, 1820–1840," *Pacific Historical Review* 31:1 (Feb. 1962), 213; Dorothy Shineberg, *They Came for Sandalwood: A Study of the Sandalwood Trade in the Southwest Pacific, 1830–1865* (London, 1967), 16–28, 215–16, 142–47; John McNeill, "From Magellan to Miti: Pacific Rim Economies and Pacific Island Ecologies since 1521," in *Pacific Centuries: Pacific and Pacific Rim History since the Sixteenth Century*, ed. Dennis O. Flynn, Lionel Frost, and A.J.H. Latham (London, 1999), 76; Dulles, *America in the Pacific*, ix.

8. Robert Aldrich, "Colonialism, Culture and Politics in the French Islands," in *Rassendiskriminierung, Kolonialpolitik und ethnisch-nationale Identität*, ed. Wilfried Wagner (Hamburg, 1992), 218; Jean Chesneaux and Nic Maclellan, *La France dans le Pacifique: De Bougainville à Morura* (Paris, 1992), 21–22, 59; Ian C. Campbell, *A History of the Pacific Islands* (Berkeley, Calif., 1989), 138–39; Jean Ingram Brookes, *International Rivalry in the Pacific Islands, 1800–1875* (Berkeley, Calif., 1941), 28–33, 62–65, 88–91.

9. Aldrich, "Colonialism, Culture and Politics in the French Islands," 218; Peter J. Hempenstall, "Imperial Manoeuvres," in *Tides of History: The Pacific Islands in the Twentieth Century*, ed. K.R. Howe, Robert C. Kiste, and Brij V. Lal (Honolulu, Hawaii, 1994), 37; Kuykendall, *Hawaiian Kingdom*, 1:150, 164–66; Louis Rollin, *Les îles marquises* (Paris, 1929), 230–37, 241–42.

10. Joyce Appleby, *Capitalism and a New Social Order: The Republican Vision of the 1790s* (New York, 1984), 47–105.

11. Richard W. van Alstyne, *The United States and East Asia* (New York, 1973), 7–39; Jacques M. Downs, "The Commercial Origins of American Attitudes toward China, 1784–1844," in *America Views China: American Images of China Then and Now*, ed. Jonathan Goldstein, Jerry Israel, and Hilary Conroy (Bethlehem, Pa., 1991), 56–64; Carl C. Cutler, *Greyhounds of the Sea: The Story of American Clipper Ships* (New York, 1930), 373–75; Thomas R. Cox, *Mills and Markets: A History of the Pacific Coast Lumber Industry to 1900* (Seattle, Wash., 1974), 3–32.

12. Ernest S. Dodge, *Islands and Empires: Western Impact on the Pacific and East Asia* (Minneapolis, Minn., 1976), 69, 115; Felix Riesenberg, *The Pacific Ocean* (New York, 1940), 237–38.

13. J.N. Tønnessen and A.O. Johnsen, *The History of Modern Whaling* (Berkeley, Calif., 1982), 111–13; David A. Chappell, "Peripheralizing the Center: An Historical Overview of Pacific Island Micro-States," in *Pacific Centuries*, ed. Flynn, Frost, and Latham, 66.

14. Riesenberg, *The Pacific Ocean*, 237–38; Arthur Power Dudden, *The American Pacific: From the Old China Trade to the Present* (New York, 1992), 14; Brookes, *International Rivalry in the Pacific Islands*, 28–33.

15. Dodge, *Islands and Empires*, 69, 115; Riesenberg, *The Pacific Ocean*, 237–38.

16. Tønnessen and Johnsen, *The History of Modern Whaling*, 111–13; Frederica

M. Bunge and Melinda W. Cooke, eds., *Oceania: A Regional Study*, 2d. ed. (Washington, D.C., 1984), 33–34; Dodge, *Islands and Empires*, 69; Dudden, *The American Pacific*, 11–15; Riesenberg, *The Pacific Ocean*, 237–38; Kuykendall, *Hawaiian Kingdom*, 1:71, 92–95.

17. Campbell, *A History of the Pacific Islands*, 4, 101; Dulles, *America in the Pacific*, ix–x, 4, 62, 201; Kuykendall, *Hawaiian Kingdom*, 1:82, 92–95; John Denis Haeger, *John Jacob Astor: Business and Finance in the Early Republic* (Detroit, Mich., 1991).

18. Herman J. Viola and Carolyn Margolis, eds., *Magnificent Voyagers: The U.S. Exploring Expedition, 1838–1842* (Washington, D.C., 1985), 4, 9–10; John H. Schroeder, *Shaping a Maritime Empire: The Commercial and Diplomatic Role of the American Navy, 1829–1861* (Westport, Conn., 1985), 40–69; James Fenimore Cooper, *History of the Navy of the United States of America*, 3 vols. (New York, 1856), 3:38–53; Norman A. Graebner, ed., *Manifest Destiny* (Indianapolis, 1968), xlii–xlvi; Dudden, *The American Pacific*, 16–17; Dulles, *America in the Pacific*, 201; Charles Wilkes, *Autobiography of Rear Admiral Charles Wilkes, U.S. Navy, 1798–1877* (Washington, D.C., 1978), 321–548; William H. Goetzmann, *New Lands, New Men: America and the Second Great Age of Discovery* (New York, 1986), 168–70, 270, 276–89, 297.

19. Viola and Margolis, eds., *Magnificent Voyagers*, 206, 221.

20. Riesenberg, *The Pacific Ocean*, 238; Goetzmann, *New Lands, New Men*, 284; Schroeder, *Shaping a Maritime Empire*, 85; Viola and Margolis, eds., *Magnificent Voyagers*, 206, 221; Graebner, *Empire on the Pacific*, 45–47, 61, 65, 70, 72–73.

21. Goetzmann, *New Lands, New Men*, 278, 284.

22. Viola and Margolis, eds., *Magnificent Voyagers*, 18.

23. Cooper, *History of the Navy*, 3:51; Viola and Margolis, eds., *Magnificent Voyagers*, 160–63, 206, 208, 214–15.

24. Dodge, *Islands and Empires*, 69, 115; Goetzmann, *New Lands, New Men*, 288–89; Dudden, *The American Pacific*, 17; Viola and Margolis, eds., *Magnificent Voyagers*, 4, 187, 196.

25. Viola and Margolis, eds., *Magnificent Voyagers*, 196.

26. Daniel Henderson, *The Hidden Coasts: A Biography of Admiral Charles Wilkes* (New York, 1953), 149–219; Viola and Margolis, eds., *Magnificent Voyagers*, 206, 221.

27. Riesenberg, *The Pacific Ocean*, 240, 244–66; Goetzmann, *New Lands, New Men*, 288–89.

28. Dudden, *The American Pacific*, 17; Viola and Margolis, eds., *Magnificent Voyagers*, 25. The scientific publications and manuscripts derived from this expedition have been cataloged in Daniel C. Haskell, *The United States Exploring Expedition, 1838–1842, and Its Publications, 1844–1874* (New York, 1942).

29. Viola and Margolis, eds., *Magnificent Voyagers*, 23.

30. For example, Robert Erwin Johnson, *Far China Station: The U.S. Navy in Asian Waters, 1800–1898* (Annapolis, Md., 1979).

2. The Great Powers in the Caribbean Basin, 1800–1890s

1. Franklin Knight, *The Caribbean: The Genesis of a Fragmented National-ism*, 2d ed. (New York, 1990), 27–158; Jan Rogozinski, *A Brief History of the Carib-bean: From Arawak and the Carib to the Present* (New York, 1994), 23–173; J.H. Parry and Philip Sherlock, *A Short History of the West Indies*, 3d ed. (New York, 1990), 13–174.

2. Walter LaFeber, *The New Empire: An Interpretation of American Expan-sion, 1860–1898* (Ithaca, N.Y., 1963), 1–16; Lester Langley, *Struggle for the Ameri-can Mediterranean: United States–European Rivalry in the Gulf-Caribbean, 1776–1904* (Athens, Ga., 1976), 25–106; Peggy K. Liss, *Atlantic Empires: The Net-work of Trade and Revolution, 1713–1826* (Baltimore, 1983), 32–33, 162–65; Rob-ert V. Remini, *Andrew Jackson and the Course of American Empire, 1767–1821* (New York, 1977), 362–365; Thomas D. Schoonover, *The United States in Central America, 1860–1911: Episodes of Social Imperialism and Imperial Rivalry in the World System* (Durham, N.C., 1991), introduction.

3. Carroll Pursell, *The Machine in America: A Social History of Technology* (Baltimore, 1995), 109–28, 179–99; Richard van Alstyne, *The Rising American Em-pire* (Chicago, 1960), 78–169; Walter LaFeber, *The American Age: United States Foreign Policy at Home and Abroad since 1750* (New York, 1989), 94, 98, 101–4; Walther Bernecker and Thomas Fischer, "Deutschland und Lateinamerika im Zeitalter des Imperialismus, 1871–1914," in *Deutsche in Lateinamerika—Lateinamerika in Deutschland*, ed. Karl Kohut, Dietrich Briesemeister, and Gustav Siebenmann (Frank-furt, 1996), 371–97; Schoonover, *The United States in Central America*, 4–10.

4. Ciro Cardoso and Héctor Pérez Brignoli, *América Central y la economía occidental (1520–1930)* (San José, Costa Rica, 1977), 113–80; Ralph Lee Woodward Jr., "Central America from Independence to c. 1870," in *The Cambridge History of Latin America*, ed. Leslie Bethell, 3:471–506; Ralph Lee Woodward Jr., *Central America: A Nation Divided*, 2d ed. (New York, 1985), 120–202; Héctor Pérez Brignoli, *Breve Historia de Centro América* (Madrid, 1985), 79–106; Thomas Schoonover, "Prussia and the Protection of German Transit through Middle America and Trade with the Pacific Basin, 1848–1851," *Jahrbuch für Geschichte von Staat, Wirtschaft und Gesellschaft Lateinamerikas* 22 (1985): 393–422; Thomas Schoonover, "Costa Rican Trade and Navigation Ties with the United States, Germany, and Europe, 1840–1885," *Jahrbuch für Geschichte von Staat, Wirtschaft und Gesellschaft Lateinamerikas* 14 (1977): 269–309.

5. Thomas D. Schoonover, "Metropole Rivalry in Central America, 1820s to 1929: An Overview," in *Central America: Historical Perspective on the Contempo-rary Crisis*, ed. Ralph Lee Woodward Jr. (Westport, Conn., 1988), 21–46.

6. LaFeber, *The American Age*, 69–147; Langley, *Struggle for the American Mediterranean*, 25–106; Thomas D. Schoonover, *Germany in Central America: Competitive Imperialism, 1821–1929* (Tuscaloosa, Ala., 1998), 34–66; Thomas D.

Schoonover, *The French in Central America: Culture and Commerce, 1820–1930* (Wilmington, Del., 2000), 1–46; Thomas Schoonover, "Competitive Imperialism: The United States Challenges the World in Middle America, 1820–1930," unpublished manuscript; Paul M. Kennedy, *The Rise and Fall of the Great Powers* (New York, 1987), 193–248.

7. Van Alstyne, *The Rising American Empire*, 1–27, 100–77; Robert May, *The Southern Dream of a Caribbean Empire, 1854–1861*, rev. ed. (Athens, Ga., 1989), 3–45; Charles Vevier, "American Continentalism: An Idea of Expansionism, 1845–1910," *American Historical Review* 65 (Jan. 1960): 323–35; Eric Foner, *Free Soil, Free Labor, Free Men* (London, 1970), 268–80.

8. May, *The Southern Dream of a Caribbean Empire*, 3–45, 259–75; Robert E. May, *Manifest Destiny's Underworld: Filibustering in Antebellum America* (Chapel Hill and London, 2002); Charles H. Brown, *Agents of Manifest Destiny: The Lives and Times of the Filibusters* (Chapel Hill, N.C., 1980), 13–18, 458–63; David M. Pletcher, *The Diplomacy of Annexation: Texas, Oregon, and the Mexican War* (Columbia, Mo., 1973); Thomas R. Hietala, *Manifest Design: Anxious Aggrandizement in Late Jacksonian America* (Ithaca, N.Y., 1985).

9. William H. Goetzmann, *New Lands, New Men: America and the Second Great Age of Discovery* (New York, 1986), 270–72; Norman A. Graebner, *Empire on the Pacific: A Study of American Continental Expansion* (1955; reprint, Santa Barbara, Calif., 1983), 1–21, 176, 217–28; Vevier, "American Continentalism," 323–35; Van Alstyne, *The Rising American Empire*, 100–146.

10. Much of the next pages comes from Thomas D. Schoonover, "Napoleon Is Coming! Maximilian Is Coming! The International History of the Civil War in the Caribbean Basin," in *The Union, the Confederacy, and the Atlantic Rim*, ed. Robert E. May (W. Lafayette, Ind., 1995), 101–30; see also Langley, *Struggle for the American Mediterranean*, 81–106; David M. Pletcher, *The Diplomacy of Involvement: American Economic Expansion across the Pacific, 1784–1900* (Columbia, Mo., 2001), 68–73.

11. Hans-Ulrich Wehler, "Industrial Growth and Early German Imperialism," in *Studies in the Theory of Imperialism*, ed. Roger Owen and Bob Sutcliffe (London, 1972), 71–92; Martin Winckler, *Bismarcks Bündnispolitik und das europäische Gleichgewicht* (Stuttgart, 1964); Schoonover, *Germany in Central America*, 1–66.

12. Published materials on colonization organizations in I Hauptabteilung, Preussisches Staatsministerium (Rep. 90), Nr. 232 Geheimes Staatsarchiv Preussischer Kulturbesitz, Berlin; Jahresberichte des Hamburger Colonisationsvereins, 1851–1855, Akten des Bundestages, DB/28, vol. 1, Bundesarchiv, Aussenstelle Frankfurt; Franz Hugo Hesse, "Andeutungen über Mittel-Amerika und seine Zukunft," [ca. 1851], AA II Rep 6, Nr. 3518, Bundesarchiv Merseburg (BAM); Hesse to Otto von Manteuffel, 30 Dec. 1852, 2. 4. 1., Abt. II, Nr 5246 (AA III, Rep. 14, Nr 534), BAM; Julio Castellanos Cambranes, "Aspectos del desarrollo socio-económico y político de Guatemala, 1868–1885, en base de materiales de archivos alemanes," *Política y Sociedad* 3 (1977): 7–

14; Herbert Schottelius, *Mittelamerika als Schauplatz deutscher Kolonisationsversuche, 1840–1865* (Hamburg, 1939); Thomas Schoonover, "Germany in Central America, 1820s–1929: An Overview," *Jahrbuch für Geschichte von Staat, Wirtschaft und Gesellschaft Lateinamerikas* 25 (1988): 33–59.

13. Schoonover, *Germany in Central America*, 1–66.

14. Cyril Allen, *France in Central America: Felix Belly and the Nicaraguan Canal* (New York, 1966); G. de Sibourg to MAE, 15 April, 21 May 1854, CCC, Panama, vol. 1, Archive du ministère des affaires étrangères, Paris; Félix Belly, *Percement de l'isthme de Panama par le canal de Nicaragua* (Paris, 1858), 121–57; Stanley J. Pincetl Jr., "France and the Clayton Bulwer Treaty of 1850," *Annales* 45 (1968): 167–94; Schoonover, *The French in Central America*, 1–46.

15. Thomas D. Schoonover, "Latin America," in *Spain's Foreign Relations in the Nineteenth Century*, ed. James W. Cortada (Westport, Conn., 1994), 113–30; Antonia Pi-Suner, *México y España durante la República Restaurada* (México, 1985), 20–21; James W. Cortada, *Spain and the American Civil War: Relations at Mid-Century, 1855–1868* (Philadelphia, 1980).

16. Knight, *The Caribbean*, 27–192; Rogozinski, *A Brief History of the Caribbean*, 44–223; Schoonover, *Germany in Central America*, 55–66; Schoonover, *The French in Central America*, 23–76.

17. Roy Franklin Nichols, *The Disruption of American Democracy* (New York, 1962), 186–87, 231–33, 325–26; Graebner, *Empire on the Pacific*, 1–21.

18. Napoleon III to Forey, 3 July 1862, quoted in Alfred H. Hanna and Kathryn A. Hanna, *Napoleon III and Mexico: American Triumph over Monarchy* (Chapel Hill, N.C., 1971), 79–80; Henry Blumenthal, *France and the United States: Their Diplomatic Relations, 1789–1914* (Chapel Hill, N.C., 1970), 66–67.

19. Schoonover, "Latin America," 113–30; Jerónimo Bécker, *Historia de las relaciones exteriores de España*, 3 vols. (Madrid, 1924–1926), 2:471–79, 513–19; Robert W. Frazer, "The Role of the Lima Congress, 1864–1865, in the Development of Pan-Americanism," *Hispanic American Historical Review* 29 (Aug. 1949): 319–48; Thomas G. Powell, "Spain and Mexico," in *The Iberian-American Connection: Implications for U.S. Foreign Relations*, ed. Howard J. Wiarda (Boulder, Colo., 1986), 253–92; Mark J. van Aken, *Pan-Hispanism: Its Origin and Development to 1866* (Berkeley, Calif., 1959), 50–58; Thomas Schoonover, *Dollars over Dominion: The Triumph of Liberalism in Mexican–United States Relations, 1861–1867* (Baton Rouge, La., 1978), 61–71, 75–77.

20. Thomas Schoonover, "Intereses británicos en Costa Rica cerca 1857," *Estudios Sociales Centroamericanos* 6 (Sept.–Dec. 1973): 152–54; Thomas Schoonover, "Imperialism in Middle America: United States Competition with Britain, Germany, and France, 1820s–1920s," in *Eagle Against Empire: American Opposition to European Imperialism, 1914–1982*, ed. Rhodri Jeffreys-Jones (Provence, France, 1983), 41–58.

21. Guy P. Palmade, *Capitalisme et capitalistes français au XIXe siècle* (Paris, 1961), 196–98; Joachim Kuhn, "Napoleon III und der Nicaraguakanal," *Historische*

Zeitschrift 208 (1969): 295–319; F.L. Hardy to MAE, 1 May 1862, CCC, Guat., vol. 7, AMAE; unsigned report, 24 Feb. 1863, Affaires divers politiques, carton 2, folder, Affaires coloniales Belgiques, AMAE; Edward Loos to Napoléon III, 18 June 1863, Analysis of Loos dispatch, July, 1863, Mémoires et Documents, Amér., vol. 68, AMAE; Blumenthal, *France and the United States*, 79–91; Marvin R. Zahniser, *Uncertain Friendship: American-French Diplomatic Relations through the Cold War* (New York, 1975), 127–47.

22. Ernest Paolino, *The Foundations of the American Empire: William Henry Seward and U.S. Foreign Policy* (Ithaca, N.Y., 1973), 25–40; Thomas Schoonover, "Black Colonization in Mexico and Central America during the Civil War: Foreign Relations and Imperialism," *Pacific Historical Review* 49 (Nov. 1980): 607–20.

23. Hanna and Hanna, *Napoleon III and Mexico*, 38–46; Arnold Blumberg, *The Diplomacy of the Mexican Empire, 1863–1867* (Philadelphia, 1971), 5–6; Paolino, *The Foundations of the American Empire*, 27–28; Schoonover, *Dollars over Dominion*, 67–71, 140–42.

24. Seward, St. Paul, Minnesota, speech, 18 Sept. 1860, Seward, Senate speech, March 11, 1850, quoted in *The Shaping of American Diplomacy: Readings and Documents in American Foreign Relations*, ed. William A. Williams, 2 vols. (Chicago, 1970) 1:314; Frederick C. Drake, *The Empire of the Seas: A Biography of Rear Admiral Robert Wilson Shufeldt, USN* (Honolulu, Hawaii, 1984), 334–53; Jean Ingram Brookes, *International Rivalry in the Pacific Islands, 1800–1875* (Berkeley, Calif., 1941), 405–16.

25. Schoonover, "Napoleon Is Coming!" 101–30.

26. Kurt Himer, *75 Jahre Hamburg-Amerika Linie. 1. Teil: Adolf Godeffroy and seine Nachfolger bis 1886* (Hamburg, 1922), 42–43; Schoonover, *Germany in Central America*, 55–84; Brenda Gayle Plummer, *Haiti and the United States: The Psychological Moment* (Athens, Ga., 1992), 85–88; Holger H. Herwig, *Politics of Frustration: The United States in German Naval Planning, 1889–1941* (Boston, 1976), 72–76; Regina Wagner, *Los Alemanes en Guatemala, 1828–1944* (Guatemala, 1995), 76–239; Ragnhild Fiebig-von Hase, *Lateinamerika als Konfliktherd der deutsch-amerikanischen Beziehungen 1890–1913*, 2 vols. (Göttingen, 1986), 1:104–93, 361–427; Nancy Mitchell, *The Danger of Dreams: German and American Imperialism in Latin America* (Chapel Hill, N.C., 1999), 9–21.

27. Thomas Schoonover, "France in Central America, 1820s to 1920s: An Overview," *Revue française d'histoire d'outre mer* 79 (1992): 161–97.

28. Eliot Grinnell Mears, *Maritime Trade of the Western United States* (Stanford, Calif., 1938), 122–25.

29. Charles Ameringer, "Bunau-Varilla, Russia, and the Panama Canal," *Journal of Interamerican Studies and World Affairs* 12 (July 1970): 328–38; Lester D. Langley, *America and the Americas: The United States in the Western Hemisphere* (Athens, Ga., 1989), 93–103; Hans-Ulrich Wehler, "Der amerikanische Imperialismus vor 1914," in *Der moderne Imperialismus*, ed. Wolfgang J. Mommsen (Stuttgart, Germ., 1971), 172–92; Langley, *Struggle for the American Mediterranean*, 152–86.

30. Schoonover, "Metropole Rivalry in Central America," 21–46.

31. Ibid.

32. Ciro Cardoso, "Central America: The Liberal Era," in *The Cambridge History of Latin America,* ed. Bethell, 5:197–227; Pérez Brignoli, *Breve Historia de Centro América,* 79–132; Cardoso and Pérez Brignoli, *América Central y la economía occidental,* 149–80, 199–320; Lester D. Langley and Thomas Schoonover, *The Banana Men: American Mercenaries and Entrepreneurs in Central America, 1880–1930* (Lexington, Ky., 1995), chaps. 1–2.

33. Woodward, *Central America,* 177–223; Cardoso, "Central America: The Liberal Era," 5:197–227.

34. Jürgen Buchenau, *In the Shadow of the Giant: The Making of Mexico's Central America Policy, 1876–1930* (Tuscaloosa, Ala., 1996), 43–44.

35. N. Ray Gilmore, "Mexico and the Spanish-American War," *Hispanic American Historical Review* 43:3 (1963): 511–25; Schoonover, *The United States in Central America,* 97–110, 130–48; de Grandprey to Min. Guerre, April 1, 1896, F^{30}393^2: Nic., Amef; Emile Joré to MAE, 24 April 1898, CP 1918, CR, Pol. extérieure, N. S. 2, Archive du ministère de l'économie et des finances, Paris; Marcelleis Pellet to Théophile Delcasse, 7 Jan. 1899, CP 1918, Amér. cent. I, N. S. 1, AMAE.

36. Michael H. Hunt, *Ideology and U.S. Foreign Policy* (New Haven, Conn., 1987), 69–90; Walter LaFeber, *The Clash: U.S.-Japanese Relations Throughout History* (New York, 1997), 3–31; Richard van Alstyne, *The United States and East Asia* (New York, 1973), 60–64, 90–92.

3. The Great Powers in East Asia and the Pacific, 1840s–1890s

1. Paul M. Kennedy, *The Rise and Fall of the Great Powers: Economic Change and Military Conflict from 1500 to 2000* (New York, 1987), 194–98; Thomas Schoonover, *Germany in Central America: Competitive Imperialism, 1821–1929* (Tuscaloosa, Ala., 1998), 55–106; Thomas Schoonover, *The United States in Central America, 1860–1911: Episodes of Social Imperialism and Imperial Rivalry in the World System* (Durham, N.C., 1991), chaps. 2, 4, and 8.

2. Jean Ingram Brookes, *International Rivalry in the Pacific Islands, 1800–1875* (Berkeley, Calif., 1941), 10–42; Thomas R. Cox, *Mills and Markets: A History of the Pacific Coast Lumber Industry to 1900* (Seattle, Wash., 1974); Charles Vevier, "American Continentalism: An Idea of Expansionism, 1845–1910," *American Historical Review* 65 (Jan. 1960): 323–35; Laurence M. Hauptman, "Westward the Course of Empire: Geography Schoolbooks and Manifest Destiny, 1783–1893," *The Historian* 40:3 (May 1978): 423–37.

3. Norman A. Graebner, *Empire on the Pacific: A Study of American Continental Expansion* (1955; reprint, Santa Barbara, Calif., 1983), 83–122, 212–28; Walt Whitman, "A Broadway Pageant," in *Walt Whitman: The Complete Poems,* ed. Francis Murphy (Baltimore, 1975), 273.

4. William A. Williams, *The Roots of the Modern American Empire: A Study*

of the Growth and Shaping of Social Consciousness in a Marketplace Society (New York, 1969), 4–46, 87–88; Thomas Schoonover, *Dollars over Dominion: The Triumph of Liberalism in Mexican–United States Relations, 1861–1867* (Baton Rouge, La., 1978), xii–xx, 263–65.

5. Brookes, *International Rivalry in the Pacific Islands*, 10–42; Chen Chi, *Die Beziehungen zwischen Deutschland und China bis 1933* (Hamburg, 1973), 79.

6. Foster Rhea Dulles, *America in the Pacific: A Century of Expansion* 2d ed. (New York, 1969), 1–2; Timothy Parsons, *The British Imperial Century, 1815–1914: A World History Perspective* (Lanham, Md., 1999); Mark Borthwick, *Pacific Century: The Emergence of Modern Pacific Asia*, 2d. ed. (Boulder, Colo., 1998), 89–93; Frederic Wakeman Jr., *The Fall of Imperial China* (New York, 1975), 125–29; Charles C. Stelle, *Americans and the China Opium Trade in the Nineteenth Century* (New York, 1981), 141–44; Jacques M. Downs, "American Merchants and the China Opium Trade, 1800–1840," *Business History Review* 42:3 (winter, 1968): 418–42; Peter W. Fay, "The Protestant Mission and the Opium War," *Pacific Historical Review* 40:3 (May 1971): 145–61.

7. John K. Fairbank, *China: A New History* (Cambridge, Mass., 1992), 201–5; Milton W. Meyer, *China: An Introduction* (Totowa, N.J., 1978), 169–73; Edward V. Gulick, *Peter Parker and the Opening of China* (Cambridge, Mass., 1973), 202–10; Murray A. Rubinstein, "American Board Missionaries and the Formation of American Opinion toward China, 1830–1860," in *America Views China: American Images of China Now and Then*, ed. Jonathan Goldstein, Jerry Israel, and Hilary Conroy (Bethlehem, Pa., 1991), 67–79.

8. Jonathan D. Spence, *The Search for Modern China* (New York, 1990), 13–14; Karl J. Rivinius, "Imperialistische Welt- und Missionspolitik: der Fall Kiautschou," in *Imperialismus und Kolonialmission: Kaiserliches Deutschland und koloniales Imperium*, ed. Klaus J. Bade (Wiesbaden, Germ., 1982), 269–88; Jürgen Osterhammel, *China und die Weltgesellschaft, vom 18. Jahrhundert bis in unsere Zeit* (Munich, 1989), 160–61; Wakeman, *The Fall of Imperial China*, 155.

9. David L. Anderson, "Anson Burlingame: American Architect of the Cooperative Policy in China, 1861–1871," *Diplomatic History* 1 (summer 1977): 239–56; David L. Anderson, *Imperialism and Idealism: American Diplomats in China, 1861–1898* (Bloomington, 1986).

10. E. Mowbray Tate, *Transpacific Steam: The Story of Steam Navigation from the Pacific Coast of North America to the Far East and the Antipodes, 1867–1941* (New York, 1986), 23–24, 31, 44–45; Kwang-Ching Liu, *Anglo-American Steamship Rivalry in China, 1862–1874* (Cambridge, Mass., 1962), 9–10, 72–79, 150–56.

11. Joseph W. Esherick, *The Origins of the Boxer Uprising* (Berkeley, Calif., 1986), 68–73; Chen, *Die Beziehungen zwischen Deutschland und China*, 79; Spence, *The Search for Modern China*, 13–14; Helmuth Stoecker, *Deutschland und China im 19. Jahrhundert: Das Eindringen des deutschen Kapitalismus* (Berlin, 1958), 16–17; P.J. Cain and Anthony Hopkins, *British Imperialism: Innovation and Expansion, 1688–1914* (London, 1994), 425–26.

12. Sherman Cochran, *Encountering Chinese Networks: Western, Japanese, and Chinese Corporations in China, 1880–1937* (Berkeley, Calif., 2000), 1–29; Sherman Cochran, *Big Business in China: Sino-Foreign Rivalry in the Cigarette Industry, 1890–1930* (Cambridge, Mass., 1980), 1–3, 201–2, 209–11; Esherick, *Origins of the Boxer Uprising,* 68–73; Paul H. Clyde and Burton F. Beers, *The Far East: A History of the Western Impact and the Eastern Response (1830–1970)* (Englewood Cliffs, N.J., 1971), 209–11.

13. Ding Jianhong, "Die Politik Li Hongzhangs gegenüber Deutschland," in *Deutsch-chinesische Beziehungen vom 19. Jahrhundert bis zur Gegenwart,* ed. Kuo Heng-yü and Mechthild Leutner (Munich, 1991), 241–44.

14. Immanuel C.Y. Hsu, *The Rise of Modern China,* 4th ed. (New York, 1990), 389–90.

15. John F. Cady, *The Roots of French Imperialism in Eastern Asia* (Ithaca, N.Y., 1954), 291–95; Milton E. Osborne, *The French Presence in Cochinchina and Cambodia: Rule and Response (1859–1905)* (Ithaca, N.Y., 1969), 277; Victor Purcell, *The Boxer Uprising: A Background Study* (1963; reprint, Hamden, Conn., 1974), 84.

16. Stoecker, *Deutschland und China,* 40, 47–56; Bernd Martin, "Die preussische Ostasienexpedition in China. Zur Vorgeschichte des Freundschafts-, Handels- und Schiffahrts-Vertrages vom 2. September 1861," in *Deutsch-chinesische Beziehungen,* ed. Kuo and Leutner, 211; Stewart G. Firth, "German Firms in the Pacific Islands, 1857–1914," in *Germany in the Pacific and Far East, 1870–1914,* ed. John A. Moses and Paul M. Kennedy (St. Lucia, Aust., 1977), 3–4.

17. Martin, "Die preussische Ostasienexpedition in China," 214–16, 220; Michael Köhler, *Akkulturation in der Südsee: Die Kolonialgeschichte der Karolinen-Inseln im pazifischen Ozean und der Wandel ihrer sozialen Organisation* (Frankfurt, 1982), 264; Helmuth Stoecker, "Preussisch-deutsche Chinapolitik in den 1860/70er Jahren," in *Imperialismus,* ed. Hans-Ulrich Wehler (Cologne, Germ., 1976), 243–58; Chen, *Die Beziehungen zwischen Deutschland und China,* 21–23.

18. Michael Fröhlich, *Imperialismus: Deutsche Kolonial- und Weltpolitik, 1880–1914* (Munich, 1994), 27, 41–42; Hans-Ulrich Wehler, *Bismarck und der Imperialismus* (Cologne, 1969), 391–407; Firth, "German Firms in the Pacific Islands," 3–4; Paul M. Kennedy, *The Samoan Tangle: A Study in Anglo-German-American Relations, 1878–1900* (Dublin, Ireland, 1974), 24–39, 133–44, 285–305; Richard P. Gilson, *Samoa, 1830 to 1900: The Politics of a Multi-Cultural Community* (Melbourne, Aust., 1970), 207–14, 391–407; Otto Riedel, *Der Kampf um Deutsch-Samoa: Erinnerungen eines Hamburger Kaufmanns* (Berlin, 1938), 35–38; Ian C. Campbell, *A History of the Pacific Islands* (Berkeley, Calif., 1989), 97.

19. Wehler, *Bismarck und der Imperialismus,* 391–407; Günther Meyer, "German Interests and Policy in the Netherlands, East Indies, and Malaya, 1870–1914," in *Germany in the Pacific and Far East,* ed. Moses and Kennedy, 40–58; Paul M. Kennedy, "Bismarck's Imperialism: The Case of Samoa, 1880–1890," *The Historical Journal* 15:2 (1972): 261, 280.

20. Klaus J. Bade, *Friedrich Fabri und der Imperialismus in der Bismarckzeit: Revolution — Depression — Expansion* (Freiburg, Germany, 1975); Wehler, *Bismarck und der Imperialismus*, 391–407; Schoonover, *Germany in Central America*, 67–69, 83–87, 105–6, 112–13.

21. Helmut Christmann, Peter Hempenstall, and Dirk Anthony Ballendorf, *Die Karolinen-Inseln in deutscher Zeit: Eine kolonialgeschichtliche Fallstudie* (Münster, Germ., 1991), 4–9; Wolfgang Reinhard, *Geschichte der europäischen Expansion*, 4 vols. (Stuttgart, Germ., 1988), 3:66, 105; Hermógenes E. Bacareza, *A History of Philippine-German Relations* (n.p., 1980), 51–54, 60–65.

22. Stewart G. Firth, "Die Bostoner Mission in den deutschen Marshall-Inseln," in *Imperialismus und Kolonialmission*, ed. Bade, 257–67; Peter J. Hempenstall, "Europäische Missionsgesellschaften und christlicher Einfluss in der deutschen Südsee: das Beispiel Neuguinea," in *Imperialismus und Kolonialmission*, ed. Bade, 228, 234.

23. Aldrich, "Colonialism, Culture and Politics," 217–30; Charles Daney, *Indochine* (Paris, 1992), 11–12; Campbell, *A History of the Pacific Islands*, 83–84; Peter J. Hempenstall, "Imperial Manoeuvres," in *Tides of History: The Pacific Islands in the Twentieth Century*, ed. K.R. Howe, Robert C. Kiste, and Brij V. Lal (Honolulu, Hawaii, 1994), 37; Jean Martin, *L'Empire triomphant, 1871–1936*, 2 vols. (Paris, 1990), 1:204, 206, 213; Rollin, *Les îles marquises*, 230–37, 241–42; Jacques Binoche-Guedra, *La France d'outre-mer, 1815–1962* (Paris, 1992), 67.

24. Neville Meaney, *The Search for Security in the Pacific, 1901–1914* (Sydney, Aust., 1976), 9; C. Hartley Grattan, *The Southwest Pacific to 1900: A Modern History* (Ann Arbor, Mich., 1963), 453–509; C. Hartley Grattan, *The United States and the Southwest Pacific* (Cambridge, Mass., 1961), 86–89, 119–27.

25. James W. Gould, "American Imperialism in Southeast Asia before 1898," *Journal of Southeast Asian Studies* 3:2 (1972): 306–14; William G. Beasley, *Japanese Imperialism, 1894–1945* (Oxford, 1987), 15.

26. Ralph S. Kuykendall, *Hawaiian Kingdom, 1778–1893*, 3 vols. (Honolulu, Hawaii, 1966–1968), 1:304–9.

27. Merze Tate, *The United States and the Hawaiian Kingdom: A Political History* (New Haven, Conn., 1965), 44; Akira Iriye, "Japan's Drive to Great-Power Status," in *The Cambridge History of Japan*, ed. Marius B. Jansen, 6 vols. (New York, 1988–1992), 5:759–65; Walter LaFeber, *The Clash: U.S.-Japanese Relations Throughout History* (New York, 1997), 53–57.

28. Hempenstall, "Imperial Manoeuvres," 35; Kuykendall, *Hawaiian Kingdom*, 1:71.

29. Jean-Baptiste Alberti, *La colonisation à la Nouvelle-Calédonie. Colonisation pénale. Colonisation libre* (Paris, 1909), 8; Arthur J. Knoll, "Zealotry among the Converted: American Board Missionaries in Micronesia, 1852–1919," in *European Impact and Pacific Influence*, ed. Hiery and MacKenzie (London, 1997), 100–118; Firth, "Die Bostoner Mission in den deutschen Marshall-Inseln," 257; Edmundo Eusebio Valera Jr., "'Imperialism of Righteousness': The Influence of the American

Protestant Social Gospel on Foreign Missions and Expansionism, 1890–1910" (Ph.D. diss., Fordham University, 1998), 224–92.

30. Alberti, *La colonisation à la Nouvelle-Calédonie*, 8, 21–23; Campbell, *A History of the Pacific Islands*, 131–32, 149; Ph. Delord, *Mon voyage d'enquête en Nouvelle-Calédonie, août-septembre 1899* (Paris, 1901); Donald Denoon, ed., *The Cambridge History of the Pacific Islanders* (Cambridge, Eng., 1997); Jean Chesneaux and Nic Maclellan, *La France dans le Pacifique: De Bougainville à Moruva* (Paris, 1992), 57–58; S. Ferdinand-Lop, *Les possessions françaises du pacifique* (Paris, 1933); Virginia Thompson and Richard Adloff, *The Pacific Islands: French Polynesia and New Caledonia* (Berkeley, Calif., 1971), 15–16; Rivinius, "Imperialistische Welt- und Missionspolitik," 269–88; John Dademo Waiko, *A Short History of Papua New Guinea* (Melbourne, Aust., 1993), 24–25.

31. Campbell, *A History of the Pacific Islands*, 97; Frederick W. Christian, *The Caroline Islands: Travel in the Sea of the Little Islands* (1899; reprint, London, 1967), 24f.

32. Firth, "Die Bostoner Mission in den deutschen Marshall-Inseln," 258; Reinhard, *Geschichte der europäischen Expansion*, 3:66; Dirk J. Ballendorf, "Agents, Alcohol and Aliens: Ancient 'Bones of Contention' in German Palau, and Their Present-Day Implications," in *Rassendiskriminierung, Kolonialpolitik und ethnisch-nationale Identität*, ed. Wilfried Wagner (Hamburg, 1992), 309–20; Hermann Hiery, "Germans, Pacific Islanders and Sexuality: German Impact and Indigenous Influence in Melanesia and Micronesia," in *European Impact and Pacific Influence: British and German Colonial Policy in the Pacific Islands and the Indigenous Response*, ed. Hermann Hiery and John M. MacKenzie (London, 1997), 300–301; Knoll, "Zealotry among the Converted: American Board Missionaries in Micronesia, 1852–1919," 100–118; Christian, *The Caroline Islands*, 24f.

33. Hsu, *The Rise of Modern China*, 388–89; Spence, *The Search for Modern China*, 204–9; Lewis H. Gann, "Western and Japanese Colonialism: Some Preliminary Comparisons," in *The Japanese Colonial Empire, 1895–1945*, ed. Ramon H. Myers and Mark R. Peattie (Princeton, N.J., 1984), 502; Lisa Joy Pruitt, "'A Looking-Glass for Ladies': American Protestant Women and the Orient in the Nineteenth Century" (Ph.D. diss., Vanderbilt University, 1998), 238–39.

34. Esherick, *Origins of the Boxer Uprising*, 68–95; Hsu, *The Rise of Modern China*, 388–89.

35. Akira Iriye, *Across the Pacific: An Inner History of American–East Asian Relations* (New York, 1967), 79–80; Charles E. Neu, *The Troubled Encounter: The United States and Japan* (New York, 1975), 29; William R. Hutchison, "Modernism and Missions: The Liberal Search for an Exportable Christianity, 1875–1935," in *The Missionary Enterprise in China and America*, ed. John K. Fairbank (Cambridge, Mass., 1974), 110–24; Valera, "'Imperialism of Righteousness,'" 293–388, 391.

36. Spence, *The Search for Modern China*, 231–34; John K. Fairbank, "The Many Faces of Protestant Missions in China and the United States," in *The Mission-*

ary Enterprise in China and America, ed. John K. Fairbank (Cambridge, Mass., 1974), 6–12; Iriye, *Across the Pacific*, 79–80; Neu, *The Troubled Encounter*, 29; Valera, "'Imperialism of Righteousness,'" 162–223; Stuart Creighton Miller, "Ends and Means: Missionary Justification of Force in Nineteenth Century China," in *The Missionary Enterprise in China and America*, ed. Fairbank, 249–83.

37. Rivinius, "Imperialistische Welt- und Missionspolitik," 269–88; Esherick, *Origins of the Boxer Uprising*, 74–95.

38. John A. Harrison, *China since 1800* (New York, 1967), 58–66; Clyde and Beers, *The Far East*, 161–62.

39. Spence, *The Search for Modern China*, 19–20; Parsons, *The British Imperial Century 1815–1914*, 96–105.

40. Meyer, *China*, 174–75; Binoche-Guedra, *La France d'outre-mer*, 65–67; Martin, *L'Empire triomphant*, 204, 206, 213; William R. Nestor, *Power Across the Pacific: A Diplomatic History of American Relations with Japan* (New York, 1996), 16–17, 57; Marilyn Blatt Young, *The Rhetoric of Empire: American China Policy, 1895–1901* (Cambridge, Mass., 1968), 78–84.

41. Iriye, "Japan's Drive to Great-Power Status," 5:721, 726–65; Mark R. Peattie, "The Nan'yo: Japan in the South Pacific, 1885–1945," in *The Japanese Colonial Empire*, ed. Ramon H. Myers and M.R. Peattie, 172–78; Mark R. Peattie, "Introduction," in *The Japanese Colonial Empire*, ed. Myers and Peattie, 6–9, 11; Marius B. Jansen, "Japanese Imperialism: Late Meiji Perspectives," in *The Japanese Colonial Empire*, ed. Myers and Peattie, 62–63, 65–66, 72, 78; LaFeber, *The Clash*, 33–60.

42. Beasley, *Japanese Imperialism*, 14, 19–20, 27; Douglas L. Oliver, *The Pacific Islands* (Honolulu, Hawaii, 1989), 57–61; Purcell, *The Boxer Uprising*, 129; E.H. Norman, *Origins of the Modern Japanese State* (New York, 1975), 236–42.

43. Iriye, "Japan's Drive to Great-Power Status," 5:733–65; Oliver, *The Pacific Islands*, 57–61; Shunsuke Kamei, "The Sacred Land of Liberty: Images of America in Nineteenth Century Japan," in *Mutual Images: Essays in American-Japanese Relations*, ed. Akira Iriye (Cambridge, Mass., 1975), 55–72.

44. Harrison, *China since 1800*, 70–76; Beasley, *Japanese Imperialism*, 4–7, 9.

45. Harrison, *China since 1800*, 70–76; Beasley, *Japanese Imperialism*, 4–7; Spence, *The Search for Modern China*, 221–24; William G. Beasley, *The Rise of Modern Japan* (London, 1990), 148.

46. Meyer, *China*, 174–77; Beasley, *The Rise of Modern Japan*, 148; Gerd Fesser, "Hunderte deutscher Kaufleute werden jauchzen," *Die Zeit*, 21 November 1997, 16.

47. Harrison, *China since 1800*, 70–76.

48. Hsu, *The Rise of Modern China*, 345; Akira Iriye, "Japan as a Competitor, 1895–1917," in *Mutual Images*, ed. Iriye, 73–77; Osterhammel, *China and die Weltgesellschaft*, 203; Christopher Howe, *The Origins of Japanese Trading Supremacy* (London, 1996), 369.

49. Seward W. Livermore, "American Naval-Base Policy in the Far East, 1850–1914," *Pacific Historical Review* 13:2 (June 1944): 113–35.

4. U.S. Domestic Developments and Social Imperialism, 1850s–1890s

1. Immanuel Wallerstein, *The Modern World System*, 3 vols. (New York, 1974–88), vol. 3; Charles Vevier, "American Continentalism: An Idea of Expansionism, 1845–1910," *American Historical Review* 65 (Jan. 1960), 323–35; Walter LaFeber, "Technology and U.S. Foreign Relations," *Diplomatic History* 24:1 (winter 2000): 1–19; Thomas McCormick, *China Market: America's Quest for Informal Empire, 1893–1901* (Chicago, 1967), 21–50; Thomas Schoonover, *The United States in Central America, 1860–1911: Episodes of Social Imperialism and Imperial Rivalry in the World System* (Durham, N.C., 1991), 2–4, 8–10.

2. Vevier, "American Continentalism," 323–35; Thomas Schoonover, "Napoleon Is Coming! Maximilian Is Coming! The International History of the Civil War in the Caribbean Basin," in *The Union, the Confederacy, and the Atlantic Rim*, ed. Robert E. May (W. Lafayette, Ind., 1995), 101–30.

3. Eric Foner, *Free Soil, Free Labor, Free Men* (New York, 1970); Thomas Schoonover, *Dollars over Dominion: The Triumph of Liberalism in Mexican–United States Relations, 1861–1867* (Baton Rouge, 1978), introduction, conclusion.

4. Charles Beard, *The Industrial Revolution* (London, 1901); William Appleman Williams, *The Contours of American History* (Chicago, 1961), 225–342; Christopher Chase-Dunn, "Core-Periphery Relations: The Effects of Core Competition," in *Social Change in the Capitalist World Economy*, ed. Barbara Hockey Kaplan (Beverly Hills, Calif., 1978), 159–76; Raimundo Luraghi, *The Rise and Fall of the Plantation South* (New York, 1978), 146–52; Harold D. Woodman, *King Cotton and His Retainers: Financing and Marketing the Cotton Crop of the South, 1800–1925* (Lexington, Ky., 1968), 141–95; Bob Sutcliffe, "Imperialism and Industrialization in the Third World," in *Studies in the Theory of Imperialism*, ed. Roger Owen and Bob Sutcliffe (London, 1972), 171–92; Robert Wiebe, *The Search for Order, 1877–1920* (New York, 1967), 224–55.

5. Schoonover, *The United States in Central America*, 3–11.

6. Schoonover, "Napoleon Is Coming!" 101–30.

7. William H. Seward, Senate speech, 11 March 1850, quoted in *The Shaping of American Diplomacy: Readings and Documents in American Foreign Relations*, ed. William A. Williams, 2 vols. (Chicago, 1970), 1:314.

8. Seward, St. Paul, Minnesota, speech, 18 Sept. 1860, quoted in *The Shaping of American Diplomacy*, ed. Williams, 1:314.

9. Ibid.; Ernest N. Paolino, *The Foundations of the American Empire: William Henry Seward and U.S. Foreign Policy* (Ithaca, N.Y., 1973), 27–28; Walter LaFeber, *The American Age: United States Foreign Policy at Home and Abroad since 1750* (New York, 1989), 131–32.

10. Paolino, *The Foundations of the American Empire*, 27–28; Vevier, "American Continentalism," 323–35; LaFeber, "Technology and U.S. Foreign Relations," 1–19.

11. Schoonover, *Dollars over Dominion*, 212–50; Thomas Schoonover, ed., *Mexican Lobby: Matías Romero in Washington, 1861–1867* (Lexington, Ky., 1986); Thomas Schoonover, "Mexican Affairs and the Impeachment of President Andrew Johnson," *East Tennessee Historical Society Publications* 46 (1974): 76–93; Thomas Schoonover, "The Mexican Minister Describes Andrew Johnson's 'Swing Around the Circle,'" *Civil War History* 19 (June 1973): 149–61.

12. Williams, *The Contours of American History*, 225–343; Leonard P. Curry, *Blueprint for Modern America* (Nashville, Tenn., 1968), 3–9, 244–52; Dana Frank, *Buy American: The Untold Story of Economic Nationalism* (Boston, 1999), 33–55; Hans-Ulrich Wehler, *Der Aufstieg des amerikanischen Imperialismus* (Göttingen, Germ., 1974), 24–73; Clifford W. Haury, "Hamilton Fish and the Conservative Tradition," in *Traditions and Values: American Diplomacy, 1865–1945*, ed. Norman A. Graebner (Lanham, Md., 1985), 1–27.

13. Robert W. Rydell, "The Culture of Imperial Abundance: World's Fairs in the Making of American Culture," in *Consuming Visions: Accumulation and Display of Goods in America, 1880–1920*, ed. Simon J. Bronner (New York, 1989), 191–216.

14. James A. Field Jr., "The 'Worst Chapter' in Almost Any Book," *American Historical Review* 83 (June 1978): 644–68; Edward P. Crapol, *James G. Blaine: Architect of Empire* (Wilmington, Del., 2000), 78–79, 116, 124, 129–30, 134.

15. Walter LaFeber, *The New Empire: An Interpretation of American Expansion, 1860–1898* (Ithaca, N.Y., 1963), 1–61; Wehler, *Der Aufstieg des amerikanischen Imperialismus*, 24–73; Martin J. Sklar, "The N.A.M. and Foreign Markets on the Eve of the Spanish-American War," *Science and Society* 23 (spring 1960): 133–62.

16. McCormick, *China Market*, 21–52; LaFeber, *The New Empire*, 176–96; William A. Williams, *The Roots of the Modern American Empire: A Study of the Growth and Shaping of Social Consciousness in a Marketplace Society* (New York, 1969), 132–235; Frederick C. Drake, *The Empire of the Seas: A Biography of Rear Admiral Robert Wilson Shufeldt, USN* (Honolulu, Hawaii, 1984), 334–53; Richard E. Welch Jr., *The Presidencies of Grover Cleveland* (Lawrence, Kans., 1988), 164–99.

17. McCormick, *The China Market*, 21–50; David M. Pletcher, *The Diplomacy of Trade and Investment: American Economic Expansion in the Hemisphere, 1865–1900* (Columbia, Mo., 1998), 23–24; Schoonover, *The United States in Central America*, 2–4, 8–10.

18. LaFeber, *The New Empire*, 1–61; Kenneth Hagan, *American Gunboat Diplomacy and the Old Navy, 1877–1889* (Westport, Conn., 1973).

19. On the U.S. economy during the late nineteenth century, Gabriel Kolko, *Main Currents in Modern American History* (New York, 1976); Wiebe, *The Search for Order*; Samuel P. Hays, *The Response to Industrialism, 1885–1914* (Chicago, 1957). On canal diplomacy, Walter LaFeber, *The Panama Canal: The Crisis in Historical Perspective*, rev. ed (New York, 1989), 3–22; Walter Edward Lowrie, "France, the United States, and the Lesseps Panama Canal: Renewed Rivalry in the Western

Hemisphere, 1879–1889" (Ph.D. diss., Syracuse University, 1976); David McCullough, *The Path Between the Seas: The Creation of the Panama Canal, 1870–1914* (New York, 1977); William Appleman Williams, *The Tragedy of American Diplomacy*, rev. ed. (New York, 1988), 18–57; Schoonover, *The United States in Central America*, 77–96.

20. Hans-Ulrich Wehler, *Grundzüge der amerikanischen Außenpolitik: 1750–1900* (Frankfurt, 1984), introduction and chapter 1; Williams, *The Roots of the Modern American Empire*, 4–46; Marvin J. Sklar, *The United States as a Developing Country: Studies in U.S. History in the Progressive Era* (New York, 1992), 1–77; Thomas Schoonover, *Germany in Central America: Competitive Imperialism, 1821–1929* (Tuscaloosa, Ala., 1998), 7–9, 135–36, 152–53; Thomas Schoonover, "Metropole Rivalry in Central America, 1820s to 1929: An Overview," in *Central America: Historical Perspective on the Contemporary Crisis*, ed. Ralph Lee Woodward Jr. (Westport, Conn., 1988), 21–46; Charles W. Calhoun, *Gilded Age Cato: The Life of Walter Q. Gresham* (Lexington, Ky., 1988), 203–12; Richard Rubinson, "Political Transformation in Germany and the United States," in *Social Change in the Capitalist World Economy*, ed. Barbara Hockey Kaplan (Beverly Hills, Calif., 1978), 39–73.

21. Resolution of the National Board of Trade, Dec. 1897, Merchant Exchange collection, Missouri Historical Association, St. Louis.

22. California State Nicaragua Canal Convention, memorial, 29 March 1892, David R. Francis papers, Missouri Historical Society; Board resolution, 9 Dec. 1895, Merchant Exchange collection; William Merry to Lewis Haupt, 17 Aug. 1898, Lewis Haupt papers, box 2, Library of Congress (LC); Lawrence A. Clayton, "The Nicaraguan Canal in the Nineteenth Century: Prelude to American Empire in the Caribbean," *Journal of Latin American Studies* 19 (November 1987): 323–52.

23. Timothy Parsons, *The British Imperial Century, 1815–1914: A World History Perspective* (Lanham, Md., 1999), 96–105; Donald Denoon, ed., *The Cambridge History of the Pacific Islanders* (Cambridge, Eng., 1997), 156.

24. Kristin L. Hoganson, *Fighting for American Manhood: How Gender Politics Provoked the Spanish-American and Philippine-American Wars* (New Haven, 1998), 200–208.

5. Three Crises: The 1893 Depression, China, and Cuba

1. Walter LaFeber, *The New Empire: An Interpretation of American Expansion, 1860–1898* (Ithaca, N.Y., 1963), 284–417; Thomas McCormick, *China Market: America's Quest for Informal Empire, 1893–1901* (Chicago, 1967), 17–125; William A. Williams, *The Tragedy of American Diplomacy* (New York, 1972), 18–89; Daniel M. Crane and Thomas A. Breslin, *An Ordinary Relationship: American Opposition to Republican Revolution in China* (Miami, Fla., 1986), 1–29; Louis A. Pérez Jr., *The War of 1898: The United States and Cuba in History and Historiography* (Chapel Hill, N.C., 1998), 1–56; Joseph Smith, *The Spanish-American War: Conflict in the Caribbean and the Pacific, 1895–1902* (London, 1994), 1–19, 77–79; John L. Offner, *An Unwanted War: The Diplomacy of the United States and*

Spain over Cuba, 1895–1898 (Chapel Hill, N.C., 1992); Ivan Musicant, *Empire by Default: The Spanish-American War and the Dawn of the American Century* (New York, 1998), 136–37. For an earlier work which combines aspects of the crises in Cuba, China, and the depression plus the Boxers and Philippine insurgents, see a special issue: "American Empire, 1898–1903," in the *Pacific Historical Review* 48:4 (November 1979).

2. Walter LaFeber, *The American Age: United States Foreign Policy at Home and Abroad since 1750* (New York, 1989), 189.

3. Akira Iriye, "Japan's Drive to Great-Power Status," in *The Cambridge History of Japan*, ed. Marius B. Jansen, 6 vols. (New York, 1988–1992), 5:765–82; Karen Wigen, *The Making of a Japanese Periphery, 1750–1920* (Berkeley, Calif., 1995), 218–19; William G. Beasley, *The Rise of Modern Japan* (London, 1990), 146; William G. Beasley, *Japanese Imperialism, 1894–1945* (Oxford, 1987), 58, 69.

4. Mark R. Peattie, "The Japanese Colonial Empire, 1895–1945," in *The Cambridge History of Japan*, ed. John W. Hall, Marius B. Jansen, Madoka Kanai, and Denis Twitchett, 6:217–27; Rudolf Hartmann, *Geschichte des modernen Japan: Von Meiji bis Heisi* (Berlin, 1996), 70, 72–79; Beasley, *The Rise of Modern Japan*, 140; Beasley, *Japanese Imperialism*, 6–7, 9; Christopher Howe, *The Origins of Japanese Trading Supremacy* (London, 1996), 339.

5. Peter Nitsche, "Der Bau einer Großmacht: Russische Kolonisation in Ostasien," in *Staatenbildung in Übersee: Die Staatenwelt Lateinamerikas und Asiens*, ed. Jürgen Elvert and Michael Salewski (Stuttgart, 1992), 160, 162; Victor Purcell, *The Boxer Uprising: A Background Study* (1963; reprint, Hamden, Conn., 1974), 89–90, 95–96; P.J. Cain and Anthony Hopkins, *British Imperialism: Innovation and Expansion, 1688–1914* (London, 1994), 433, 440–41, 470.

6. Immanuel C.Y. Hsu, *The Rise of Modern China*, 4th ed. (New York, 1990), 346–49; Helmuth Stoecker, *Deutschland und China im 19. Jahrhundert: Des Eindringen des deutschen Kapitalismus* (Berlin, 1958), 246–47, 251; Chen Chi, *Die Beziehungen zwischen Deutschland und China bis 1933* (Hamburg, 1973), 21–23, 25; Raimund Lammersdorf, *Anfänge einer Weltmacht: Theodore Roosevelt und die transatlantischen Beziehungen der USA 1901–1909* (Berlin, 1994), 369; Michael Fröhlich, *Imperialismus: Deutsche Kolonial- und Weltpolitik, 1880–1914* (Munich, 1994), 27, 42; John E. Schrecker, *Imperialism and Chinese Nationalism* (Cambridge, Mass., 1971), 29–30, 33.

7. Gerd Fesser, "Hunderte deutscher Kaufleute werden jauchzen," *Die Zeit*, 21 November 1997, 16.

8. Ibid.

9. Chi, *Die Beziehungen zwischen Deutschland und China*, 29; Fröhlich, *Imperialismus*, 27, 42; John A. Harrison, *China since 1800* (New York, 1967), 76–77; Karl J. Rivinius, "Imperialistische Welt- und Missionspolitik: der Fall Kiautschou," 277–78.

10. Fesser, "Hunderte deutscher Kaufleute werden jauchzen," 16; Fröhlich, *Imperialismus*, 27, 42; Rivinius, "Imperialistische Welt- und Missionspolitik," 280.

11. Rivinius, "Imperialistische Welt- und Missionspolitik," 279.

12. Nitsche, "Der Bau einer Großmacht," 160, 162; Purcell, *The Boxer Uprising,* 89–90, 95–96; Hans-Ulrich Wehler, *Deutsche Gesellschaftsgeschichte,* 3 vols. (Munich, 1987–1995) 3:1142.

13. Cain and Hopkins, *British Imperialism,* 435–36.

14. Hsu, *The Rise of Modern China,* 346–49; John K. Fairbank, Edwin O. Reischauer, and Albert M. Craig, *East Asia: The Modern Transformation* (Boston, 1965), 470–76; Jacques Binoche-Guedra, *La France d'outre-mer, 1815–1962* (Paris, 1992), 66; Paul A. Cohen, *History in Three Keys: The Boxers as Event, Experience, and Myth* (New York, 1997), 20–21, 27; Purcell, *The Boxer Uprising,* 84–97.

15. Charles Denby, quoted in LaFeber, *The American Search for Opportunity,* 138.

16. Spence, *The Search for Modern China,* 14.

17. Harrison, *China since 1800,* 78–86; Jean Chesneaux, "La place des sociétés secrètes dans l'évolution historique de la Chine aux XIXe–XXe siècles," in *Mouvements populaires et sociétés secrètes en Chine aux XIXe et XXe siècles,* ed. Jean Chesneaux, Feiling Davis, and Nguyen Nguyet Ho (Paris, 1970), 13–40.

18. Clyde and Beers, *The Far East,* 192–220; Cohen, *History in Three Keys,* 19–21, 27, 41.

19. Clyde and Beers, *The Far East,* 192–220; Paul A. Varg, *The Making of a Myth: The United States and China, 1897–1912* (East Lansing, Mich., 1968), 11, 171.

20. Paul M. Kennedy, *The Rise and Fall of the Great Powers: Economic Change and Military Conflict from 1500 to 2000* (New York, 1987), 195–96.

21. Holger H. Herwig, *The Politics of Frustration: The United States in German Naval Planning, 1889–1941* (Boston, 1976), 11–66; Jürgen Buchenau, *In the Shadow of the Giant: Making Mexico's Central American Policy, 1876–1930* (Tuscaloosa, Ala., 1996), 22–79; Thomas D. Schoonover, *Germany in Central America: Competitive Imperialism, 1821–1929* (Tuscaloosa, Ala., 1998), 85–136; Lewis H. Gann, "Western and Japanese Colonialism: Some Preliminary Comparisons," in *The Japanese Colonial Empire, 1895–1945,* ed. Ramon H. Myers and M.R. Peattie (Princeton, N.J., 1984), 503, 524–25; Warren I. Cohen, *America's Response to China: An Interpretive History of Sino-American Relations,* 2d ed. (New York, 1980), 77.

22. Theodore Roosevelt, *The Autobiography of Theodore Roosevelt,* ed. Wayne Andrews (New York, 1975), 142–43.

23. William J. Pomeroy, *American Neo-Colonialism: Its Emergence in the Philippines and Asia* (New York, 1970), 27; Brooks Adams, *The Law of Civilization and Decay* (1896; reprint, New York, 1955), esp. 289–92.

24. Merze Tate, *The United States and the Hawaiian Kingdom: A Political History* (New Haven, Conn., 1965), 299; Charles E. Neu, *The Troubled Encounter: The United States and Japan* (New York, 1975), 35; John Dobson, *Reticent Expansionism: The Foreign Policy of William McKinley* (Pittsburgh, Pa., 1988), 35–36.

25. Kennedy, *The Rise and Fall of the Great Powers*, 233–36; Harry Thurston Peck, *Twenty Years of the Republic, 1885–1905* (New York, 1924), 546–59, 574–75.

26. Hans Delbrück, "Deutschlands internationale Lage und Amerika," *Preußische Jahrbücher* 112 (April 1903): 184–88; Ernst Francke, "Weltpolitik und Sozialreform," in *Handels- und Machtpolitik*, ed. Gustav Schmoller, Max Sering, and Adolph Wagner (Stuttgart, 1900), 103–32; Schoonover, *Germany in Central America*, 135–36, 152–53.

27. "Memorandum über die strategische Bedeutung eines Schiffahrt-Kanals durch Mittelamerika für die Vereinigten Staaten, England und Deutschland," Gustav Adolf von Götzen, 1 March 1898, enclosed with Theodor von Holleben to Hohenlohe-Schillingsfürst, 1 March 1898, IA, Amer. Gen. 12, Bd 1, Politisches Archiv des Auswärtigen Amts, Bonn; Oberst a.D. Kürchhoff, "Flottenstützpunkte," *Beiträge zur Kolonialpolitik, Kolonialrecht und Kolonialwirtschaft* 4 (1902–1903): 63–66.

28. Hans-Peter Ullmann, *Das Deutsche Kaiserreich, 1871–1918* (Frankfurt, 1995), 154–63, quotations from 158–59.

29. Emile Joré to Ministère des affaires étrangères (MAE), 9 Oct. 1899, CP 1918, C.R., Politique intérieure, N. S. 1, Archive du ministère des affaires étrangères (AMAE), Paris; Joré to MAE, 7 Nov. 1899, "Mission française au San Carlos et au Rio Frio, 1898–1899," CP 1918, Pan., Canal interocéanique, I, N. S. 9, AMAE; Christopher Andrew and A.S. Kanya-Forstner, "French Business and the French Colonialists," *Historical Journal* 19:4 (1976): 981–1000; Stuart M. Persell, *The French Colonial Lobby, 1889–1938* (Stanford, 1983), 37–39; Christopher M. Andrew and A.S. Kanya-Forstner, "The French 'Colonial Party': Its Composition, Aims and Influence, 1885–1914," *Historical Journal* 14 (1971): 99–128.

30. James M. Skinner, *France and Panama: The Unknown Years, 1894–1908* (New York, 1988), 27–97; David McCullough, *The Path Between the Seas: The Creation of the Panama Canal, 1870–1914* (New York, 1977), 45–241; Paul Lefébure, "A la conquête d'un isthme: les États Unis et l'Europe," *Annales des sciences politiques* 16 (Sept. 1901): 600–619.

31. McCormick, *China Market*, 107.

32. Tennant S. McWilliams, *Hannis Tayler: The New Southerner as an American* (University, Ala., 1978), 21–41, 86–89; Richard E. Welch Jr., "William McKinley: Reluctant Warrior, Cautious Imperialist," in *Traditions and Values: American Diplomacy, 1865–1945*, ed. Norman A. Graebner (Lanham, Md., 1985), 29–52; Robert C. Hilderbrand, *Power and the People: Executive Management of Public Opinion in Foreign Affairs, 1897–1921* (Chapel Hill, N.C., 1981), 8–71; Claude G. Bowers, *Beveridge and the Progressive Era* (Cambridge, Mass., 1932), 68–70.

33. H. Wayne Morgan, *America's Road to Empire: The War with Spain and Overseas Expansion* (New York, 1968), 74.

34. Theodore Roosevelt to Henry Cabot Lodge, 12 June 1898, and Lodge to Roosevelt, 15 June, 12 July 1898, in Theodore Roosevelt and Henry Cabot Lodge, *Selections of the Correspondence of Theodore Roosevelt and Henry Cabot Lodge*,

1884–1918, 2 vols. (New York, 1925), 1:306–12, 323–25; Morgan, *America's Road to Empire*, 74; Smith, *The Spanish-American War*, 188–208.

35. Pérez, *The War of 1898*, 1–56, 81–107; Stuart Anderson, *Race and Rapprochement: Anglo-Saxonism and Anglo-American Relations, 1895–1904* (Rutherford, N.J., 1981), 62–72, 174–178; Reginald Horsman, *Race and Manifest Destiny: The Origins of American Racial Anglo-Saxonism* (Cambridge, Mass., 1981), 1–6, 298–303; Louis A. Pérez Jr., *Cuba: Between Reform and Revolution*, 2d ed. (New York, 1995), 173–79; Musicant, *Empire by Default*, 580–85.

36. Louis A. Pérez Jr. *Cuba and the United States: Ties of Singular Intimacy* (Athens, Ga., 1990), 97–98; Michael Zeuske, *Kleine Geschichte Kubas* (Munich, 2000), 144; Richard Morris, ed., *Encyclopedia of American History* (New York, 1953), 290.

37. Whitelaw Reid, *Making Peace with Spain: The Diary of Whitelaw Reid (September–December 1898)*, ed. H. Wayne Morgan (Austin, Tex., 1965), 291; Musicant, *Empire by Default*, 617–21.

38. Grover Cleveland to Richard Olney, 8 July 1898, Olney Papers, vol. 83, in Tate, *The United States and the Hawaiian Kingdom*, 299, 314; Robert L. Beisner, *Twelve Against Empire: The Anti-Imperialists, 1898–1900* (New York, 1968), 146–48. One or more anti-imperialists wanted every major U.S. acquisition between 1898 and 1916.

39. Elihu Root to James G. Bailey, 14 May 1906, Robert Bacon to Bailey, 13 June 1906, DI, CA: 22 (M 77/r 34), National Archives (NA).

40. Foster Rhea Dulles, *America in the Pacific: A Century of Expansion*, 2d ed. (New York, 1969), 199; Moorfield Storey and Marcial P. Lichauco, *The Conquest of the Philippines by the United States, 1898–1925* (New York, 1926), 21–30, 261; James C. Thomson Jr., Peter W. Stanley, and John Curtis Perry, *Sentimental Imperialists: The American Experience in East Asia* (New York, 1981), 111–13.

41. Smith, *The Spanish-American War*, 182–87, 216–26; Storey and Lichauco, *The Conquest of the Philippines*, 21–30, 261; Klaus Hildebrand, "Europäisches Zentrum, überseeische Peripherie und Neue Welt: über den Wandel des Staatsystems zwischen dem Berliner Kongreß (1878) und dem Pariser Frieden (1919/20)," *Historische Zeitschrift* 249 (1989): 74, 81; Thomas D. Schoonover, *The United States in Central America, 1860–1911: Episodes of Social Imperialism and Imperial Rivalry in the World System* (Durham, N.C., 1991), 28–76, 130–48.

42. Thomson, Stanley, and Perry, *Sentimental Imperialists*, 101, 103; Schoonover, *The United States in Central America*, 57–58; William H. Moody to Commander, Caribbean Division, 4 Oct. 1902, RG 45, VP, Box 1, VP file: Miscellaneous data, NA; William H. Becker, *The Dynamics of Business-Government Relations: Industry and Export, 1893–1921* (Chicago, Ill., 1982), 1–47.

43. State Dept, April 1898, in Williams, *The Tragedy of American Diplomacy*, 28.

44. Frederick B. Pike, *Hispanismo, 1898–1936: Spanish Conservatives and*

Liberals and Their Relations with Spanish America (Notre Dame, Ind., 1971); Smith, *The Spanish-American War*, 209–11.

6. The War of 1898 in the Pacific Basin

1. Gerald F. Linderman, *The Mirror of War: American Society and the Spanish-American War* (Ann Arbor, Mich., 1974), 201–2; Julius W. Pratt, *America's Colonial Experiment: How the United States Gained, Governed, and in Part Gave Away a Colonial Empire* (New York, 1950), 76.

2. Henry Adams, *The Education of Henry Adams* (Boston, 1918), 363–64.

3. Claude G. Bowers, *Beveridge and the Progressive Era* (Cambridge, Mass., 1932), 74; Foster Rhea Dulles, *America in the Pacific: A Century of Expansion*, 2d ed. (New York, 1969), 9, 254–55; Alfred W. McCoy and Ed. C. de Jesús, eds., *Philippine Social History: Global Trade and Local Transformation* (Quezon City, Philippines, 1982), 159–61.

4. Charles Fanning, *Finley Peter Dunne and Mr. Dooley: The Chicago Years* (Lexington, Ky., 1978), 204–5.

5. George F. Hoar, *Autobiography of Seventy Years*, 2 vols. (New York, 1903), 2:304; McCoy and de Jesús, eds., *Philippine Social History*, 159–61, 169–73, 176–79, 324–25.

6. Richard O'Connor, *Pacific Destiny: An Informal History of the United States in the Far East, 1776–1968* (Boston, 1969), 261.

7. Barbara Tuchman, *The Proud Tower: A Portrait of the World Before the War, 1890–1914* (New York, 1996), 158–60.

8. Fanning, *Finley Peter Dunne*, 205.

9. Tuchman, *The Proud Tower*, 163.

10. Brian McAllister Linn, *The U.S. Army and Counterinsurgency in the Philippine War, 1899–1902* (Chapel Hill, N.C., 1989), 26–27; James C. Thomson Jr., Peter W. Stanley, and John Curtis Perry, *Sentimental Imperialists: The American Experience in East Asia* (New York, 1981), 113, 115.

11. Linn, *The U.S. Army and Counterinsurgency*, 26–27; Stanley Karnow, *In Our Image: America's Empire in the Philippines* (New York, 1989), 190–92; O'Connor, *Pacific Destiny*, 277–78.

12. Linn, *The U.S. Army and Counterinsurgency*, 26–27; John Morgan Gates, *Schoolbooks and Krags: The United States Army in the Philippines, 1898–1902* (Westport, Conn., 1973), 260–65.

13. Karnow, *In Our Image*, 194; O'Connor, *Pacific Destiny*, 256, 280, 291–98.

14. Linn, *The U.S. Army and Counterinsurgency*, 26–27; Karnow, *In Our Image*, 190–92.

15. Peter G. Gowing, *Muslim Filipinos—Heritages and Horizon* (Quezon City, Philippines, 1979), 34–37.

16. Gowing, *Muslim Filipinos*, 34–37; Samuel K. Tan, *Sulu Under American*

Rule, 1899–1913 (Quezon City, Philippines, 1968), 18–36, 55–87; Donald Smythe, "Pershing and the Disarmament of the Moros," *Pacific Historical Review* 31:3 (1962): 241–56; Donald Smythe, "Pershing and the Mount Bagsak Campaign of 1913," *Philippine Studies* 12:1 (1964): 3–31; Wayne Wray Thompson, "Governors and the Moro Province: Wood, Bliss, and Pershing in the Southern Philippines, 1903–1913" (Ph.D. diss., University of California at San Diego, 1975).

17. Gowing, *Muslim Filipinos*, 38–40; Tan, *Sulu Under American Rule*, 149–56.

18. John Dobson, *America's Ascent: The United States Becomes a Great Power, 1880–1914* (DeKalb, Ill., 1978), 102; Bowers, *Beveridge and the Progressive Era*, 74.

19. O'Connor, *Pacific Destiny*, 242, 247.

20. Jim Zwick, ed., *Mark Twain's Weapons of Satire! Anti-Imperialist Writings on the Philippine-American War* (Syracuse, N.Y., 1992), xvii–xxvii; Richard E. Welch Jr., *Response to Imperialism: The United States and the Philippine-American War, 1899–1902* (Chapel Hill, N.C., 1979), 152–55.

21. Zwick, ed., *Mark Twain's Weapons of Satire!*, xvii–xxvii.

22. O'Connor, *Pacific Destiny*, 259.

23. Henry Adams, *Letters of Henry Adams (1892–1918)*, 2 vols. (Boston, 1938), 2:359–60; Moorfield Storey and Marcial P. Lichauco, *The Conquest of the Philippines by the United States, 1898–1925* (New York, 1926), v.; Judith Papachristou, "American Women and Foreign Policy, 1898–1905: Exploring Gender in Diplomatic History," *Diplomatic History* 14:4 (fall 1990): 498–502.

24. H. William Brands, *Bound to Empire: The United States and the Philippines* (New York, 1992), 28.

25. Brands, *Bound to Empire*, 32–33; John Dobson, *Reticent Expansionism: The Foreign Policy of William McKinley* (Pittsburgh, Pa., 1988), 101; O'Connor, *Pacific Destiny*, 274–75.

26. Louis A. Pérez Jr., *The War of 1898: The United States and Cuba in History and Historiography* (Chapel Hill, N.C., 1998), 97–98; Linderman, *The Mirror of War*, 235; Graham A. Cosmas, *An Army for Empire: The United States Army in the Spanish-American War* (Columbia, Mo., 1971), 241–42; Joseph Smith, *The Spanish-American War: Conflict in the Caribbean and the Pacific, 1895–1902* (London, 1994), 114–18; David R. Sturtevant, *Popular Uprisings in the Philippines, 1840–1940* (Ithaca, N.Y., 1976), 124–38.

27. O'Connor, *Pacific Destiny*, 274–75.

28. McCoy and de Jesús, eds., *Philippine Social History*, 12–25, 109–10, 117, 135.

29. Carl Schurz, *Speeches, Correspondence, and Political Papers of Carl Schurz*, 6 vols. (New York, 1913), 5:503.

30. Ibid., 6:77–120.

31. O'Connor, *Pacific Destiny*, 283–84.

32. Ibid., 248, 277–78.

33. Ibid., 628; Schurz, *Speeches*, 5:508.

34. Pratt, *America's Colonial Experiment*, 68; Fritz Klein, *Deutschland, 1897/*

98–1917 (Berlin, 1977), 68–69; Michael Köhler, *Akkulturation in der Südsee: Die Kolonialgeschichte der Karolinen-Inseln im pazifischen Ozean und der Wandel ihrer sozialen Organisation* (Frankfurt, 1982), 275; Michael Fröhlich, *Imperialismus: Deutsche Kolonial- und Weltpolitik, 1880–1914* (Munich, 1994), 73–82, 97–98; Hans-Peter Ullmann, *Das Deutsche Kaiserreich, 1871–1918* (Frankfurt, 1995), 160–61; Hans-Ulrich Wehler, *Deutsche Gesellschaftsgeschichte*, 3 vols. (Munich, 1987–1995), 3:1142.

35. Stewart G. Firth, "German Firms in the Pacific Islands, 1857–1914," in *Germany in the Pacific and Far East, 1870–1914*, ed. John A. Moses and Paul M. Kennedy (St. Lucia, Australia, 1977), 17–19, 21; Klein, *Deutschland*, 72–73; Seward W. Livermore, "American Strategy Diplomacy in the South Pacific, 1890–1914," *Pacific Historical Review* 12:1 (March 1943): 33–51.

36. Welch, *Response to Imperialism*, 150; Thomson, Stanley, and Perry, *Sentimental Imperialists*, 106.

37. Rebecca E. Karl, "Creating Asia: China in the World at the Beginning of the Twentieth Century," *American Historical Review* 103:4 (Oct. 1998): 1105; George F. Hoar, *Autobiography of Seventy Years*, 2 vols. (New York, 1903), 2:325; Walter LaFeber, *The Clash: U.S.-Japanese Relations Throughout History* (New York, 1997), 57–62; Michael Montgomery, *Imperialist Japan: The Yen to Dominate* (London, 1987), 165.

7. The Legacy of the Crises of the 1890s

1. Kenton J. Clymer, *John Hay: The Gentleman as Diplomat* (Ann Arbor, Mich., 1975), 142.

2. Howard William Brands, *Bound to Empire: The United States and the Philippines* (New York, 1992), 34.

3. Operations-Plan gegen die Ver. St. von Nordamerika, 1899–1908, RM 5/vols. 5960–5964, Bundesarchiv, Militärarchiv, Freiburg (BAMF); Herbert von Rebeur-Paschwitz to Alfred Tirpitz, 18 Jan. 1901, IA, Amer. Gen. 13, Bd 1, Politisches Archiv des Auswärtigen Amts (PAAA); Rebeur-Paschwitz to Tirpitz, 21 Jan. 1902, RM 5/vols. 5910, BAMF; Holger H. Herwig, *The Politics of Frustration: The United States in German Naval Planning, 1889–1941* (Boston, 1976), 85–92; Volker R. Berghahn, "Zu den Zielen des deutschen Flottenbaus unter Wilhelm II," *Historische Zeitschrift* 210 (1970): 34–100; Peter Overlack, "German War Plans in the Pacific, 1900–1914," *The Historian* 60:3 (1998): 579–93. Nancy Mitchell argues that Germany's challenge in Latin America disappeared after 1903: Nancy Mitchell, "The Height of the German Challenge: The Venezuela Blockade, 1902–3," *Diplomatic History* 20:2 (1996): 185–209; Nancy Mitchell, *The Danger of Dreams: German and American Imperialism in Latin America* (Chapel Hill, 1997), 64–107, 216–28.

4. Thomas D. Schoonover, *The United States in Central America, 1860–1911: Episodes of Social Imperialism and Imperial Rivalry in the World System* (Durham,

N.C., 1991), 97–110; Thomas Schoonover, *France in Central America, 1821–1929: Commerce and Culture* (Wilmington, Del., 2000), 83–132, esp. 115–19.

5. Camille Blondel to Delcassé, 10 Feb. 1904, CP 1918, Panama, pol. étrangère, I, N. S. 3, Archive du ministère des affaires étrangères (AMAE); Jürgen Buchenau, *In the Shadow of the Giant: The Making of Mexico's Central America Policy, 1876–1930* (Tuscaloosa, Ala., 1996), 1–48; Gabriela Pulido Llano, *Desde Cuba: escenas de la diplomacía porfirista* (México, DF, 2000), chap. 3.

6. David McCullough, *The Path Between the Seas: The Creation of the Panama Canal, 1870–1914* (New York, 1977), 137–52, 161, 165–71, 405–26, 589–615.

7. José de Olivares to Assistant Secretary of State, 6 April 1909, RG 84, AmLeg. Nic., vol.-Desp. 1908–9, National Archives (NA); Ponsignon to Ministère des affaires étrangères, 28 May 1909, CP 1918, Pan., Canal de Panama V, N. S. 13, AMAE; Schoonover, *The United States in Central America*, 130–48.

8. Juan Barrios to Luis Toledo Herrarte, 5 and 11 June, 5 Aug. 1907, Joaquín Méndez to Toledo Herrarte, 16 July 1907, B99-6-3/4458/93414, Ministro de Relaciones Exteriores (MRE), Archivo General de Centro América (AGCA), Guatemala City; Charles L. Stansifer, "José Santos Zelaya: A New Look at Nicaragua's 'Liberal' Dictator," *Revista/Review Interamericana* 7 (fall 1977): 468–85; Buchenau, "A Challenge to the 'Big Stick,'" 154–206; Schoonover, *The United States in Central America*, 130–48, 152–53.

9. Lester D. Langley, *Struggle for the American Mediterranean: United States–European Rivalry in the Gulf-Caribbean, 1776–1904* (Athens, Ga., 1976), 81–189; Thomas Schoonover, "Los intereses europeos y estadounidenses en las relaciones entre México-Guatemala (1850–1930)," *Secuencia* 34 (Jan.–April 1996): 7–30; Schoonover, *The United States in Central America*, chap. 7.

10. Kenton J. Clymer, *Protestant Missionaries in the Philippines, 1898–1916: An Inquiry into the American Colonial Mentality* (Urbana, Ill., 1986), 3–7, 191–92, 196.

11. Ibid., 191–92, 196, 199; June Hunter, *The Gospel of Gentility: American Women Missionaries in Turn-of-the-Century China* (New Haven, Conn., 1984), 8–9, 169.

12. Robert McClellan, *The Heathen Chinee: A Study of American Attitudes toward China, 1890–1905* (Columbus, Ohio, 1971), 178–79; Hunter, *The Gospel of Gentility*, 5; Helmuth Stoecker, *Deutschland und China im 19. Jahrhundert: Das Eindringen des deutschen Kapitalismus* (Berlin, 1958), 30, 35; Joseph W. Esherick, *The Origins of the Boxer Uprising* (Berkeley, Calif., 1986), xiii–xvii.

13. Karl J. Rivinius, "Imperialistische Welt- und Missionspolitik: der Fall Kiautschou," in *Imperialismus und Kolonialmission: Kaiserliches Deutschland und koloniales Imperium*, ed. Klaus J. Bade (Wiesbaden, Germ., 1982), 282; Esherick, *The Origins of the Boxer Uprising*, xiv.

14. Sabine Dabringhaus, "Der Boxeraufstand in China (1900/1901): Die Militarisierung eines kulturellen Konflikts," in *"Barbaren" und "Weiße Teufel": Kulturkonflikte und Imperialismus in Asien vom 18. bis zum 19. Jahrhundert*, ed.

Eva-Marie Auch and Stig Förster (Paderborn, Germ., 1997): 143; Harrison, *China since 1800*, 86–88; Hsu, *The Rise of Modern China*, 390; Esherick, *The Origins of the Boxer Uprising*, xiii–xvii, 1, 38–39; Walter LaFeber, *The Clash: U.S.-Japanese Relations Throughout History* (New York, 1997), 65–73; Helwig Schmidt-Glintzer, *Das neue China. Von den Opiumkriegen bis heute* (Munich, 1999), 26.

15. Paul A. Cohen, *History in Three Keys: The Boxers as Event, Experience, and Myth* (New York, 1997), 15–17, 54–55, 89–90, 94–95, 184–85, 227; Esherick, *The Origins of the Boxer Uprising*, 74–95, 153–166; Chester C. Tan, *The Boxer Catastrophe* (New York, 1967), 34–36, 237; Konrad Seitz, *China: Eine Weltmacht kehrt zurück* (Berlin, 2000), 102. .

16. Cohen, *History in Three Keys*, 15–17, 54–55, 89–90, 94–95, 184–85, 227; Spence, *The Search for Modern China*, 230–35.

17. Harrison, *China since 1800*, 86–88.

18. Schmidt-Glintzer, *Das neue China*, 37; Fesser, "Hunderte deutscher Kaufleute werden jauchzen," *Die Zeit*, 21 November 1997, 16; Esherick, *The Origins of the Boxer Uprising*, 290–313; Henry Keown-Boyd, *The Fists of Righteous Harmony: A History of the Boxer Uprising in China in the Year 1900* (London, 1991), 191–93, 204.

19. Fritz Klein, *Deutschland, 1897/98–1917* (Berlin, 1977), 74–76; Fesser, "Hunderte deutscher Kaufleute werden jauchzen," 16; William G. Beasley, *The Rise of Modern Japan* (London, 1990), 149–50; Raimund Lammersdorf, *Anfänge einer Weltmacht: Theodore Roosevelt und die transatlantischen Beziehungen der USA 1901–1909* (Berlin, 1994), 10–11, 16, 18, 29, 32, 369.

20. Klein, *Deutschland, 1897/98–1917*, 74–76; Fesser, "Hunderte deutscher Kaufleute werden jauchzen," 16; Seitz, *China: Eine Weltmacht kehrt zurück*, 104.

21. Spence, *The Search for Modern China*, 230–35.

22. Harrison, *China since 1800*, 86–88; Spence, *The Search for Modern China*, 230–35; Fesser, "Hunderte deutscher Kaufleute werden jauchzen," 16.

23. Spence, *The Search for Modern China*, 230–35; John E. Schrecker, *Imperialism and Chinese Nationalism* (Cambridge, Mass., 1971), 251–52.

24. Hunter, *The Gospel of Gentility*, 8.

25. Ibid., 171.

26. Hsu, *The Rise of Modern China*, 349–50.

27. Ibid.; William A. Williams, *The Tragedy of American Diplomacy*, 2d ed. (New York, 1972), 27–64; Thomas J. McCormick, *China Market: America's Quest for Informal Empire* (Chicago, 1967); Michael H. Hunt, *Frontier Defense and the Open Door: Manchuria in Chinese-American Relations, 1895–1911* (New Haven, Conn., 1973); Michael H. Hunt, "Americans in the China Market: Economic Opportunities and Economic Nationalism, 1890s–1931," *Business History Review* 51 (autumn 1977): 277–307.

28. Harrison, *China since 1800*, 76–77; John Dobson, *America's Ascent: The United States Becomes a Great Power, 1880–1914* (DeKalb, Ill., 1978), 16; Jerry

Israel, *Progressivism and the Open Door: America and China, 1905–1921* (Pittsburgh, 1971).

29. Clyde and Beers, *The Far East*, 219; Akira Iriye, *Across the Pacific: An Inner History of American–East Asian Relations* (New York, 1967), 82; LaFeber, *The Clash*, 65–73.

30. Iriye, *Across the Pacific*, 80–81.

31. Lammersdorf, *Anfänge einer Weltmacht*, 10–11, 16, 18, 29, 32, 369.

32. Henry Adams, *The Education of Henry Adams* (Boston, 1918), 363–64.

33. Lloyd Gardner, "A Progressive Foreign Policy," in *From Colony to Empire: Essays in the History of American Foreign Relations*, ed. William A. Williams (New York, 1972), 216–18; Robert Wiebe, *The Search for Order, 1877–1920* (New York, 1967), chap. 9; Walter Scholes and Marie V. Scholes, *The Foreign Policy of the Taft Administration* (Columbia, Mo., 1970), 45–67; Lejeune Cummins, "The Origin and Development of Elihu Root's Latin American Diplomacy" (Ph.D. diss., University of California, Berkeley, 1964); Philip M. Brown, "American Intervention in Central America," *Journal of Race Development* 4 (1913–1914): 409–26.

34. Ragnhild Fiebig-von Hase, *Lateinamerika als Konfliktherd der deutsch-amerikanischen Beziehungen, 1890–1913*, 2 vols. (Göttingen, Germ., 1986), 1:320–428; John Barrett, "England, America, and Germany as Allies for the Open Door," *Engineering Magazine* 18 (Oct. 1899): 1–10; Edgar Jaffe, "Volkswirtschaft. Deutschland und die amerikanische Konkurrenz," *Preußische Jahrbücher* 108 (April 1902): 146–52; Ernst Daenell, *Das Ringen der Weltmächte um Mittel- und Südamerika* (Berlin, 1919), 20–22; Friedrich Katz, *The Secret War in Mexico: Europe, the United States, and the Mexican Revolution* (Chicago, 1981).

35. Albert Ballin to Bernhard Bülow, 2 Sept. 1899, enclosing Koch to Ballin, 30 Aug. 1899, Alfons Mumm von Schwarzenstein to For. Min., 9 Oct. 1899, Alfred von Tirpitz to For. Min., 29 Oct. 1899, IA, Amer. Gen. 12, Bd. 1, PAAA; Vorbereitung zu dem Operations-Plan gegen die Ver. St. von Nordamerika, 1899–1908, RM 5/vols. 5960–5964, BAMF; Alfred von Tirpitz, *Erinnerungen* (Leipzig, 1920) [translated as *My Memoirs*, 2 vols. (New York, 1919)]; Alfred Jacobssohn, "Zur Entwicklung des Verhältnisses zwischen der deutschen Volkswirtschaft und dem Weltmarkt in den letzten Jahrzehnten," *Zeitschrift für die gesamte Staatswissenschaft* 64 (1908): 292; Paul Voight, "Deutschland und der Weltmarkt," in *Handels- und Machtpolitik* (1900); Lamar Cecil, *Albert Ballin: Business and Politics in Imperial Germany, 1888–1918* (Princeton, N.J., 1967); Herwig, *The Politics of Frustration*, 68–92.

36. Richard D. Challener, *Admirals, Generals, and American Foreign Policy, 1898–1914* (Princeton, N.J., 1973), 28–31.

37. Schoonover, *France in Central America*, 99, 107, 118, 123, 145, 150, 163, 171, 193.

38. Walter LaFeber, *The American Search for Opportunity, 1865–1913*, vol. 2 of *The Cambridge History of American Foreign Relations*, 4 vols. (New York, 1993), 83–182; Thomas J. McCormick, *The China Market: America's Quest for Informal Empire 1893–1901* (Chicago, 1967), 17–52: Walter LaFeber, *The American Age:*

United States Foreign Policy at Home and Abroad since 1750 (New York, 1989), 218–30; Walter LaFeber, *The Panama Canal: The Crisis in Historical Perspective* (New York, 1978), 3–22; Hans-Ulrich Wehler, *Grundzüge der amerikanischen Außenpolitik, vol. 1, 1750–1900* (Frankfurt, 1984), 216–19; and an angry condemnation of U.S. intervention, Guillermo Toriello Garrido, *Tras la cortina de bananos* (Mexico, 1976).

39. William H. Moody to Commander, Caribbean Division, 4 Oct. 1902, RG 45, VP, box 1, VP file: Miscellaneous data, NA; Wilfrid Hardy Callcott, *The Caribbean Policy of the United States, 1890–1920* (Baltimore, Md., 1942); Challener, *Admirals, Generals, and American Foreign Policy,* 16–17; Schoonover, *The United States in Central America,* 46–61, 97–148.

40. Langley, *Struggle for the American Mediterranean,* 25–106; Lester D. Langley and Thomas Schoonover, *The Banana Men: American Mercenaries and Entrepreneurs in Central America, 1880–1930* (Lexington, Ky., 1995), esp. 6–32, 167–75.

41. Robert L. Beisner, *From the Old Diplomacy to the New, 1865–1900,* 2d ed. (Arlington Heights, Ill., 1986), 96–119; Elisabeth Glaser-Schmidt, *"Die Philippinen den Filipinos!": Die amerikanische Debatte über die Wirtschafts- und Verwaltungspolitik auf den Philippinen, 1898–1906* (Frankfurt, 1986).

42. Glaser-Schmidt, *"Die Philippinen den Filipinos,"* 17; Willard B. Gatewood Jr., *Black Americans and the White Man's Burden, 1898–1903* (Urbana, Ill., 1975), 259, 320, 324; Francis L. Broderick, *W.E.B. Du Bois: Negro Leader in a Time of Crisis* (Palo Alto, Calif., 1959), 123–49; Eric C. Lincoln, "The Race Problem and International Relations," in *Racial Influences on American Foreign Policy,* ed. George W. Shepherd Jr. (New York, 1970), 39–59.

43. Louis A. Pérez Jr., *The War of 1898: The United States and Cuba in History and Historiography* (Chapel Hill, N.C., 1998), 97–98; Louis A. Pérez Jr., *Cuba: Between Reform and Revolution,* 2d ed. (New York, 1995), 181–83, 188.

44. Pérez, *Cuba: Between Reform and Revolution,* 181–83, 188.

45. Robert Aldrich, "Colonialism, Culture and Politics in the French Islands," in *Rassendiskriminierung, Kolonialpolitik und ethnisch-nationale Identität,* ed. Wilfried Wagner (Hamburg, 1992), 221–22; Donald Denoon, ed., *The Cambridge History of the Pacific Islanders* (Cambridge, Eng., 1997), 214–15; Deryck Scarr, *Fragments of Empire: A History of the Western Pacific High Commission, 1877–1914* (Canberra, Aust., 1968), 292.

46. David Hanlon, "Patterns of Colonial Rule in Micronesia," in *Tides of History: The Pacific Islands in the Twentieth Century,* ed. K.R. Howe, Robert C. Kiste, and Brij V. Lal (Honolulu, Hawaii, 1994), 93–95, 101, 112; Jean Martin, *L'Empire triomphant, 1871–1936,* 2 vols. (Paris, 1990), 1:403–5, 423.

47. Robert W. Rydell, John E. Findling, and Kimberly D. Pelle, *Fair America: World's Fairs in the United States* (Washington, D.C., 2000), 1–71; Robert W. Rydell, "The Culture of Imperial Abundance: World's Fairs in the Making of American Culture," in *Consuming Visions: Accumulation and Display of Goods in America, 1880–1920,* ed. Simon J. Bronner (New York, 1989), 191–216; Burton Benedict, "Ritu-

als of Representation: Ethnic Stereotypes and Colonized Peoples at World's Fairs," in *Fair Representations: World Fairs and the Modern World*, ed. Robert W. Rydell and Nancy Glenn (Amsterdam, 1994), 28–31, 55–58; Aram A. Yengoyran, "Culture, Ideology and World's Fairs: Colonizer and Colonized in Comparative Perspectives," in *Fair Representations: World Fairs and the Modern World*, ed. Robert W. Rydell and Nancy Glenn (Amsterdam, 1994), 81–83.

48. U.S. Department of Commerce, Bureau of the Census, *Historical Statistics of the United States: Colonial Times to 1970*, 2 vols. (Washington, D.C., 1975), 2:903–7; Hunt, "Americans in the China Market," 277–307.

49. Rebecca E. Karl, "Creating Asia: China in the World at the Beginning of the Twentieth Century," *American Historical Review* 103:4 (Oct. 1998): 1096–98, 1102, 1114–17; Frank Gibney, *The Pacific Century: America and Asia in a Changing World* (New York, 1992), 108–15.

50. Paul A. Varg, *The Making of a Myth: The United States and China, 1897–1912* (East Lansing, Mich., 1968), 172; Louis A. Pérez Jr., *Cuba and the United States: Ties of Singular Intimacy* (Athens, Ga., 1990), 149–69.

Selected Bibliography

Agoncillo, Teodoro A. "The Filipino Point of View." In *American Imperialism in 1898: The Quest for National Fulfillment,* edited by Richard H. Miller, 138–47. New York: John Wiley, 1970.

Aguilar, Luis E. "Cuba, c. 1860–1934." In *The Cambridge History of Latin America,* edited by Leslie Bethell, 5:229–263. 11 vols. Cambridge: Cambridge Univ. Press, 1985–1999.

Aldrich, Robert. *The French Presence in the South Pacific, 1842–1940.* Honolulu: Univ. of Hawaii Press, 1990.

———. *Greater France: A History of French Overseas Expansion.* New York: St. Martin's, 1996.

"American Empire, 1898–1903," special issue of the *Pacific Historical Review* 48:4 (November 1979).

Anderson, Stuart. *Race and Rapprochement: Anglo-Saxonism and Anglo-American Relations, 1895–1904.* Rutherford, N.J.: Fairleigh Dickinson Univ. Press, 1981.

Bailey, Thomas A. "America's Emergence as a World Power: The Myth and the Verity." *Pacific Historical Review* 30 (Feb. 1961): 1–16.

Barrett, John. "America's Interest in Eastern Asia." In *Creating an American Empire, 1865–1914,* edited by Milton Plesur, 94–110. New York: Pitman, 1971.

Beale, Howard K. *Theodore Roosevelt and the Rise of America to World Power.* New York: Collier, 1956.

Beasley, William G. *Japanese Imperialism, 1894–1945.* Oxford: Clarendon, 1987.

———. *The Rise of Modern Japan.* London: Weidenfeld and Nicolson, 1990.

Becker, William H. *The Dynamics of Business-Government Relations: Industry and Export, 1893–1921.* Chicago: Univ. of Chicago Press, 1982.

Beisner, Robert L. *From the Old Diplomacy to the New, 1865–1900.* 2d ed. Arlington Heights, Ill.: Harlan Davidson, 1986.

———. *Twelve Against Empire: The Anti-Imperialists, 1898–1900.* New York: McGraw-Hill, 1968.

Betts, Raymond F. *The False Dawn: European Imperialism in the Nineteenth Century.* Minneapolis: Univ. of Minnesota Press, 1975.

——. *Tricouleur: The French Overseas Empire.* London: Gordon and Cremonesi, 1978.

Binoche-Guedra, Jacques. *La France d'outre-mer, 1815–1962.* Paris: Masson, 1992.

Blumenthal, Henry. *France and the United States: Their Diplomatic Relations, 1789–1914.* Chapel Hill: Univ. of North Carolina Press, 1970.

Borthwick, Mark. *Pacific Century: The Emergence of Modern Pacific Asia.* 2d ed. Boulder, Colo.: Westview, 1998.

Brands, Howard William. *Bound to Empire: The United States and the Philippines.* New York: Oxford Univ. Press, 1992.

Breslin, Thomas A. *China, American Catholicism, and the Missionary.* University Park: Pennsylvania State Univ. Press, 1980.

Breslin, Thomas A., and Daniel M. Crane. *An Ordinary Relationship: American Opposition to Republican Revolution in China.* Miami: Florida International Univ. Press, 1986.

Brookes, Jean Ingram. *International Rivalry in the Pacific Islands, 1800–1875.* Berkeley: Univ. of California Press, 1941.

Cady, John F. *The Roots of French Imperialism in Eastern Asia.* Ithaca, N.Y.: Cornell Univ. Press, 1954.

Cain, P.J., and Anthony Hopkins. *British Imperialism: Innovation and Expansion, 1688–1914.* London: Longman, 1994.

Calhoun, Charles W. *Gilded Age Cato: The Life of Walter Q. Gresham.* Lexington: Univ. Press of Kentucky, 1988.

Campbell, Ian C. *A History of the Pacific Islands.* Berkeley: Univ. of California Press, 1989.

Cardoso, Ciro, and Héctor Pérez Brignoli. *América Central y la economía occidental (1520–1930).* San José: Editorial universidad de Costa Rica, 1977.

Challener, Richard D. *Admirals, Generals, and American Foreign Policy, 1898–1914.* Princeton, N.J.: Princeton Univ. Press, 1973.

Checkland, Olive. *Britain's Encounter with Meiji Japan, 1868–1912.* London: Macmillan, 1989.

Chesneaux, Jean. *Geschichte Ost- und Südostasiens im 19. und 20. Jahrhundert.* Cologne, Germ.: Schäuble, 1969.

Chesneaux, Jean, and Nic Maclellan. *La France dans le Pacifique: de Bougainville à Moruva.* Paris: La Découverte, 1992.

Chi, Chen. *Die Beziehungen zwischen Deutschland und China bis 1933.* Hamburg: Mitteilungen des Institutes für Asienkunde, 1973.

Christmann, Helmut, Peter Hempenstall, and Dirk Anthony Ballendorf. *Die Karolinen-Inseln in deutscher Zeit: Eine kolonialgeschichtliche Fallstudie.* Münster, Germ.: Lit, 1991.

Clyde, Paul H., and Burton F. Beers. *The Far East: A History of the Western Impact and the Eastern Response (1830–1970)*. 5th ed. Englewood Cliffs, N.J.: Prentice-Hall, 1971.

Clymer, Kenton J. *John Hay: The Gentleman as Diplomat*. Ann Arbor: Univ. of Michigan Press, 1975.

——. *Protestant Missionaries in the Philippines, 1898–1916: An Inquiry into the American Colonial Mentality*. Urbana: Univ. of Illinois Press, 1986.

Cohen, Paul A. *History in Three Keys: The Boxers as Event, Experience, and Myth*. New York: Columbia Univ. Press, 1997.

Cohen, Warren I. *America's Response to China: An Interpretive History of Sino-American Relations*. 2d ed. New York: Wiley, 1980.

Cosmas, Graham A. *An Army for Empire: The United States Army in the Spanish-American War*. Columbia: Univ. of Missouri Press, 1971.

Cox, Thomas R. *Mills and Markets: A History of the Pacific Coast Lumber Industry to 1900*. Seattle: Univ. of Washington Press, 1974.

Crapol, Edward P. *James G. Blaine: Architect of Empire*. Wilmington, Del.: Scholarly Resources, 2000.

Dabringhaus, Sabine. *"Barbaren" and "Weiße Teufel": Kulturkonflikte und Imperialismus in Asien vom 18. bis zum 19. Jahrhundert*. Paderborn, Germ.: Ferdinand Schöningh, 1997.

Denoon, Donald, ed. *The Cambridge History of the Pacific Islanders*. Cambridge, Eng.: Cambridge Univ. Press, 1997.

Dobson, John. *America's Ascent: The United States Becomes a Great Power, 1880–1914*. DeKalb: Northern Illinois Univ. Press, 1978.

——. *Reticent Expansionism: The Foreign Policy of William McKinley*. Pittsburgh, Pa.: Duquesne Univ. Press, 1988.

Dodge, Ernest S. *Islands and Empires: Western Impact on the Pacific and East Asia*. Minneapolis: Univ. of Minnesota Press, 1976.

Drake, Frederick C. *The Empire of the Seas: A Biography of Rear Admiral Robert Wilson Shufeldt, USN*. Honolulu: Univ. of Hawaii Press, 1984.

Dudden, Arthur Power. *The American Pacific: From the Old China Trade to the Present*. New York: Oxford Univ. Press, 1992.

Dulles, Foster Rhea. *America in the Pacific: A Century of Expansion*. 2d ed. New York: DeCapo, 1969.

Esthus, Raymond A. *Theodore Roosevelt and International Rivalries*. Waltham, Mass.: Ginn-Blaisdell, 1970.

Fairbank, John K. *China: A New History*. Cambridge, Mass.: Harvard Univ. Press, 1992.

——. *China: The People's Middle Kingdom and the U.S.A.* Cambridge, Mass.: Harvard Univ. Press, 1967.

——. *The Great Chinese Revolution, 1800–1985*. New York: Harper and Row, 1985.

Fairbank, John K., Edwin O. Reischauer, and Albert M. Craig. *East Asia: The Modern Transformation*. Boston: Houghton Mifflin, 1965.

Fesser, Gerd. "Hunderte deutscher Kaufleute werden jauchzen." *Die Zeit*, 21 November 1997, p. 16.

Fiebig-von Hase, Ragnhild. *Lateinamerika als Konflktherd der deutsch-amerikanischen Beziehungen, 1890–1913.* 2 vols. Göttingen, Germ.: Vandenhoeck und Ruprecht, 1986.

Firth, Stewart G. "German Firms in the Pacific Islands, 1857–1914." In *Germany in the Pacific and Far East, 1870–1914*, edited by John A. Moses and Paul M. Kennedy, 2–25. St. Lucia, Australia: Univ. of Queensland Press, 1977.

Foner, Philip S. "Why the United States Went to War with Spain in 1898." *Science and Society* 32 (1968): 39–65.

Frank, Dana. *Buy American: The Untold Story of Economic Nationalism.* Boston: Beacon, 1999.

Friedel, Frank. *The Splendid Little War.* Boston: Little, Brown, 1958.

Fröhlich, Michael. *Imperialismus: Deutsche Kolonial- und Weltpolitik, 1880–1914.* Munich: dtv, 1994.

Fry, Joseph A. "From Open Door to World Systems: Economic Interpretations of Late Nineteenth Century American Foreign Relations." *Pacific Historical Review* 65:2 (May 1996): 277–303.

——. "William McKinley and the Coming of the Spanish-American War: A Study of the Besmirching and Redemption of an Historical Image." *Diplomatic History* 3:1 (winter 1979): 77–97.

Gann, Lewis H. "Western and Japanese Colonialism: Some Preliminary Comparisons." In *The Japanese Colonial Empire, 1895–1945*, edited by Ramon H. Myers and M.R. Peattie, 497–525. Princeton, N.J.: Princeton Univ. Press, 1984.

Gates, John Morgan. *Schoolbooks and Krags: The United States Army in the Philippines, 1898–1902.* Westport, Conn.: Greenwood, 1973.

Gatewood, Willard B., Jr. *Black Americans and the White Man's Burden, 1898–1903.* Urbana: Univ. of Illinois Press, 1975.

——. *"Smoked Yankees" and the Struggle for Empire: Letters from Negro Soldiers, 1898–1902.* Urbana: Univ. of Illinois Press, 1971.

Gerber, James. "Gold Rushes and the Trans-Pacific Wheat Trade: California and Australia, 1848–1857." In *Pacific Centuries: Pacific and Pacific Rim History since the Sixteenth Century*, edited by Dennis O. Flynn, Lionel Frost, and A.J.H. Latham, 125–51. London: Routledge, 1999.

Gibney, Frank. *The Pacific Century: America and Asia in a Changing World.* New York: Macmillan, 1992.

Gilmore, N. Ray. "Mexico and the Spanish-American War." *Hispanic American Historical Review* 43:3 (1963): 511–25.

Glaser-Schmidt, Elisabeth. *"Die Philippinen den Filipinos!": Die amerikanische Debatte über die Wirtschafts- und Verwaltungspolitik auf den Philippinen, 1898–1906.* Frankfurt, Germ.: Lang, 1986.

Goeztmann, William H. *New Lands, New Men: America and the Second Great Age of Discovery.* New York: Viking, 1986.

Gould, James W. "American Imperialism in Southeast Asia before 1898." *Journal of Southeast Asian Studies* 3:2 (1972): 306–14.

Gould, Lewis L. *The Spanish-American War and President McKinley*. Lawrence: Univ. Press of Kansas, 1982.

Gowing, Peter G. *Muslim Filipinos—Heritage and Horizon*. Quezon City, Philippines: New Day, 1979.

Graebner, Norman A. *Empire on the Pacific: A Study in American Continental Expansion*. 1955. Reprint, Santa Barbara, Calif.: Regina, 1983.

———. "The Year of Transition: 1898." In *An Uncertain Tradition: American Secretaries of State in the Twentieth Century*, edited by Norman A. Graebner, 1–21. New York: McGraw Hill, 1961.

Grattan, C. Hartley. *The Southwest Pacific to 1900: A Modern History*. Ann Arbor: Univ. of Michigan Press, 1963.

———. *The United States and the Southwest Pacific*. Cambridge, Mass.: Harvard Univ. Press, 1961.

Gray, Jack. *Rebellions and Revolutions: China from the 1800s to the 1980s*. Oxford: Oxford Univ. Press, 1990.

Grenville, John A.S., and George Berkeley Young. *Politics, Strategy, and American Diplomacy: Studies in Foreign Policy, 1873–1917*. New Haven, Conn.: Yale Univ. Press, 1966.

Harrison, John A. *China since 1800*. New York: Harcourt, Brace and World, 1967.

Headrick, Daniel R. *The Invisible Weapon: Telecommmunications and International Politics, 1851–1945*. New York: Oxford Univ. Press, 1991.

———. *The Tentacles of Progress: Technology Transfer in the Age of Imperialism, 1850–1940*. New York: Oxford Univ. Press, 1988.

———. *The Tools of Empire: Technology and European Imperialism in the Nineteenth Century*. New York: Oxford Univ. Press, 1981.

Healy, David F. *Drive to Hegemony: The United States in the Caribbean, 1898–1917*. Madison: Univ. of Wisconsin Press, 1988.

———. *The United States in Cuba, 1898–1902: Generals, Politicians, and the Search for Policy*. Madison: Univ. of Wisconsin Press, 1963.

Herwig, Holger H. *Politics of Frustration: The United States in German Naval Planning, 1889–1941*. Boston: Little, Brown, 1976.

Hoar, George F. *Autobiography of Seventy Years*. 2 vols. New York: Charles Scribner's Sons, 1903.

Hoganson, Kristin L. *Fighting for American Manhood: How Gender Politics Provoked the Spanish-American and Philippine-American Wars*. New Haven, Conn.: Yale Univ. Press, 1998.

Horsman, Reginald. *Race and Manifest Destiny: The Origins of American Racial Anglo-Saxonism*. Cambridge: Harvard Univ. Press, 1981.

Howe, Christopher. *The Origins of Japanese Trading Supremacy*. London: Hurst, 1996.

Hoyt, Edwin P. *Pacific Destiny: The Story of America in the Western Sea from the Early 1800s to the 1980s*. New York: W.W. Norton, 1981.

Hsu, Immanuel C.Y. *The Rise of Modern China.* 4th ed. New York: Oxford Univ. Press, 1990.

Hunt, Michael H. "Americans in the China Market: Economic Opportunities and Economic Nationalism, 1890s–1931." *Business History Review* 51 (autumn 1977): 277–307.

———. *Ideology and U.S. Foreign Policy.* New Haven, Conn.: Yale Univ. Press, 1987.

———. *The Making of a Special Relationship: The United States and China to 1914.* New York: Columbia Univ. Press, 1983.

Hutchison, William R. "Modernism and Missions: The Liberal Search for an Exportable Christianity, 1875–1935." In *The Missionary Enterprise in China and America,* edited by John K. Fairbank, 110–34. Cambridge, Mass.: Harvard Univ. Press, 1974.

Iriye, Akira. *Across the Pacific: An Inner History of American–East Asian Relations.* New York: Harcourt, Brace, and World, 1967.

———. "Japan as a Competitor, 1895–1917." In *Mutual Images: Essays in American-Japanese Relations,* edited by Akira Iriye, 74–98. Cambridge, Mass.: Harvard Univ. Press, 1975.

———. "Japan's Drive to Great-Power Status." In *The Cambridge History of Japan,* vol. 5, *The Nineteenth Century,* edited by Marius B. Jansen, 6 vols. New York: Cambridge Univ. Press, 1988–1992. 5:721–82.

Jansen, Marius B. "Japanese Imperialism: Late Meiji Perspectives." In *The Japanese Colonial Empire, 1895–1945,* edited by Ramon Myers and Mark R. Peattie, 61–79. Princeton: Princeton Univ. Press, 1984.

Karl, Rebecca E. "Creating Asia: China in the World at the Beginning of the Twentieth Century." *American Historical Review* 103:4 (Oct. 1998): 1096–118.

Karnow, Stanley. *In Our Image: America's Empire in the Philippines.* New York: Random House, 1989.

Karp, Walter. *The Politics of War: The Story of Two Wars Which Altered Forever the Political Life of the American Republic (1890–1920).* New York: Harper and Row, 1979.

Kennedy, Paul M. *The Rise and Fall of the Great Powers: Economic Change and Military Conflict from 1500 to 2000.* New York: Random House, 1987.

———. *The Samoan Tangle: A Study in Anglo-German-American Relations, 1878–1900.* Dublin: Irish Univ. Press, 1974.

Keown-Boyd, Henry. *The Fists of Righteous Harmony: A History of the Boxer Uprising in China in the Year 1900.* London: Leo Cooper, 1991.

Kindermann, Gottfried-Karl. *Der Aufstieg Ostasiens in der Weltpolitik, 1840–2000.* Stuttgart: Deutsche Verlags-Anstalt, 2001.

Knight, Franklin. *The Caribbean: The Genesis of a Fragmented Nationalism.* 2d ed. New York: Oxford Univ. Press, 1990.

Kuykendall, Ralph S. *Hawaiian Kingdom, 1778–1893.* 3 vols. Honolulu: Univ. of Hawaii Press, 1966–1968.

LaFeber, Walter. *The American Age: United States Foreign Policy at Home and Abroad since 1750.* New York: W.W. Norton, 1989.

——. *The American Search for Opportunity, 1865–1913.* Vol. 2 of *The Cambridge History of American Foreign Relations.* 4 vols. New York: Cambridge Univ. Press, 1993.

——. *The Clash: U.S.-Japanese Relations Throughout History.* New York: W.W. Norton, 1997.

——. *The New Empire: An Interpretation of American Expansion, 1860–1898.* Ithaca, N.Y.: Cornell Univ. Press, 1963.

——. "That 'Splendid Little War' in Historical Perspective." *Texas Quarterly* 11 (1968): 89–98.

Langley, Lester D. *America and the Americas: The United States in the Western Hemisphere.* Athens: Univ. of Georgia Press, 1989.

——. *Struggle for the American Mediterranean: The United States–European Rivalry in the Gulf-Caribbean, 1776–1904.* Athens: Univ. of Georgia Press, 1976.

Langley, Lester D., and Thomas Schoonover. *The Banana Men: American Mercenaries and Entrepreneurs in Central America, 1880–1930.* Lexington: Univ. Press of Kentucky, 1995.

Linderman, Gerald F. *The Mirror of War: American Society and the Spanish-American War.* Ann Arbor: Univ. of Michigan Press, 1974.

Linn, Brian McAllister. "The Struggle for Samar." In *Crucible of Empire: The Spanish-American War and its Aftermath,* edited by James C. Bradford, 158–82. Annapolis, Md.: Naval Institute, 1993.

——. *The U.S. Army and Counterinsurgency in the Philippine War, 1899–1902.* Chapel Hill: Univ. of North Carolina Press, 1989.

Liss, Peggy K. *Atlantic Empires: The Network of Trade and Revolution, 1713–1826.* Baltimore: Johns Hopkins Univ. Press, 1983.

Livermore, Seward W. "American Naval-Base Policy in the Far East, 1850–1914." *Pacific Historical Review* 13:2 (June 1944): 113–35.

Lodge, Henry Cabot. *The War with Spain.* New York: Harper and Brothers, 1899.

Lukacs, John. "Our War with Spain Marked the First Year of the American Century." *American Heritage* 49:3 (1998): 72–80.

Mahan, Alfred T. "The United States Looking Outward." In *Creating an American Empire, 1865–1914,* edited by Milton Plesur, 82–91. New York: Pitman, 1971.

Martin, Jean. *L'Empire triomphant, 1871–1936.* 2 vols. Paris: Denoël, 1990.

May, Ernest R., and James C. Thompson Jr. *American–East Asian Relations: A Survey.* Cambridge, Mass.: Harvard Univ. Press, 1972.

May, Glenn A. *Battle for Batanga: A Philippine Province at War.* New Haven, Conn.: Yale Univ. Press, 1991.

McCormick, Thomas J. *America's Half Century.* Baltimore, Md.: Johns Hopkins Univ. Press, 1990.

Rystad, Göran. *Ambiguous Imperialism: American Foreign Policy and Domestic Politics at the Turn of the Century.* Lund, Sweden: Esselte Studium, 1975.

——. "Republic or Empire? The Philippine-American War and American Expansionism at the Turn of the Century." In *La République impérialiste: l'expansionisme et la politique extérieure des Etats-Unis, 1885–1909,* edited by Serge Ricard and James Bolner, 132–58. Provence, France: Université de Provence, 1987.

Schmidt-Glintzer, Helwig. *Das neue China. Von den Opiumkriegen bis heute.* Munich: C.H. Beck, 1999.

Schoonover, Thomas D. *The French in Central America: Culture and Commerce, 1820–1930.* Wilmington, Del.: Scholarly Resources, 2000.

——. *Germany in Central America: Competitive Imperialism, 1821–1929.* Tuscaloosa: Univ. of Alabama Press, 1998.

——. "Latin America." In *Spain's Foreign Relations in the Nineteenth Century,* edited by James W. Cortada, 113–30. Westport, Conn.: Greenwood, 1994.

——. "Metropole Rivalry in Central America, 1820s to 1929: An Overview." In *Central America: Historical Perspective on the Contemporary Crisis,* edited by Ralph Lee Woodward Jr., 21–46. Westport, Conn.: Greenwood, 1988.

——. "Napoleon Is Coming! Maximilian Is Coming! The International History of the Civil War in the Caribbean Basin." In *The Union, the Confederacy, and the Atlantic Rim,* edited by Robert E. May, 101–30. W. Lafayette, Ind.: Purdue Univ. Press, 1995.

——. *The United States in Central America, 1860–1911: Episodes of Social Imperialism and Imperial Rivalry in the World System.* Durham, N.C.: Duke Univ. Press, 1991.

Schroeder, John H. *Shaping a Maritime Empire: The Commercial and Diplomatic Role of the American Navy, 1829–1861.* Westport, Conn.: Greenwood, 1985.

Seitz, Konrad. *China: Eine Weltmacht kehrt zurück.* Berlin: Siedler, 2000.

Shineberg, Dorothy. *They Came for Sandalwood: A Study of the Sandalwood Trade in the Southwest Pacific, 1830–1865.* London: Melbourne Univ. Press, 1967.

Silverberg, Robert. *Stormy Voyager: The Story of Charles Wilkes.* Philadelphia: J.B. Lippincott, 1968.

Sklar, Martin J. "The N.A.M. and Foreign Markets on the Eve of the Spanish-American War." *Science and Society* 23 (spring 1960): 133–62.

Smith, Ephraim. "William McKinley's Enduring Legacy: Debate on the Taking of the Philippine Islands." In *Crucible of Empire: The Spanish-American War and its Aftermath,* edited by Richard H. Bradford, 205–49. Annapolis, Md.: Naval Institute, 1993.

Smith, Joseph. *The Spanish-American War: Conflict in the Caribbean and the Pacific, 1895–1902.* London: Longman, 1994.

Spector, Ronald. *Admiral of the New Empire: The Life and Career of George Dewey.* Baton Rouge: Louisiana State Univ. Press, 1974.

——. *Professors of War: The Naval War College and the Development of the Naval Profession.* Newport, R.I.: Naval War College Press, 1977.

Spence, Jonathan D. *The Search for Modern China.* New York: W.W. Norton, 1990.

Stelle, Charles Clarkson. *Americans and the China Opium Trade in the Nineteenth Century.* New York: Arno, 1981.

Stoecker, Helmuth. *Deutschland und China im 19. Jahrhundert: Das Eindringen des deutschen Kapitalismus.* Berlin: Rütten und Loening, 1958.

Storey, Moorfield, and Marcial P. Lichauco. *The Conquest of the Philippines by the United States, 1898–1925.* New York: G.P. Putnam's Sons, 1926.

Tan, Chester C. *The Boxer Catastrophe.* New York: W.W. Norton, 1967.

Tate, Merze. *The United States and the Hawaiian Kingdom: A Political History.* New Haven, Conn.: Yale Univ. Press, 1965.

Thomson, James C., Jr., Peter W. Stanley, and John Curtis Perry. *Sentimental Imperialists: The American Experience in East Asia.* New York: Harper and Row, 1981.

Tirpitz, Alfred von. *Erinnerungen.* Leipzig: R.F. Koehler, 1920. [Translated as *My Memoirs.* 2 vols. New York: Dodd, Mead, 1919.]

Tompkins, E. Berkeley. *Anti-Imperialism in the United States: The Great Debate, 1890–1920.* Philadelphia: Univ. of Pennsylvania Press, 1970.

Tønnessen, Johan Nicolay, and A.O. Johnsen. *The History of Modern Whaling.* Berkeley: Univ. of California Press, 1982.

Trask, David F. *The War with Spain in 1898.* New York: Macmillan, 1981.

Valera, Edmundo Eusebio, Jr. "'Imperialism of Righteousness': The Influence of the American Protestant Social Gospel on Foreign Missions and Expansionism, 1890–1910." Ph.D. diss., Fordham University, 1998.

Van Alstyne, Richard W. *The Rising American Empire.* Chicago: Quadrangle, 1960.

——. *The United States and East Asia.* New York: W.W. Norton, 1973.

Varg, Paul A. *The Making of a Myth: The United States and China, 1897–1912.* East Lansing: Michigan State Univ. Press, 1968.

——. *Missionaries, Chinese, and Diplomats: The American Protestant Missionary Movement in China, 1890–1952.* Princeton, N.J.: Princeton Univ. Press, 1958.

Vevier, Charles. "American Continentalism: An Idea of Expansion, 1845–1910." *American Historical Review* 65 (Jan. 1960): 323–35.

Viola, Herman J., and Carolyn Margolis, eds. *Magnificent Voyagers: The U.S. Exploring Expedition, 1838–1842.* Washington, D.C.: Smithsonian Institution Press, 1985.

Wakeman, Frederic, Jr. *The Fall of Imperial China.* New York: Free Press, 1975.

Wallerstein, Immanuel. *Historical Capitalism.* New York: Verso, 1983.

——. *The Modern World-System III: The Second Era of Great Expansion of the Capitalist World-Economy, 1730s-1840s.* Orlando, Fla.: Academic Press, 1988.

Wehler, Hans-Ulrich. *Bismarck und der Imperialismus.* Cologne, Germ.: Kiepenheuer und Witsch, 1969.

———."Der amerikanische Imperialismus vor 1914." In *Der moderne Imperialismus*, edited by Wolfgang J. Mommsen, 172–92. Stuttgart, Germ.: W. Kohlhammer, 1971.

———. *Der Aufstieg des amerikanischen Imperialismus*. Göttingen, Germ.: Vandenhoeck und Ruprecht, 1974.

———. *Deutsche Gesellschaftsgeschichte*. 3 vols. Munich: C.H. Beck, 1987–1995.

———. *Grundzüge der amerikanischen Außenpolitik*. Vol. 1, *1750–1900*. Frankfurt, Germ.: Suhrkamp, 1984.

Welch, Richard E., Jr. *The Presidencies of Grover Cleveland*. Lawrence: Univ. of Kansas Press, 1988.

———. *Response to Imperialism: The United States and the Philippine-American War, 1899–1902*. Chapel Hill: Univ. of North Carolina Press, 1979.

———. "William McKinley: Reluctant Warrior, Cautious Imperialist." In *Traditions and Values: American Diplomacy, 1865–1945*, edited by Norman Graebner, 29–52. Lanham, Md.: Univ. Press of America, 1985.

Wiebe, Robert. *The Search for Order, 1877–1920*. New York: Wang and Hill, 1967.

Williams, William A. *America Confronts a Revolutionary World*. New York: William Morrow, 1976.

———. *The Contours of American History*. Chicago: Quadrangle, 1961.

———. *The Roots of the Modern American Empire: A Study of the Growth and Shaping of Social Consciousness in a Marketplace Society*. New York: Vintage, 1969.

———. *The Tragedy of American Diplomacy*. 2d ed. New York: Dell, 1972.

Wolff, Leon. *Little Brown Brother: How the United States Purchased and Pacified the Philippine Islands at the Century's Turn*. Garden City, N.Y.: Doubleday, 1961.

Young, Marilyn Blatt. *The Rhetoric of Empire: American China Policy, 1895–1901*. Cambridge, Mass.: Harvard Univ. Press, 1968.

Zwick, Jim, ed. *Mark Twain's Weapons of Satire! Anti-Imperialist Writings on the Philippine-American War*. Syracuse, N.Y.: Syracuse Univ. Press, 1992.

Index

"a fair field and no favor," 114

Accessory Transit Company, 22, 28

accumulation of wealth, 4, 5, 6, 36, 55, 58, 63

Adams, Brooks, 21, 74, 97

Adams, Henry, x, 89, 97, 114

Adams, John Quincy, 14

Adams [John Quincy]–Luis de Onís Continental Treaty (1819), 7–8, 20

Admiralty Inlet, 15

adventurers, 8, 15, 21, 23

Afghanistan, ix

age of discovery, 8

age of diversified economic, religious, strategic, and political ventures and conflict, 8

Age of Imperialism, 61

agrarian businessmen, 10, 54

Aguinaldo, Emilio, 8, 84, 85, 90, 91, 92, 101; returns to Philippines in U.S. vessel, 85

Alaska, 34, 44, 62, 117

Aleutians Islands, 83

Alexander II, 72

Alsace-Lorraine, 43

Amazon River basin, 24

Amelia, 12

American Bible Society, 105

American Board of Commissioners for Foreign Missions, 45

American empires, xi

American entrepreneurs, 18; control material value in circum-Caribbean, 56

American missionaries, 45

American power, 91

American suspicions of Germany, 115

American System of Henry Clay, 58

Anglo-Saxon "division of the world's markets," 78; competition, 103; powers, 43; preeminence, 58; superiority, 119; white, Protestant imperialism, 15

Antarctica, 14, 16

anti-Chinese outrages, 70

anti-foreign elements, 31

anti-foreign reactions, 3, 108

Anti-Imperialist League, 96

anti-slavery movements, 19

Anzer, Johann Baptist (German bishop), 67, 68

Apia, Samoa, 13

Asia, 1, 3, 5, 6, 7, 12, 22, 23, 26, 29, 31, 35, 40, 43, 44, 45, 52, 63, 65, 73, 86, 87, 100, 101, 116; anti-foreign reaction, 2; foreign penetration of, 121; markets, ix; trade, 12; wealth, 9; western businessmen in, 3

"Asia": term a product of the western-dominated world system, 121

"Asia for the Asians," 3

Asian nationalists, 2, 8; responses to encroaching foreign powers, 121

Asian Solidarity Society, 121

Asiatic Humanitarian Brotherhood, 121

Astor, John Jacob, 8, 9, 14

astronomical observatory, U.S., 17

Atlantic, 10, 69
Atlantic whales, 12
Atrato River, 9, 104
Auckland (New Zealand), 30
Australia, 3, 8, 9, 39, 43
Australian annexationism, 44
Australian nationalism, 43
Austria-Hungary, 26, 33, 41, 50, 73

bacteria and mosquitoes, 83
Balangiga on Samar Island, 92
baleen. *See* whalebone
Ballin, Albert, 115
"banana men": agents of private enterprise, 117
banana plantations, 32; trade, 60
Baptist, 105
Barrios, Justo Rufino, 32
Barry, David, xiv
Bay Islands, 18
bêche-de-mer (tepang or sea cucumber), 11, 51
beet sugar, 19
Beijing, 30, 50, 109, 110 foreign compound, 109;
Beijing-to-Hankou (Hankow) railroad, 69
Belgium, 18, 22, 26, 40
Belize. *See* British Honduras
Bell, J. Franklin, 92
Belly, Félix, 25
Bernecker, Walther, xiii
Beveridge, Albert, 77, 95
Bidlack Treaty (1846), 26
"big stick" policy, 114
Billy Budd, 13
Binoche-Guedra, Jacques, 43
Bismarck, Otto von, 29
black Americans, 118; accept U.S. colonialism, 28, 118; soldiers, 118
Blaine, James G., 58
Blair, Montgomery, 28
"blood tribute," 119
Boer War, 96
Bogue (Boca del Tigre) treaty with the British, 37
Bolln, Michael, xiv, 89, 110
Bombay, 5

Boston Mission, 46
Bougainville, Louis Antoine de, 9
Boxer Rebellion (1898–1901), 69, 95, 96, 106, 107, 109, 119, 121; expelling European powers, 107; causes, 106–8; costs, 109–11; indemnity agreement, 111; siege of Beijing, 109–10; western and Japanese troops brutal, 110
Boxers, 64, 70, 100, 108, 109; atrocities, 112; attacks upon foreigners and converts, 107
Braudel, Fernand, xiii
Brauer, Kinley, xiii
Brazil, 34, 73
Bremen, 40
British and Foreign Bible Society, 105
British Honduras, 18, 28
British interests, ix; imperialism, 26, 97; navy, 16; Protestants, 106; chief traders in China, 37
British-German treaty on Samoa (1899), 100
Brownell, Cornelius, 96
Brownsville, 20
Bryan, William Jennings, 103
Buchenau, J_rgen, xiii
Bud Bagsak (1913), 95
Bud Daho (1906), 95
Buddhism, 47
Buffalo World's Fair (1901), 119–20
Bülow, Bernhard von, 67, 100
Bunau-Varilla, Philippe, 114
Burlingame, Anson, 38
Burma, 49

California, 24, 73; and Japanese immigration, 33
canal access, 79; agreements, 23; enthusiasts, 54. *See also* isthmian transit
canal route, 9, 36, 63, 74, 75; to produce great wealth, 31
Canton, 30. *See also* Guangzhou
Cape Horn, 14
Caribbean, 1, 12, 20, 34, 36, 43, 52, 71, 73, 86, 88, 102, 118; colonies, 18; naval stations, 116
Caribbean basin, 2, 10, 18, 21, 22, 23, 24, 76, 84, 113; U.S. efforts to stabilize, 77
Caribbean colonial empires, 19

Caribbean islands, 19, 54; markets for fish, lumber, flour, and cheap textiles, 19

Caribbean–Central American region, ix, x, xi, 20, 23, 31, 59, 77, 115

Carlotta, Princess of Belgium, 26

Carnegie, Andrew, 97, 105

Caroline Islands, 42, 75, 99, 100

Carriker, Robert, xiv

cartography, 17

Caspian Sea, ix

Central America, x, 18, 19, 22, 23, 24, 54, 75, 105; Caribbean coast of, 22; union, 32

Central American Federation (1823–1847), 21

Central Asia, ix

Central Pacific islands, 42, 43, 74, 99

Central Pacific–Union Pacific railroad, 24

Chaffee, Adna R., 92

Challener, Richard, 115

Changijang, 69

cheap labor, 20, 101

Chefoo Convention of 1876, 49

Chekiang province. See Zhijiang province

Chile, 34, 83

China, ix, 1, 7, 8, 9, 33, 35, 36, 37, 40, 50, 51, 52, 62, 64, 65, 68, 71, 74, 76, 80, 84, 85, 96, 102, 107, 109, 112, 119, 121; access to China, 74; anti-missionary activity, 70; civil disorder, 37; compulsory religious freedom, 38; diplomatic relations with the world, 39; disrupted domestic economy, 39; division imagery, 71–72, 89, 112–13; division of, 1894–1898, 5, 65, 66; expansion eastward, 45; expels foreigners, 107; financial burden of war, 51; first resident minister abroad in London, 40; foreign intrusions, 37; lure to westerners, 37–40; market, 3, 11, 12; military revitalized, 70; northern, 34; origins of debt problems in 1895, 51; partial division of, 1897–1898, 2, 69; post–Opium War turmoil, 39; reduced customs revenue, 39; "special relationship" with, 52; suffers a stream of foreign encroachment, 39; trade, 51; traders, 10; unfavorable trade balances, 37; U.S.

policy to prevent spheres of influence, 113; western concession-grabbing after 1895, 106

Chinese celebrate defeat of Germany in World War I, 111

Chinese Christian converts, 70, 110; special privileges, 107

Chinese debt: corruption, 51

Chinese economy, 39; wrecked by borrowing for war reparations, 51

Chinese financial and economic woes, 40, 69

Chinese forces, 50; defeated in two brief wars, 40

Chinese government, 38, 40, 68; blames foreign influence for banditry and secret societies, 40; declares war on western powers, 109; difficulties raising funds in 1895, 108; overview of four hundred years of American history, xi

Chinese hatred of foreigners, 68, 106

Chinese immigrants, 44, 70; vigilante attacks on, in the U.S. west, 70

Chinese labor, 33, 45; builds west coast railroads in Latin America, 45

Chinese nationalism, 3

Chinese nationalists oppose a Manchu-led reform movement, 111

Chinese political cartoon, 107

Chinese Revolution (1910–1919), 3

Chinese society, 70; in crisis, 48

Chinese view of U.S. foreign policy motivation, xi

Chinese villages, 7, 47

Chinese weakness, 67

"Christian butchers," 96

Christian missionary activity, 4, 45, 52, 63, 87; fervor, 48; objectives, 95; visions, 105

Christian Science Society, 105

Christianity, 70

circum-Caribbean, 6, 18, 21, 22, 26, 56, 60, 62, 66; nationalist disgust over the loss of sovereignty, 62

Civil War, 36, 53; and Reconstruction, 54–55, 57, 63; blockade runners, 56; postwar years, 31

civilizing mission, ill-defined, 12, 120

Cixi, Empress Dowager, 50, 69, 70, 109, 110, 111

Clark, George Rodgers, 7, 9, 14

class conflict, 4, 98

Clayton-Bulwer Treaty, 24, 26, 103

Cleveland, Grover, 84; ashamed of Hawaiian annexation, 84

Clymer, Kenton, 105, 106

coconut plantations, 41

Cocos Islands, 84

coffee, 32

collaborators, 31, 62

Colombia, 18, 33, 104; U.S. subversion of its sovereignty in 1903, 103

Colón, 62

Columbia River, 14; mouth, 15

Columbus, Christopher, x, 1, 86

Columbus's (and Uncle Sam's) dream, 3, 7, 8, 14, 22, 24, 36, 52, 58, 62, 64, 86, 122; of a reliable route to East Asia, 29, 59, 102

Columbus-European vision, 3

commerce, 5, 17

communications, 4, 59

comparative advantage, politically constructed, 21

competition, 63; and conflict are integral to laissez-faire liberal order, 102

competitive imperialism, 7, 21, 33, 52, 67

compradors, 34; intermediaries between metropole and periphery, 49, 62

Comte, Aguste, 34

Confederacy, 28, 53; activity in the Caribbean, 56; relations with Europe, 56

Confucianism, 47, 111; and traditional thought, 40; history, 68

Confucius's birthplace, 67, 71

Conger, Sarah, 112

Congo, 74

Congregationalist, 105

Cook, James, 9, 10, 119

cooped leaders, 31

Cooper, Edward E., 118

Cooper, James Fenimore, 13, 15, 36

copra (dried coconut meat), 41, 100

core, 6. *See also* metropole

Corinto, Nicaragua, 29

Corwin, Thomas, 28

Costa Rica, 22, 26, 28, 30, 32, 73, 84; Prussia pursues naval station, 41; resistance to Central American union, 32; fear of U.S. isthmian canal, 33; opposes U.S. in Cuba, 33

Costa Rican railroad, 3; transisthmian railroad, 29, 31

Cotton South: economic dependence on Europe, 55

Crimean War of 1854, 38

Crocker, Charles, 39

Cuba, 18, 19, 23, 26, 54, 58, 65, 71, 73, 79, 84, 88, 96, 102; U.S. occupations (1898–1902, 1906–1909, 1917–1920), 117; U.S. role aggressive, 33

Cuban autonomists, 79

Cuban government, 104

Cuban insurgents, 3, 5, 77, 80; alienation of, 83; denied victory by U.S. government, 80; flag, 90

Cuban people, 76

Dalian (Darien, Dalny, or Lüda), 68

Darien region, 62

Davis, Jefferson, 26

Day, William, 79

Declaration of Independence, 96

Denby, Charles, 69

Denmark, 18

Denver, Colorado, 90

dependency theory, 7

depression, 1780s, 12

depression, 1873, 58, 85, 116

depression, 1873–1898, 5, 58, 63, 65; ethical and moral bankruptcy, 59; explained, 7, 59

depression, 1893, 4, 7, 12, 65, 76; "exporting the unemployment," 61; fabled China market, 76; recovery, 77

Deutsche Handels- und Plantagen Gesellschaft, 100

Dewey, George, 98, 115

Dewey, John, 98

Díaz, Porfirio, 33, 104

Dieterichs, Otto von, 115

Disciples of Christ, 105

discovery and exploration, 4, 7, 9, 14

disorder from low wages and unemployment, 54

Dobson, John, 97, 113

Dooley, Mr., 90, 91. *See also* Dunne

Dormon, Jim, xiv

Dulles, Foster Rhea, 10, 89

Dunne, Peter Finley, 89, 90, 91, 92

Dupetit-Thouars, Abel, 11, 46

East Asia, x, 1, 8, 12, 14, 17, 24, 30, 35, 36, 51, 61, 67, 117; Prussian East Asia expedition, 1859–1861, 41; Prussia pursues naval station, 41

east-west relationship, 48

economic growth, 53

Ecuador, 84

Edward VII, 71

El Salvador, 22, 30, 105

Empress Dowager. *See* Cixi

Empress of China, 12

England, 73

Engstrand, Iris, xiv

entrepreneurs, 8, 12, 21

Episcopalian, 105

Esherick, Joseph, 47

Estrada Cabrera, Manuel, 104

ethnocentric, 53, 98

Eurasian heartland theory, ix

Europe, ix, 1, 3, 13, 25, 26, 55, 104, 114; quest for the wealth of Asia, 2

European expansion, 29; in the 1890s, x

European liberalism, 63

European powers, 6, 18, 30, 36, 50, 88; interest in the isthmus, 22; settlement in North America, 10

expansionism, 78, 101; motivation, 3

exploration and discovery, 7, 9, 10, 14, 15

extraterritoriality, 7, 84; disrespect of, 106; in China, 118; in Hawaii, 11

Fabri, Friedrich, 42

factors of production, 6, 21, 36

Febvrier-Despointes, Auguste, 45

Feng, Guilang, xiv

Fiero, Gloria, xiv

Fiji, 43

filibusterers, 23, 56, 117

Filipino War (1899–c.1920), 95. *See also* Philippine insurrection

Filipinos, 84, 91; Christians, 95; resistance, 85; wealthy distrust democracy, 98

Fischer, Thomas, xiii

Fonseca Bay, 105

Forey, Elie, 27

Formosa, 67, 73

France, x, 11, 18, 22, 26, 28, 32, 37, 40, 42, 43, 50, 67, 68, 73, 75, 115, 116; Gulf-Caribbean ventures, 30; intervention in Mexico, 26–29; opposes U.S. expansion, 75; Pacific squadron, 11; uses colonial forces in World War I, 119; whaling, 13

Franco-Belgian syndicate, 69

Franco-Chinese War, 43, 49

Franco-Prussian War of 1870–1871, 43

Frémont, John C., 29

French acquisitions: in North Africa, 25; in Oceania, 25; in Southeast Asia, 25; in the Caribbean, 25

French Caribbean interests, revived, 30

French Catholics, 106; priests, 11

French colonies, 43

French empire, 12; imperial glory, resurrected, 25

French merchant operations, 11

French military mission in Guatemala, 30

French missionary activity, 11, 45; control missionary passports in China, 48

"friars" claims, 96

Frye, William P., 79

fur-gathering and trading activity, 4, 8, 9, 12, 15, 17, 24, 51

Gadsden Purchase (1854), 26

Galápagos Islands, 84

Galveston, 20

García, Calixto, 83

"generation of 1898," 86

geopolitics, 4, 35, 77

German actions at Manila Bay, 75

German colonies, 99, 100

German commerce, 41

German emigration, 25

German entrepreneurs and investors, 25, 30, 42, 46, 100, 115

German expansionism, 29, 42, 48, 75, 99
German leaders, 24, 114
German missionaries, 46, 68; in Shandong, 107; killed, 68
German naval building program, 111
German-Spanish dispute in Central Pacific, papal mediation of, 42
German states, 22, 24; and whaling, 13; and trade problems with Spanish tariff law in Central Pacific, 42
German war plans against the United States, 103
German flag on Yap, 42
Germans control missionary passports, 48
Germany, x, 18, 40, 42, 43, 49, 50, 67, 69, 71, 73, 74, 83, 85, 88; acquires remaining Spanish possessions in Central Pacific, 99; activity in Costa Rica, 29; activity on the isthmus, 29–30; Customs Union (Zollverein), 41; "governmental imperialism," 75; "grossdeutsch" or "kleindeutsch" unification, 41; in Central America, 74–75; naval and coaling stations envisioned, 67, 75; objectives in Samoa, 74; "place in the sun," 68; sale of U.S. pork, 74; seeks European agreement to curtail U.S. in 1898, 74; share of Central Pacific trade, 42; share of South Pacific trade, 41; world aspirations, 99
Gilberts, 100
glut. See overproduction
Godeffroy, Johann Cesar, 41
Godeffroy company (Hamburg): in Apia (Samoa), 41, 100; sends its first trading vessel to the South Pacific, 41
Goetzmann, William, 15, 16
gold rush of 1849, 8
Graebner, Norman A., 4
Gran Colombia, 18–19
Granger, Jean-Michel, xiv
Grant, Ulysses S., 26
Great Britain, x, 11, 12, 18, 26, 32, 33, 37, 40, 43, 49, 55, 67, 68, 73, 74, 83, 88, 89; and indigenous people, 95; opposes isthmian canal, 26; whaling, 13; world's major investing nation, 26

great powers, 17; chain of coaling, cable, and naval stations, 75; comparative colonial rule, 95; competition, 31; material culture, 58; in the Pacific basin, 35
Guadeloupe, 30
Guam, 79, 103, 117; seized in War of 1898, 89
Guangdong, 67
Guangdong Bay, 69
Guangdong-Guangxi-Yunnan province, 69
Guangxi, 67
Guangzhou, 37. See also Canton
guano islands, 100, 117
Guantánamo Bay, 103, 117
Guatemala, 22, 26, 28, 30, 31, 34, 73; leads Central American union project, 32; government, 32; liberal elites, 32
"guerra de la reforma," 25
Guevara, Che, 104
Gulf of Mexico ports, 20
Gulf-Caribbean basin, 1, 3, 4, 54, 99
Guy, John, 108

Haiti, 19, 30, 73, 75, 102, 117; U.S. intervention (1915–1934), 101, 117
Hamburg, 40, 41
Hamburg-America Passenger Company, 115
Hankow-Beijing railroad: concession to a Belgian syndicate, 113
Hanlon, David, 119
Hansa cities, 24, 41; merchants, 40, 42
HAPAG. See Hamburg-America Passenger Company
Harrison, Benjamin, 106
Hart, Robert, 51
Hawaii, 8, 10, 11, 12, 13, 14, 34, 42, 44, 51, 58, 73, 74, 75, 79, 83, 84, 88, 96, 102, 103, 117; affairs, 41; and Japanese immigration, 33; annexation, 84; Asian migrants, 44; foreign trade, 44
Hay, John, 4, 102, 112
Hay-Pauncefote Treaty of 1901, 103
Haymarket massacre of 1884, 65
Henry Cabot Lodge Corollary (1912), 105, 114
Hesse, Franz Hugo, 25

Hildebrand, Klaus, 85
Hindu scholar, 101
hispanismo movements, 29; a revival of His-
    panic and Latin cultural ties, 86
Hispano-American conference in Madrid
    (1901), 86
historical processes, long term, 1
Hitler, Adolf: pursues Mackinder heartland
    theory, ix
Ho Chi Minh, 8, 122
Hoar, George, 83, 91, 103; anti-imperialism,
    83
Hobson, John, 50
holding company, 60, 61
Homestead Act, 12
Homestead strike of 1892, 65
Honduras, 18, 26, 28, 102, 105, 117; north
    coast of, 7
Hong Kong, 30
Honolulu, 13, 30
Hood's Canal, 15
Hopkins, Mark, 39
Horowitz, David, xiii
Hsu, Immanuel, 40, 47
Huangpu: Chinese treaty with the French
    (1844), 37
Huntington, Collis P., 39
hydrography, 17

idealism, 12, 63, 86
I-ho ch'uan. *See* Yi He Tuan
imperial competition, 75; in East Asia, 85
Imperial Maritime Customs Administration,
    51, 69
"imperialism of righteousness," 47
imports: undercounting, under weighing,
    and undervaluing, 60
India, 5, 26
Indian Ocean, 10, 52
Indian wars, 8
Indochina, 67
industrial powers, 6, 21
industrialization, 4; empire building, 88; raw
    materials and markets, 88
Inland Waters Steam Navigation Act, 113
international balance of power, 85
international competition, 4, 54

Internet, 5
Interoceanic Canal Commission, 103, 105
Iriye, Akira, xiii, 113
isthmian leaders, 31
isthmian territory, 3, 7, 23; ransacked for
    wealth, 117
isthmian transit, 19, 20, 22, 25, 26, 33, 35,
    52, 56, 62, 71, 77, 78, 86, 103, 114; ac-
    cess to, 29; need for, 17, 19
Italy, 22, 33, 40, 52, 73; demands naval sta-
    tion in China, 69, 108

Jackson, Andrew, 14
Jaluit GmbH, 100
Jansen, Marius, 49
Japan, 1, 6, 8, 9, 33, 34, 36, 40, 41, 44, 49,
    69, 66, 73, 74, 75, 85, 104; Christian
    missionaries, 47; competes for transit, 33;
    imperial expansion, 45, 49, 50, 66;
    Kotoku Shusui on imperialism of, 50;
    modernization, 66; Russia as a problem
    in Korea, 51; sphere of influence in
    Fujian (Fukien) province, 69, 85
Japanese immigrants, 44, 74
Japanese Imperial armory: ships materiel to
    Aguinaldo, 101
Japanese socialists, 121
Japanese-Mexican project, 114
Jefferson, Thomas, 7, 9; agrarian world, 7
Jilin (Chihli), 107, 108
"John Bull" (Great Britain), 89
Johnson, Andrew, 57
Jolo, 94, 95
Juan de Fuca Straits, 15
Juárez, Benito, 28

Kanagawa (Yokohama), 39
Kaoru, Inoue, 50
Karnow, Stanley, 94
Keith, Minor C., 31
Kennedy, Paul, 73
kerosene, 6
"King Cotton," 55
Korean War (1950–1953), 121
Korea, 34, 44, 49, 50, 51, 73
Kowloon, 69
Kristof, Nicholas, 8

Kuykendall, Ralph, 45
Kwangsi. *See* Guangxi
Kwangtung. *See* Guangdong

La Paz, 114
labor exploitation, 4
LaFeber, Walter, xiii, 8, 66
Lahaina (Maui), 13
Lake lanao, 95
Lake Nicaragua, 22
Lammersdorf, Raimund, 114
Lan, Ke, xiv
"large policy" imperialism, 76
Latin America, 24, 28, 29, 31
Ledyard, John, 7, 8, 9
Lesseps, Ferdinand de, 30; Panama canal project, 30, 43
Lewis, Meriwether, 9, 14
Leyte, 92
Li Hongzhang: China's most prominent leader, 39, 51
Liaodong (Liaotung), 50, 51, 68
liberal imperialism, 103, 119
liberalism, 34, 55, 58, 78; classical (or the free market economic system), 19; development program in U.S., 57; free labor system, 55; free-market changes, 53; free-market economics, 57; free-market rhetoric, 60–61; free soil land policy, 8; industrializing states, 21; ideologies, 6, 54; laissez-faire, 5, 63, 105; promises material progress, 34; replaces mercantilism, 53–54; system of industrial capitalism, 5, 23, 58
Lichauco, Marcial, 97
Lincoln, Abraham, 26, 97; administration, 27, 57
Linderman, Gerald, 97
Liverpool, 30
Lodge, Henry Cabot, 79, 97; *See also* Henry Cabot Lodge Corollary
London Missionary Society, 45, 46
London, 5
Louisiana Purchase (1803), 7, 20
Lübeck, 40
lumbering and timbering activity, 8, 12, 24, 51
Luzon, 92

Macao, 49
Mackinder, Halford, ix
Magdalena Bay (in La Paz, Baja California), 84, 105
Mahan, Alfred Thayer, 96, 99; use of distorting language, 99
Malay Archipelago, 3; peninsula, 42
maldistribution of wealth, 57
Malthus, Thomas Robert, 21
Manchuria, 51, 69
Mangin, Charles, 119
"manifest design," 23
Manifest Destiny, 4, 23, 43, 61, 76
Manila, 30, 52, 79, 83, 85, 89, 115; surrender to U.S., 85
Mao Zedong, x, 1, 3, 8, 122
Maori resist British, 119
Marco Polo, 66
Marianas, 42, 100
Mariscal, Ignacio, 104
maritime activity, 4, 10; adventurers, 8; services, 62
markets, 10, 21, 36; for manufactured products, 8; foreign markets needed, 57; in Europe, Latin America, and Asia, 59
Marotta, Gary, xiv
Marquesas Islands, 11; annexed by French government, 12
Marshall Islands, 42, 43, 46, 100
Martin, Jean, 119
Martinique, 30
Mary D. Hume, 13
mass production, 4, 7, 20
Massachusetts, 12
"material progress," 58
materialism, 12, 63, 120
Maui, 13
Mauru, 100
Maury, Matthew Fontaine, 54; geopolitics, 54
Maximilian, Archduke of Hapsburg empire, 26; executed in Querétaro, 29
May, Ernest, 1
McCormick, Thomas, xiii, 76
McKinley, William, 64, 66, 83, 97, 103; administration, 79, 95; claims that prayer assisted decision making, 64; "conception of duty, humanity, civilization," 90

Meiji leaders, 49

Melanesia, 2, 42; indigenous people resist the French in 1878 and 1917, 119

Melville, Herman, 10, 13, 36

mercantilistic agrarian order, 23, 53

merchants, 1, 4, 8, 11, 12, 15, 23; capitalists, 54

Meriwether, Lewis, 7

Merritt, Wesley, 98

Methodist Episcopal, 105

metropole, 6, 20, 32, 70; and periphery, 7, 54; and semi-peripheral powers, 19; competition, 21; development, 7; economies, 22; entrepreneurs, 31; firms, 61; leaders, 63; states, 7, 59, 61, 62; growth to, status, 55; unemployment, 6. *See also* peripheral states *and* semi-periphery

metropolitan France, 119

Mexican Clubs, 28

Mexican conservatives, 25, 28

Mexican leaders, 103

Mexican Revolution (1910–1920), 117

Mexican society, 19

Mexican War, 8, 24

Mexico, 1, 18, 19, 22, 23, 26, 27, 30, 33, 34, 54, 73, 102, 103, 117; Britain withdraws, 27; costly war of independence, 19; European intervention, 25, 28; fears a U.S. canal, 33; foreign monarch for, 27; French military intervention, 27; opposes U.S. expansionism, 103–5; resistance to Central American union, 32; Spain withdraws, 27

Miami, 20

Micronesia, 1, 42, 100; societies, 119

"Micronesian gold," 100. *See also* copra

Middle America. *See* Central America

middle class, 34

Middle East, 76

Mikado, 71

Midway, 34, 44, 117

Mill, John Stuart, 55

Mindanao, 94, 95, 99

mining, 21, 23; and railroad concessions, 69; in Central America, 32

missionaries, 1, 4, 11, 14, 15, 23, 35, 63, 105, 121; diplomatic burden, 48; gunboat protection, 48; protection, 37

Mississippi River valley, 23, 54, 116

Mobile, 20, 117

Moby Dick, 13

Moltke, Helmuth von, 111

Mondwurf, Georg, xiv

Mongolia, 49

Monroe, James, 20

Monroe Doctrine, 4, 20, 22, 28, 35, 43, 44, 61, 73, 84, 105, 114, 115

Monroe Doctrine leagues, 28

Mormon, 105

Moroland, 19, 85 119; U.S. efforts to govern , 94–95; U.S. policy similar to Spanish, 95

Moros, 85, 94, 95; resist United States, 95, 119. *See also* Muslims

multinational corporations, 60, 61, 62; collectivized, bureaucratic, planning organizations, 61

Muslims, 38, 85, 94, 119. *See also* Moros

Nanjing (Nanking) Treaty with the British in 1842, 37

Nantucket (Mass.), 12, 15

Nantucketers, 13

Napoleon III, 12, 25, 26, 27; imperial dream defeated, 29; government seeks acquisitions in foreign lands, 25; government, 28; Mexican mistake, 30

national banking system, 57

National Board of Trade, 62

naval bases and coaling stations, 11, 20, 36, 42, 63, 74, 88, 99, 117; Far East, 52; in Pago Pago, 83; German and U.S. interest in, 19

Navy's General Board, 115, 116

Netherlands, 12, 18, 22, 37, 40, 52; and indigenous people, 95

New Bedford (Mass.), 12

New Caledonia, 12

New Grenada, 22

New Guinea, 43, 67; German colony, 42

New Orleans, 20, 30, 117

New Panama Canal Company, 76, 103

New World, 29, 116; development, 33; independence movements, 26

New York, 5, 30; railroad investors, 22

New York–Honduras Rosario Mining Company, 32

New Zealand, 3, 9, 39, 43

Nicaragua, 18, 25, 26, 28, 29, 32, 33, 62, 73, 75, 102, 105, 117; fears a U.S. canal, 33; German military intervention, 29; north coast of, 7; transit route, 23; U.S. interventions (1906–1932), 101, 117

Nicaraguan Canal, 62; U.S. canal project in Nicaragua cancelled, 104

Nicholas II, 67, 71; coronation in 1896, 51

"no transfer principle," 20

Nootka Sound, 9

North American continent, 10, 35

North Americans: expansionists since 1607, 56

North Atlantic communities (states), 1, 5, 7, 17, 36, 86; intruders, 121; merchants, 37; political economies, 19

North Pacific Exploring Expedition, 17

Novick, Peter, 1

"objectivity," 1

Occidental and Oriental Steamship Company, 39

Oceania, 1, 11, 17, 23, 24, 26, 30, 31, 35, 36, 40, 44, 45, 51, 52, 61, 88, 101, 118; trade, 41

Ohio River valley, 23

Omaha World's Fair (1898), 119

"open door," 6, 61; imperialism, 59; in China, 114; restricted Chinese sovereignty, 113; trade, 112

open door notes, 113; first notes (1899), 112; second notes preserving Chinese territorial and administrative unity (1900), 112

opium, 37; western governments compel sales in China, 37

"opium of the masses," 37

Opium Wars, 2, 44; after the First Opium War, 39; complicated Chinese culture and politics, 39; during 1838–1842, 37; during 1856–1858, 38, 41

Oregon territory: acquisition, 14–15, 17; settlement, 8, 16

Orient, 11

Ostend Manifesto (1854), 26

overproduction, 59, 61, 69, 74, 86, 85, 88

Pacific, 11, 15, 16, 22, 29, 34, 43, 71, 83, 118; indigenous populations, 15; indigenous resistance, 119; theater of World War II (1941–1945), 121; trade basin, 23; whaling, 12

Pacific basin, 1, 2, 4, 7, 8, 10, 11, 12, 14, 17, 18, 21, 24, 30, 34, 35, 36, 37, 40, 42, 52, 58, 66, 69, 73, 76, 83, 88, 97, 99, 101; empire, 120; resources, 30; share of U.S. trade grows, 120; trade with, 120

Pacific coast, 7

Pacific islands, 1, 8, 9, 12, 30, 33, 35, 36, 42, 47; charts, 16; German language training, 46; inhabitants, 3, 119; labor, 45

Pacific Mail Steamship Company, 24, 38, 39; starts service to China in 1867, 38–39

Pacific Northwest, 15

Pacific Ocean, x, 16, 69; image, 10; made into an American lake, 83

Pago Pago (Samoa), 43, 52, 58, 83

Palau, 99

Pan American Conference (1864), 28

Pan Americanism, 29

Panama, 26, 32, 102, 105; after 1903, 101; U.S. protection of, 84; U.S. intervention (1899–1903), 116, 117; U.S. role in, aggressive, 33

Panama Canal, 1, 2, 10, 12, 34, 101, 115, 118, 120, 121; compared to Suez Canal for trade, 30; completed, 120–21; massive technological and scientific project, 104; U.S. canal project at Panama, 104; zone, 103, 117

Panama City, 62

Panama Railroad, 22, 23; Company, 24

Pan-Americanism, 61, 86, 116; Mexico City meeting in 1901, 102

Pauncefote, Julian, 112. *See also* Hay-Pauncefote Treaty of 1901

Pearl Harbor, 52, 83

Peit'ang Cathedral, 109

People's Daily (Chinese newspaper), xi

Pérez, Louis, Jr., xiii, xix, 77, 78, 79, 80, 81, 82, 118
peripheral states (periphery), 6, 7, 55, 61, 62, 63, 70, 88; underdevelopment of, 7. *See also* metrople *and* semi-periphery
Perouse, Jean François de la, 9
Perry, John Curtis, 85, 100
Perry, Matthew C., 23
Pershing, John J., 94
Philippine insurgents, 3, 101; desire for self-government, 97
Philippine insurrection (1899–c.1920), 3, 5, 93, 94, 119, 120, 121; costs, 93; public relations nightmare for U.S. forces, 92–93; torture common, 84. *See also* Filipino War
Philippine republic: crushed by U.S. troops, 91
Philippines, 41, 42, 64, 65, 73, 74, 78, 79, 80, 83, 84, 89, 96, 99, 102, 103, 113, 117, 119, 120; acquisition of, 90; annexation of, 97; cruelty of Spanish friars, 84; excursion, 97; forced conversions to Christianity, 95; U.S. conduct, 92; pillaging of the region, 117; U.S. wants entrepôt harbor in East Asia, 79; world's fair images, 119–20
"pivot of history," ix
plantations, 19
Platt River valley, 23
PMSS. *See* Pacific Mail Steamship Company
Pohnpei resist Germans, 119
political economy, 6, 63
Polk, James, 15
Polynesia, 1, 42
populism, 63
Port Arthur, 68
Portugal, 12, 18, 37, 40, 49, 52; officials, 48
positivists, 34
post-Taibei (Taiping) years (1861–1895), 39
Presbyterian, 105
price transferring, 60, 61
productionism, 58
"progress," 6
progressives, 47; search for order and opportunity, 66

protective tariff, 57
protectorates, 66, 74, 84, 117
Protestants, 1, 45, 105; disruptive in China, 47; distrust Spanish Catholicism, 105
Prussia, 24, 25, 29, 33, 40, 41, naval expedition to East Asia, 41
"psychic crisis," 76
Puerto Limón (Costa Rica), 31; naval station site, 29
Puerto Rico, 18, 58, 79, 89, 103, 117
Puget Sound, 15
Pullman strike of 1894, 65

Qing (Ch'ing) regime, 40, 67; pursued a modest reform program, 39
Qing-Dao, 67, 68, 75, 100, 111; as "the Empire's Hongkong," 68
Qu-Fu, 67. *See also* Confucius's birthplace

racism, 4, 58, 85, 98, 114, 120; dehumanize the opponent, 99; inhumanity and abusive geopolitics of U.S. action, 97; racial and cultural superiority over the periphery, 58; toward blacks and Hispanics, 53
radio, 4
railroad magnates, 54
railroads, 10; agreements, 23; at Panama isthmus, 22; concessions in China, 113; concessions in China, U.S., and Belgium, 69
raw materials, 8, 20
reciprocal most-favored-nation rights, 38
Reed, Thomas, 91, 92
Reid, Whitelaw, 83
Reinsch, Paul, 106
religion, 63; challenges to, by Darwinism and science, 64; revivalism, 63. *See also* "opium of the masses"
religious-cultural clash, 20, 111
"Resource Raiding," 11
restricted sovereignty. *See* extraterritoriality
Reynolds, William, 15
"righteousness of imperialism," 47
Rivinius, Karl, 106
Roberts, Edmund, 23
Roman Catholic Church: in Shandong, 48; French protection of worship, 11; in the

Philippines, 105; missionaries, 46; power, 20

Roman Catholicism, 105

Roosevelt, Theodore, 71, 73, 79, 110, 111, 114; Corollary to Monroe Doctrine, 35, 114

Root, Elihu, 84, 118

route from the North Atlantic to Asia, 102

Royal Geographic Society, ix

rum, 19

Russia, ix, 8, 9, 37, 40, 49, 50, 51, 52, 67, 68, 73, 85; as China's hero in 1896, 51

Russian Pan-Slavic policies, 50

Russo-Chinese Bank, 69

Russo-Japanese War, 113

Samar, 94

Samoa, 41, 42, 44, 46, 51, 58, 73, 74, 75, 88, 99, 103, 117; division of, 100; resists Germans, 119; tripartite protectorate, 43

San Diego, 24, 105

San Francisco, 13, 14, 15, 17, 24, 30, 39, 88

San Juan River, 9, 22

San Luis d'Apra: chief port on Guam, 89

sandalwood, 11, 51

Santiago de Cuba, 83

Santo Domingo, 19, 25, 26, 27, 102, 117; U.S. intervention (1916–1924), 101, 117

Santo Tomás (Guatemala), 22; Belgian colony, 28

Schoonover, Ebba Wesener, xv

Schurz, Carl, 98

scientific and geographical labors, 11, 16

scientific instruments, 17

sea transportation, 8

sealers, 9, 12, 24

"search for order," 63

Second Opium War (1856–1858), 38, 41; foreign diplomats to reside in Beijing, 38

sectional crisis, 36, 53, 57, 63

security issues, 4, 12

semi-periphery, 55, 59. See also metropole and peripheral states

Seventh-Day Adventist, 105

Seward, George, 48

Seward, William, ix, x, 26, 28, 56, 57

Shandong peninsula, 46, 49, 67, 68, 70–71, 107, 108, 109, 111

Shanghai, 30

Shanxi (Sanmen) Bay, 69, 108; north of Fuzhou (Foochow) on the Fujian coast, 113

shells, 11, 51

Sherman, John, 74

Sherman, William T., 26

Shimonoseki Treaty, 51, 66

Shinto, 49

shipbuilding, 10

Shusui, Kotoku, 50

Sino-Japanese War (1894-1895), 51, 65, 66, 70, 106; Triple Intervention (Russia, France, and Germany), 50, 69

slave plantation economy, 22, 23

slave trade, 20

slavery, 5, 19, 54

Smith, Adam, 55

Smith, Jacob H. "Howling Wilderness," 92, 99; court-martialed and retired, 92

Smithsonian "Castle on the Mall," 16

social Darwinism, 50, 63, 78

social imperialism, 6, 7, 53, 54, 58, 59, 63, 65, 78, 98, 112, 114, 117

socialism, 63

Solomon Islands, 67, 119

Sombart, Werner, 36

South America, 10, 21

South Asia, 26, 36

South Pacific, 12, 14, 74; islands, 11, 41, 43, 49

Southeast Asia, 9, 43, 76

southern dreams of a Caribbean empire, 23

Soviet policy, ix

Spain, x, 1, 12, 18, 22, 25, 26, 37, 40, 64, 65, 76, 85, 102; and indigenous people, 95; conflict with Peru and Chile, 27; conduct in Cuba, 77; distress in 1895–1898, 3; intellectuals, 86; royal house, 25, 26

Spanish colonial years, 21

Spanish-American War, 1. See also War of 1898

Spence, Jonathan, 38

Spengler, Otto, 21

sperm whale oil, 13

spheres of influence, 66, 112

spirit or martial arts societies, 70, 106. *See also* Boxers

St. Louis Merchant Exchange, 62

St. Louis World's Fair (1904), 120

Standard Oil, 6

Stanford, Leland, 39

Stanley, Peter W., 85, 86, 100

Stapenhorst and Hoffschläger firm, 46

state-dominated internationalism, 121

Storey, Moorfield, 85, 97

Strong, Josiah, 74

Student Volunteers for Foreign Missions, 47

submarine cables, 1, 69, 89; technology, 20

Suez Canal, 1, 26, 30, 52, 84, 121

sugar, 19, 20

Sultan of Sulu (Philippines), 15

Sulu Archipelago, 75, 94, 99

Sulu region, 95

Sulu Sea, 94

Sumner, Samuel S., 94

Sweden, 18

Sydney (Australia), 30

Tahiti, 46; Queen Pomare IV, 46

Taiwan. *See* Formosa

Tampa, 20

Taoism, 47

Tarawa, battle of (1943), 16

technological and manufacturing economies, 6

technological change, rapid, 2, 54, 55

technologically and industrially based economy, 53

technology, 1, 4, 48, 54, 55, 58, 66, 104; agriculture, 21; clipper ships and steam vessels, 1, 20, 35, 36, 39; coal and petroleum, 20; consequences of, 5, 20; draws Asia and the North Atlantic closer, 105; military, 5; early telegraphy, 5; steamships, 20, 36; transportation, 20; steel, inexpensive and high quality, 20

Tehuantepec Isthmus, 9, 62

telegraph, 4, 5, 84

telephone, 4

Thailand, 67

"that splendid little war," 4. *See also* War of 1898

"The New Empire," 36

"the social gospel," 48

Thomson, James C., Jr., 85, 100

"Three World Empires," 35; theory of, 73

Tian, Haiyan, xiv

Tianjin (Tientsin), 109; Pact of 1858, 38; Treaty of, 48

Tirpitz, Alfred von, 67, 68, 73, 100, 115

Tonga, 42, 46

Tonkin, 43

transcultural history, x

transisthmian roads, 10

transnational history, x

trans-Siberian railroad, 51

Treaty of Paris, 96

Treaty of Wangxia (Wanghia), 23, 37

treaty port system, U.S. introduces: to Japan (1858), 44; to Korea (1882), 44; to Siam (1855), 44

Tsingtao. *See* Qing-Dao

Tsingtao brewery, 46

Turkestan, 49

Turner, Frederick Jackson, 10

Twain, Mark, 96; vice-president of Anti-Imperialism League, 96

"Two Crises, One War," 66

Tyler, John, 15, 16

Typee, 13

U.S. adopts Spanish repression methods, 96

U.S. aid to filibustering, 25

U.S. alarm, German and Japanese expansion, 73

U.S. anti-imperialists, 84

U.S. avoids transfer of authority to indigenous people, 79, 98

U.S. black colonies in circum-Caribbean, 28

U.S. economic interests lead to involvement in conflict, 87

U.S. economy: power of, x; proposed use of communications to link, to world, 57

U.S. empire, 84, 99; desires for, on the Pacific, 36; distribution base in East Asia, 88; "empire of the seas," 56

U.S. entrepreneurs, 8, 12, 24, 51

U.S. expansion, 10, 23, 24, 29, 56–57, 58. 73; by war, 91; goals, 34; historians misrepresent, 100; in the 1890s, x; mastery of the Pacific, 10; promotion rather than protection of U.S. economic interests, 85

U.S. Exploring Expedition (1836–1842), 14, 16–17, 41, 83; contributions to natural science overlooked, 16–17; specimens gathered, 16

U.S. generals suffer only short-term disadvantages, 93

U.S. geopoliticians, 10, 22, 23, 24; interests on the isthmus, 115

U.S. government, 3, 7, 18; acts to bind the North Atlantic area to the Pacific basin, 116; promotion of U.S. interests abroad, 116; allows overthrow of Hawaiian government, 74; demands equal treatment in Asia, 38; domestic development, 22, 63; hegemony in the New World, 114

U.S. growth, 4

U.S. interest in East Asia and the Pacific, 12, 44, 120

U.S. intervention, 1, 4; most commonly for access, 86

U.S. leaders, 29; mostly Protestant, 20

U.S. material and spiritual needs, 78

U.S. military governance, 94; hospital, Philippines, 93

U.S. mission, 20, 63; costs, 95

U.S. missionaries, 48, 51, 64, 106; aggressive, 105

U.S. Naval Academy, 16

U.S. naval strategist, 96

U.S. Navy, 15, 16, 83; Black Plan (aimed at Germany), 115; creates a Caribbean Division, 116; General Board, 113; Orange Plan (aimed at Japan), 113

U.S. policy, ix; attitude toward foreign competition abroad, 61; of acquisitions and protectorates, 96

U.S. political economy, 1, 23, 53, 117

U.S. politics, 57, 63; leaders, 59

U.S. racism: in Cuba, 118; in the Philippines, 99

U.S. recovery from the depression of 1893, 77

U.S. rejects independent Philippines, 85

U.S. repression of revolutions, 102

U.S. rogue conduct, 104

U.S. security, 20; Britian refuses to challenge, 27; management of the Caribbean basin, 101; Napoleon III challenges, 27

U.S. self-image of a democratic, Christian, benevolent people, 6

U.S. sense of insecurity, 75

U.S. society, 53, 65

U.S. soldiers-of-fortune, 117

U.S. steamships dominate China's inland waterways, 38

U.S. superpower, ix

U.S. tariffs, 60

U.S. trade with Oceania and Asia 1821–1945, 120

U.S. unemployment, 7

U.S. well-being and progress, 23

U.S. well-being and security, 74, 86

U.S.-Asian relations, 11

U.S.-Colombian canal pact (1846), 26

U.S.-German competition, worldwide, 103

U.S.-German treaty on Samoa (1900), 100

U.S.-Hawaiian reciprocity, 42

Ullmann, Hans-Peter, 75

underconsumption, 59

Union Coloniale Française, 75, 76

United Brethren in Christ, 105

United Fruit Company, 32, 86

United States, 6, 13, 18, 40, 43, 52, 61, 65, 68, 73, 102; and indigenous people, 95; becoming overseas imperialist power, x

Universal Interoceanic Canal Company, 76

University of Erlangen-Nürnberg, xiii

USS *Maine* sunk in Havana harbor, 76

utopianism, 63

Valparaiso (Chile), 11, 30, 41

Van Buren, Martin, 14, 16

Van Buren–Tyler dispute, 16, 17

Vanderbilt, Cornelius, 22
Varg, Paul, 71, 121
Vava'u harbor as a coaling station, 42
Venezuela, 30, 73, 75
Vevier, Charles, 10
victims of imperialism, 121
Victoria, 72
Vietnam, 49; U.S. intervention 1950–1974, 121
Vincendon-Doumoulins (Calif.), 9
violence, 4
Virgin Islands, 19, 75, 84, 103, 117
Vladivostok, 51

Wake Island, 79, 103, 117; annexed, 89
Waldersee, Alfred von, 110
Walker, John G., 62, 103
Walker, William, 22
Wallerstein, Immanuel, xiii
Wangxia (Wanghia). *See* Treaty of Wangxia
War of 1812, 7
War of 1898, 1, 2, 3, 4, 5, 34, 63, 85, 91, 95, 98, 102, 105, 118, 121; aftermath in the Caribbean, 102–6, 113–18; aftermath in the Philippines, 89–101; casualties and costs, 83; causes, 4; in the making, 77–86; in the Pacific, 78–79, 83–89; linked to China and the Boxers, 106–13, 118–22; military force and racism, 101; Paris Peace Commission, 83; postwar trade, 99; trans-Mississippi west joins war, 90; U.S. peace commissioners, 79
water: importance in North American history, 10; centrality of the sea, 36
Watterson, Henry, 98
Wehler, Hans-Ulrich, xiii, 42
Weihaiwei (Shandong peninsula), 49, 69
Welch, Richard, 100
Weltpolitik (an integrated world policy), 75
west coast: of New World, 21, 23, 30; of North America, 74; of South America, 11, 62
West Indian islands, 56
Western Europe, x
Western Hemisphere, x
western imagination, 37

western imperialism, 37, 49, 50, 51; reshaping Asian cultures, 3
western industrializing states: increasingly competitive and acquisitive, 59
western merchants, 37
western missionaries, 45–49; demands, 1; disrupt Chinese society, 47
western powers export Christianity, 105
western technology, 39, 40
westward expansion, 4, 7, 10, 12, 14
Weyler, Valeriano "Butcher," 79, 92, 93
whale oil, 11, 13
whalebone (baleen), 13
whalers, 4, 9, 15, 16
whaling, 8, 10, 11, 12, 14, 17, 23, 24, 35, 51; communities, 15; industry, 8, 13–14; Japanese sperm whale fields, 10; major U.S. economic activity, 13; peak in 1830–1861, 13; U.S., fleet, 11, 13; vessels, 13
white man's burden, 91
Wilkes, Charles, 9, 14, 15, 16, 17, 23, 89; charts used in World War II, 16; court-martial a fiasco, 16
Willamette Valley, 8
William II, 67, 68, 71, 72, 73, 110, 111
Williams, T. Harry, xiii
Williams, William A., xiii
Winks, Robin, xiii
Women's Christian Temperance Union, 97
Wood, Leonard, 94, 118
Woodward, Ralph Lee, xiii
workers in liberal economic order, 5, 7, 34; protest, 62
world depression. *See* depression
world economy, 22, 33, 55, 56; disparity among nations, 59; harbors, 15; markets, 19
World War II, ix
world wars, 7
world's fairs, 58, 119; at Buffalo (1901), 119–20; at Omaha (1898), 119; at St. Louis (1904), 120

Yalu River, 68
Yangzi valley, 49, 69
Yi He Tuan ("Righteous and Harmonious

Fists"), 106, 108, 109. *See also* Boxers *and* Boxer Rebellion
Yingkou (Yingkow), 68
Yokohama, 30.
Yunnan province, 43, 49, 67

Zelaya, José Santos, 104; canal negotiations with European and Japanese interests, 104
Zhijiang province, 69
Zou Rong, 111